W9-BDZ-533

Classroom Strategies *for* Interactive Learning

INTERNATIONAL
Reading Association
800 BARKSDALE ROAD, PO BOX 8139
NEWARK, DE 19714-8139, USA
www.reading.org

Doug Buehl

The International Reading Association attempts, through its publications, to provide a forum for a wide spectrum of opinions on reading. This policy permits divergent viewpoints without implying the endorsement of the Association.

Executive Editor, Books	Corinne M. Mooney
Developmental Editor	Charlene M. Nichols
Developmental Editor	Tori Mello Bachman
Developmental Editor	Stacey Lynn Reid
Editorial Production Manager	Shannon T. Fortner
Design and Composition Manager	Anette Schuetz

Project Editors   Stacey Lynn Reid and Rebecca A. Stewart

Cover Design   Lise Holliker Dykes

The publisher would appreciate notification where errors occur so that they may be corrected in subsequent printings and/or editions.

Library of Congress Cataloging-in-Publication Data

Buehl, Doug.
  Classroom strategies for interactive learning / Doug Buehl. -- 3rd ed.
      p. cm.
  Includes bibliographical references.
  ISBN 978-0-87207-686-0 (alk. paper)
  1. Reading comprehension. 2. Content area reading. 3. Active learning. I. Title.
  LB1050.45.B84 2008
  371.3--dc22
                                                                                          2008037120

This book is dedicated to three voracious readers: my wife, Wendy, and sons, Jeremy and Christopher. Their encouragement, support, good humor, and love have made this edition possible.

Contents

About the Author vii
Foreword ix
Preface xi

SECTION 1
Developing Strategic Readers and Learners
CHAPTER 1 Teaching for Comprehension 3
CHAPTER 2 Frontloading: The Key to Comprehension 15
CHAPTER 3 Guiding Comprehension Through Text Frames 22
CHAPTER 4 Consolidating Understanding With Fact Pyramids 30

SECTION 2
Classroom Strategies for Teaching and Learning
Integrating Strategies and Instruction 39

Analogy Charting 42
Anticipation Guides 45
   Prediction Guides 47
Author Says/I Say 49
   Say Something Read-Aloud 51
B/D/A Questioning Chart 52
Brainstorming Prior Knowledge 55
   LINK 55
   List-Group-Label 56
   Alphabet Brainstorming 57
Chapter Tours 59
Character Quotes 62
   Reading With Attitude 64
Concept/Definition Mapping 66
Connect Two 70
   Possible Sentences 71
Different Perspectives for Reading 73
Discussion Web 76
Double-Entry Diaries 79
First-Person Reading 82
   Eyewitness Testimony Charts 82
   First Impressions 83
   You Ought to Be in Pictures 83
Follow the Characters 86
Guided Imagery 90
Hands-On Reading 93
History Change Frame 96
History Memory Bubbles 99
Inquiry Charts 101
Interactive Reading Guides 104
K-W-L Plus (Know/Want to Know/Learned) . . . 107
Magnet Summaries 111
Math Reading Keys 115
Mind Mapping 118

Paired Reviews 121
   3-Minute Pause 121
   Paired Verbal Fluency 122
   Think/Pair/Share 122
   Reflect/Reflect/Reflect 122
   Line-Up Reviews 123
Power Notes 125
   Power Notes and Concept Maps 127
   Power Notes and Pattern Puzzles 127
Problematic Situations 129
Pyramid Diagram 131
Question–Answer Relationships 133
Questioning the Author 137
   Elaborative Interrogation 139
Quick Writes 141
   Learning Logs 142
   Admit and Exit Slips 143
RAFT (Role/Audience/Format/Topic) 144
Role-Playing as Readers 148
   Point-of-View Study Guides 148
   Readers Theatre 149
Save the Last Word for Me 151
Science Connection Overview 153
Self-Questioning Taxonomy 157
   Self-Questioning for Literary Fiction 158
Story Impressions 162
Story Mapping 166
Structured Note-Taking 170
   Proposition/Support Outlines 172
Student-Friendly Vocabulary Explanations 175
Template Frames 178
Text Coding 180
Vocabulary Overview Guide 183
Word Family Trees 186
Written Conversations 190

APPENDIX Reproducibles 193

About the Author

Doug Buehl is a teacher, staff developer, and adolescent literacy consultant. During his 33 years in the Madison Metropolitan School District in Madison, Wisconsin, USA, Doug was a social studies teacher, reading teacher, and reading specialist at Madison East High School and a district adolescent literacy support teacher. In addition to presenting at literacy workshops, his experiences include collaborating with teachers as a school literacy coach, teaching struggling readers, coordinating a schoolwide content area tutoring program, teaching college preparatory advanced reading, and teaching night school students returning for their high school diploma.

He is the coauthor of *Reading and the High School Student: Strategies to Enhance Literacy* (2nd ed., 2007) and *Strategies to Enhance Literacy and Learning in Middle School Content Area Classrooms* (3rd ed., 2007). In addition, Doug has for nearly two decades written a column on literacy strategies for *OnWEAC*, published by the Wisconsin Education Association Council and available online. He was the first editor of the adolescent literacy newsletter *The Exchange*.

Doug has been an active literacy professional at the local, state, and national levels. He was a founding member of the International Reading Association's (IRA) Commission on Adolescent Literacy and served as president of the Wisconsin State Reading Association (WSRA), the IRA Secondary Reading Interest Group, and the Madison Area Reading Council. Doug was the 1996 recipient of IRA's Nila Banton Smith Award and was inducted to the WSRA Friends of Literacy Hall of Fame in 2000. Recently Doug served as cochair of the Wisconsin Department of Public Instruction Adolescent Literacy Task Force.

Doug is currently an educational consultant and works with school districts to provide professional development for teachers. He is an instructor in adolescent literacy at Edgewood College in Madison, and he is the parent of two sons: Jeremy, a social studies teacher, and Christopher, a biochemist. He lives on the near east side of Madison with his wife, Wendy, a professional violinist and middle school orchestra teacher.

He can be contacted at drbuehl@sbcglobal.net.

Foreword

I am so grateful to Doug Buehl for providing us with a third edition of his immensely useful and popular book of classroom strategies and for his new, insightful framework for developing proficient readers. I know I speak for classroom teachers, specialists and coaches, and college faculty who use his guide regularly when I thank him for this wonderful updated resource.

When I received the draft of this new edition, I quickly looked at the table of contents to see which strategies he had included and how he had organized this edition. I noted the two sections: Section 1, "Developing Strategic Readers and Learners," and Section 2, "Classroom Strategies for Teaching and Learning." I then looked more carefully to see which strategies had survived the test of teachers' evaluation and use. I was happy to see some familiar favorites as well as many new additions—some I was familiar with and others that were intriguing. To accommodate some of the new strategies, he has grouped some that provide variations on a basic strategy focus. This seems a thoughtful way to help teachers adapt their approaches for particular texts and purposes. What treasures in this rich and full collection of strategies!

Then I did what I hope all readers will do: I went to the first section and began reading. It is easy to be tempted to skip ahead to the strategy descriptions and guides; however, I strongly suggest readers begin with the first section and read the first four chapters carefully before exploring the second section. These first chapters provide an important foundation on which decisions about the use of particular strategies can be made. You might want to return to these chapters later and try out some of the reading strategies with them. (For example, Author Says/I Say, B/D/A Questioning Chart, and Paired Reviews can work well with these meaty chapters.)

Buehl gives us a fresh look at comprehension in this edition, grounded in a clear understanding of the various components and processes involved in building understanding. Using characteristics of proficient readers, he clarifies the kinds of thinking that deserve focus—from making connections to prior knowledge and generating questions to synthesizing and self-monitoring. A new chapter on frontloading helps us link the nature of proficient reading with the role of teachers in guiding and developing students' thinking. His explanations of how teachers can model strategic reading, create metacognitive language around reading, use the strategies as scaffolding, and set their goal for student independence provide a clear and thoughtful instructional guide. In addition, within these foundational chapters, Buehl captures what teachers need to think about when working with students to deepen their engagement with texts and to help them become independent, metacognitive learners.

The strategy guides themselves make this book a treasure. They are clearly explained, easy to use, and, most important, they work for students. The variety of guides also makes clear why students deserve scaffolds in reading challenging texts. There are many different ways readers approach texts and many different kinds of thinking that are required in the diversity of text formats read—from mathematical explanations to personal point of view narratives in literature. The wide variety of strategies and the Strategy Indexes make visible the various decisions teachers face when determining how to support students in their negotiation with texts. Reading well is not a simple act; teaching well isn't either. Teachers have received another important "scaffold" in this third edition.

Donna M. Ogle
Past President, International Reading Association
(2001–2002)
Professor of Reading and Language
National-Louis University
Chicago, Illinois, USA

Preface

The first edition of *Classroom Strategies for Interactive Learning* (1995) was an outgrowth of my ongoing collaboration with the Wisconsin Education Association Council (WEAC). Since 1990, I have been the author of the strategies column The Reading Room in WEAC's monthly publication, which circulates to Wisconsin public school teachers and is available online at the WEAC website at www.weac .org/News/reading.htm. This third edition adapts many of those strategies, which were culled from a variety of sources including professional journals, books, and presentations. The book is not intended to be an exhaustive compendium of classroom strategies but aims to streamline strategy discussion so that teachers can readily discern benefits to their students and implement these ideas in their instruction. Teachers who want more in-depth treatment of a strategy can consult the resources listed at the end of each strategy description.

This third edition represents a number of substantial changes from the previous edition. Most obviously, some strategies have been added, others have been dropped, and many have been reworked to reflect new ways of integrating them into instruction. The discussion of each strategy has been heavily influenced by much of the scholarship of the last decade, which has emphasized explicit teaching of comprehension strategies.

As a result, Chapters 1 and 2 are essentially new "territory" and, together with Chapters 3 and 4, provide the foundation for effective use of the 45 strategies outlined in Section 2. Because of these changes, the Strategy Index presented in Section 2 for each classroom strategy has also been updated. Now, each strategy is correlated with the specific comprehension processes that students are engaged in as they are guided through learning from classroom texts. In addition, the Strategy Indexes reveal the instructional focus of each strategy and, as in the second edition, reveal which text frames correlate with each strategy (see Chapter 3).

It was exciting to revisit strategies that have been "old friends" to discover fresh ways to mine their effectiveness with students and to experiment with new methods to support learning from classroom texts. Enjoy, and good luck working with your students!

Acknowledgments

A number of individuals deserve recognition for their roles in this publication. Through his support for my monthly column, Bill Hurley, editor at WEAC, has allowed these strategies to be shared with teachers for nearly two decades. I have also relished many collegial relationships with my fellow teachers during 33 years as a reading specialist and teacher in Madison, Wisconsin, USA. Two former colleagues with the Madison Metropolitan School District deserve special mention. Sharon McPike, the other "half" of our reading team at Madison East High School, has been a constant source of professional input for reality-testing these strategies with our students. Sharyn Stumpf, my co-collaborator as district adolescent literacy support teacher, has added insight and additional perspective toward integrating strategy instruction across the curriculum. My years working with Sharon and Sharyn have been invigorating and greatly rewarding.

My wife, Wendy Buehl, reviewed this manuscript with a keen eye for detecting wayward prose and unclear description. In addition, I have appreciated the spirited discussions about pedagogy that seem to unfold inevitably with the fellow teachers in my family: Wendy, middle school orchestra teacher; my son Jeremy, high school history teacher; and his wife, Mandi, high school chemistry teacher. My son Christopher tolerates all this "teacher talk" with whimsical patience at family gatherings. Finally, I owe a special debt of gratitude to the over three decades' worth of students I was privileged to work with at Madison East High School. I learned much from you and I thank you most humbly.

Developing
Strategic
Readers
and Learners

CHAPTER 1

Teaching for Comprehension

Picture yourself as a reader. Perhaps you see yourself relaxing in the evening, burrowed into a comfortable chair, relishing a good book. Or sipping your morning coffee and perusing the daily newspaper, as you tune into the outside world before you head to work. Or poised in front of a computer monitor, as you navigate your way through an progression of possible websites, quickly inventorying content as you track down a needed snippet of information. It is easy to visualize yourself in a multitude of settings, interacting with a wide spectrum of texts, engaged in the act we call "reading."

Of course, we see people reading all the time, and it is easy to describe the overt behaviors of reading—eyes focusing, pages turning, onscreen texts scrolling. But how would you describe the mental behaviors of reading—what happens in the mind of a reader, the part we cannot see? Pause for a moment and try to put it into words—how would you describe the action "to read"?

Now consider the following "reads":

- The police officer quickly *reads* the situation and decides upon an appropriate response.
- The park ranger is always careful to *read* the skies when escorting hikers into the mountains.
- The coach *reads* the opponents' defense and immediately adjusts the next play.
- The child tries to *read* his mother's reaction to see if he will be permitted to play with his friends.

How well did your definition coincide with these "reads"? Very likely, you conceptualized reading as an activity that focused on the ability to identify written words, recognize their meanings, and create an understanding of an author's message. Yet if we consider read in its broader meaning, we realize that reading is a process that involves strategic examination of some form of information to achieve an understanding. We read to make sense of what we are observing. Making sense—of human interactions, of weather patterns, of competitor's moves, of facial expressions, and of course, of written language—is the purpose of reading.

Our students are expected to read from an impressive array of texts on a daily basis in our classrooms. It is sometimes easy for students, and their teachers,

to lose sight of why they read. Students do not read to complete assignments. They do not read to be prepared for tests. And they do not read to meet standards. They read to understand.

Reading comprehension is fundamental to learning in the subjects we teach. Although some students appear to handle school reading demands successfully, many students experience breakdowns in their attempts to make sense of the texts they encounter in the classroom. How can we explain the dynamics of effective reading? What happens in a reader's mind when comprehension results? How can we use classroom strategies to develop readers who can learn from a wide variety of texts, both print and electronic?

Reading Comprehension: What Do Proficient Readers Do?

Imagine the following episode in your life as a reader. You are spending enjoyable minutes immersed in a national news magazine. As you page through it, you quickly size up articles and make instant decisions whether to continue on or linger a while and read. Suddenly the headline "Caution: Killing Germs May Be Hazardous to Your Health" (Adler & Interlandi, 2007) catches your attention. You are intrigued. Aren't germs harmful, you wonder? Isn't that why we need antibiotics? Before you realize it, you have launched into reading this article.

The authors refer to microbes, and you briefly ponder what you remember about these microscopic creatures. Bacteria, you think, and maybe viruses. You remember that your body harbors "good" bacteria, so you theorize that the author might focus on killing the wrong germs. You also recall concerns about doctors overprescribing antibiotics. As you read on, some of your questions are answered and new ones surface. The authors do emphasize that attacks on microbes impel them to mutate into stronger and deadlier forms. You revise your definition of microbes to include fungi and protozoa.

Some paragraphs are stuffed with unfamiliar scientific terminology, and these you rapidly glance over to extract the gist of the message: Serious microbe-causing ailments are on the rise. You are particularly struck by the vivid descriptions of the human body as a colony consisting of tens of trillions of microbes, which help define us as well as facilitate our abilities to function as living organisms. (I should start referring to myself as "we" rather than "I," you whimsically muse.) Images are constantly triggered by the text: bacteria in the teeth, salmonella in the digestive tract, friendly microbes inhabiting our skin.

As you finish the article you still have questions: How dangerous might some microbes become? What will it take for people to adopt more common-sense practices with their "co-inhabitants"? How should I change my behavior? As you pause for a few moments, you realize your understanding of germs has significantly changed as you now have an image of yourself as a "considerate host" who needs these fellow travelers as much as they need you.

The description in the preceding scenario illustrates a reader thoughtfully engaged with a written text. This scenario parallels what proficient readers do as a matter of habit. Research reveals that proficient readers employ a host of comprehension strategies as they read and learn. These comprehension strategies provide the bedrock for learning in our classrooms, from the early grades through high school and college.

However, the reality in our classrooms is that many students do not regularly exhibit proficient reader behaviors with school reading tasks. Teachers often feel resigned to the fact that, when it comes to reading comprehension, some students will inevitably "get it," and some students won't. Instead of thoughtful engagement with text that works toward understanding, many students resort to the following three typical ineffective reading practices.

1. **Skimming for answers.** Much of what we call "school reading" falls into this category. Students are preoccupied with completing an assignment, and if an activity overemphasizes locating literal information rather than comprehension, they can in effect bypass reading and skim for details that can be copied down. Although homework might appear to be acceptable, students have only taken a superficial look at the text and comprehension has not occurred.

2. **Surface processing.** Another common ineffective practice is reading without thinking about what an author is trying to communicate. Students may dutifully read the assigned text, but although their eyes are looking at words, they do not engage in an inner dialogue with the author and themselves. As a result, students essentially read "to get done," and teachers hear the familiar refrain: "I read it but I didn't understand it."

3. **Reading and forgetting.** Finally, students who do not employ proficient reader strategies are unlikely to

learn from their reading. Because they have not personalized an understanding of what an author is telling them, new learning is highly vulnerable to rapid forgetting. Consequently, students are able to demonstrate little carry-over from their reading to class discussions, follow-up activities, and assessments.

So what do proficient readers do? What are the characteristics of proficient reading, and how can we get our students to exhibit these behaviors when they read?

Comprehension Processes of Proficient Readers

Proficient reading abilities are integral to the literacy challenges and choices we make as adults each day of our lives. Likewise, proficient reading abilities are integral for learning. For students to achieve success in learning in social studies and science, literature and mathematics, in fact, in all curricular areas, they need to develop strategic comprehension behaviors. In particular, the increasing availability of a vast reservoir of information from Internet sources mandates that students develop proficient reader characteristics.

In their seminal work on comprehension instruction, Keene and Zimmermann (2007) frame the rich vein of research on proficient readers around seven characteristic modes of thinking that are in constant interplay when an individual is engaged in understanding (see Table 1). As you examine these essential components of comprehension, notice how each was integral to the dynamics of reading described in the "germs" example.

Making Connections to Prior Knowledge

Instructional activities that prompt students to reflect upon existing knowledge about a topic, especially before starting to read, can help them effectively read even confusing or challenging material. Researchers argue that prior knowledge—what a person already knows—may be the most important variable for understanding. This search for meaningful connections activates previous learning and taps into past experiences, which help readers understand new information and establish interest, motivation, and purpose for reading a specific text. Many students, especially struggling readers, tend to dive into a reading assignment without assessing how their background knowledge can help them make sense of what an author is saying.

Generating Questions

Instructional activities that elicit self-questioning spark a highly active mindset during learning. Self-questioning, of course, is very different from answering

Table 1
Comprehension Processes of Proficient Readers

Comprehension Process	Description
Making Connections to Prior Knowledge	Reading comprehension results when readers can match what they already know (their schema) with new information and ideas in a text. Proficient readers activate prior knowledge before, during, and after reading and they constantly evaluate how a text enhances or alters their previous understandings.
Generating Questions	Comprehension is, to a significant degree, a process of inquiry. Proficient readers pose questions to themselves as they read. Asking questions is the art of carrying on an inner conversation with an author, as well as an internal dialogue within one's self.
Creating Mental Images	Comprehension involves breathing life experiences into the abstract language of written texts. Proficient readers use visual, auditory, and other sensory connections to create mental images of an author's message.
Making Inferences	Much of what is to be understood in a text must be inferred. Authors rely on readers to contribute to a text's meaning by linking their background knowledge to information in the text. In addition to acknowledging explicitly stated messages, proficient readers "read between the lines" to discern implicit meanings, make predictions, and read with a critical eye.
Determining Importance	Our memories quickly overload unless we can pare down a text to its essential ideas. Texts contain key ideas and concepts amidst much background detail. Proficient readers strive to differentiate key ideas, themes, and information from details so that they are not overwhelmed by facts.
Synthesizing	Proficient readers glean the essence of a text (determine importance) and organize these ideas into coherent summaries of meaning. Effective comprehension leads to new learning and the development of new schema (background knowledge). Proficient readers make evaluations, construct generalizations, and draw conclusions from a text.
Monitoring Reading and Applying Fix-Up Strategies	Proficient readers "watch" themselves as they read and expect to make adjustments in their strategies to ensure that they are able to achieve a satisfactory understanding of a text.

Source: Buehl, D. (2007). A professional development framework for embedding comprehension instruction into content classrooms. In J. Lewis & G. Moorman (Eds.), *Adolescent literacy instruction: Policies and promising practices* (p. 200). Newark, DE: International Reading Association.

someone else's questions. Rather than "leaning back" to receive information, learners who raise their own questions are personally interacting with new ideas and using questions to try to make sense of what they are encountering. When readers wonder about something—wonder why, wonder if, wonder where, wonder whether, wonder what, wonder how—they are raising questions that a written text may address. They also use self-questioning to check their progress: Did this make sense? Should I double-check information in that last paragraph to ensure that I did not misread it? Did I satisfactorily figure out the probable meaning of that unfamiliar term? Do I need to clarify anything in this passage?

Creating Mental Images

Instructional activities that stimulate student imaginations help them picture in their mind's eye what an author represents in written language. When readers are deeply engaged in imagining what a text is describing, it is as if the words disappear and instead a personal DVD is playing in their heads. Visualizing involves linking cues from the author's words with personal experiences as readers mentally craft their own versions of scenes and events. Visualizing is quite idiosyncratic because no two individuals bring exactly the same set of experiences to draw upon when creating mental images from suggested language. Students who become bogged down in the words on the page may forget to visualize, and as a result have trouble relating to what is being portrayed by an author.

Making Inferences

Instructional activities that assist students in identifying and analyzing implied meanings in a text enable them to merge clues from an author with their prior knowledge to construct a more complete understanding of a text. Facility with inferential thinking develops from an awareness that authors expect readers to fill in the gaps between what they are able to put into writing and what readers themselves should bring to a text. In addition, inferences are necessary to flesh out the beliefs, attitudes, and perspectives that influence an author's message. Predicting—encouraging readers to take stock of what they have read so far to think ahead and anticipate what an author might say—is a particularly critical inferential reading behavior.

> *"Given knowledge about what good readers do when they read, researchers and educators have addressed the following question: Can we teach students to engage in these productive behaviors? The answer is a resounding yes." (Duke & Pearson, 2002, p. 206)*

Determining Importance

Instructional activities that help students sort key ideas and concepts from background details focus attention on questions such as, What is the point of this? or Why is the author telling me this? Students often miss the point an author may be sharing in a written text and instead find themselves lost in a maze of factual detail. Comprehension depends on readers' making reflective decisions as to what is worthy of remembering over time. Classroom strategies that help students perceive the structure of a text—the relationships between ideas and information—are a prerequisite for determining importance.

Synthesizing

Instructional activities that engage students in summarizing what they read into personal understandings are absolutely necessary if learners are to reduce a mass of material into a manageable distillation. Synthesizing is the culmination of comprehension—to synthesize, learners must make connections, raise questions, visualize, make inferences, and determine importance. Because of the transcendent nature of synthesizing, most students find summarizing to be a difficult process. Synthesis is that "Aha! I get it!" moment, which allows readers to develop their personal interpretation of an author's message and to establish their "take" on what a text might mean to them.

Monitoring Reading and Applying Fix-Up Strategies

The 45 classroom strategies in Section 2 all model proactive methods for successfully reading challenging texts so that students become comfortable with problem-solving options for understanding a text and achieving their purposes for reading. When proficient readers encounter breakdowns in their comprehension—difficult vocabulary, unfamiliar references—they pause to make a determination whether to adjust their reading, or to use additional strategies to make sense of the unclear passage. Proficient readers do not proclaim, "I read it, but I didn't understand it." They know that reading *means* you understood it.

Constructing Meaning

These proficient reader characteristics represent a marked contrast with former ways of conceptualizing reading comprehension, which was described more as a skill than as an active mental process. Reading was conceived to be the skill of recognizing letters and words, which led to the ability to connect words into sentences, sentences into paragraphs, and paragraphs into longer passages that represented various themes or ideas. If a student could recount what was in the text—in other words, reproduce what an author had written—then we concluded that comprehension had occurred. If a student could not recount, then we explained that the student was lacking in reading ability, the student had poor study skills, or the text was too difficult.

Instead, current research on reading comprehension underscores that a reader constructs meaning from a text rather than merely reproduces the words on the page. Comprehension happens when readers actively create meaning; they do not passively receive it. No two people will have exactly the same comprehension of a text because no two people will be reading a text under exactly the same conditions. According to the RAND Reading Study Group (2002), the interactions among the following four conditions determine what meaning a reader will construct from a text:

1. What the *reader* brings to the reading situation
2. The characteristics of the written *text*
3. The *activity* that defines the task and purpose of the reader
4. The *context* within which the reading occurs

The Reader

Teachers know that every student brings certain skills as a reader to the classroom. Too often, we might over-attribute comprehension breakdowns to skill deficits: word identification ("this student does not apply phonics skills"), fluency ("this student reads slowly and word-by-word"), or reading technique ("this student lacks study skills"). Although these are certainly facets of what it means to be a reader, it is too simplistic to focus solely on whether students have developed specific reading skills. Because comprehension relies on a mental construction that intertwines what is on the page with what is already known, the background knowledge and experiences of the reader are primary determinants of how a text will be understood. The more students already know about a topic, the better they will be able to comprehend texts about that topic. If their background knowledge includes much of the content vocabulary that appears, for instance, in a passage on medieval cathedrals or in an article on creatures that live in the ocean, then comprehension is enhanced correspondingly. Additionally, students may have developed the facility to read materials typical of some content disciplines but may struggle with texts in other subject areas. Finally, comprehension is influenced greatly by personal reasons for reading a particular text and the willingness or motivation to do so.

The Text

What are students expected to read in our classrooms? A textbook...a short story...a magazine article...a website? As the RAND Reading Study Group (2002) concluded,

> The texts that children read in today's schools are substantially more diverse than those in use several decades ago.... We now live in a world that is experiencing an explosion of alternative texts that vary in content, readability levels, and genre. They incorporate multimedia and electronic options and pertain to a variety of cultures and groups. This variety makes it much more difficult for teachers to select appropriate texts for individual readers. (p. 24)

Traditionally, teachers have relied upon readability formulas and grade-level designations to gauge difficulty of reading material. Currently, computerized evaluations of a text's vocabulary load and sentence complexity provide teachers with Lexile scores, which can be used to better match reading materials to students. But Lexile scores are not available for many of the texts students read, and factors such as how content is presented, density of concepts, and available study features need careful consideration. In addition, the author's language and the text's organizational structure—from the sentence level up through entire chapters or units—play a critical role in the process of constructing meaning. (See Chapter 3 for a discussion of the impact of organizational text frames on reading.) Clearly, some texts are written and organized in ways that are more reader-friendly than others, as anyone who has struggled through a computer manual can attest. Finally, the unique nature of hypertexts, that require readers to select their pathway through the text according to individual needs and priorities, present special concerns and challenges.

The Activity

Why does a person read a specific text? Comprehension is significantly affected by the nature of the reading activity. Did students select the reading material, or did someone else? Are they reading to enhance their knowledge about a topic, to discover how to accomplish a task, to experience a kind of thinking, or to appreciate and enjoy an author's craft? Who determines what constitutes adequate comprehension—the reader or someone else? In the classroom, teacher expectations and instructions determine the way a student approaches reading. Does the assignment require a careful examination for mastery of details, or will a general understanding of the major ideas suffice? Will the information be discussed the next day, tested a week later, or used to complete a project? After the reading, will students complete a worksheet, answer inferential questions, develop their interpretations, write an essay, or conduct a lab experiment? Are students expected to do independent work, or can they collaborate in their reading with others? Student comprehension of a text will vary considerably depending on the messages the teacher sends through the parameters of a reading assignment.

The Context

Reading, of course, does not occur in a vacuum. A reader's comprehension is influenced by a variety of contextual factors: physical conditions such as noise level and comfort (on the bus, in a classroom, in bed), time elements (early morning, late in the school day, midnight), and the support, encouragement, and attitudes of others (family members, peers, teachers). In the classroom, a teacher assumes primary responsibility for creating the environment for reading. Is reading emphasized primarily as an isolated, solitary act, or are students constantly provided opportunities to interact as they develop their understandings? How have students been mentored to respect and assist each other as they collaborate on classroom tasks? How are the multiple perspectives that individual readers bring to specific texts honored and encouraged? Are students comfortable risking the interjection of their ideas and viewpoints into the classroom conversation? Are discussions of text open to a range of possible interpretations as students grapple with their understandings, or are students conditioned to supply a "correct" response?

Readers as Apprentices

As proficient readers meaningfully negotiate this sophisticated interaction among the reader, a specific text, a focusing activity, and the context for reading, they automatically shift into the characteristic modes of thinking outlined as comprehension processes. Proficient readers might employ a number of effective study tactics as they strive to achieve an understanding: previewing a selection, rereading a difficult passage, adjusting reading rate, underlining pertinent information, tracking thoughts in the margin, using context to figure out new vocabulary, creating a graphic representation, jotting down notes, and periodically summing up understanding. Of course, which study tactics readers select depend on why they are reading a selection, how familiar they are with its content, and which tactics they are skilled in applying.

> *"Numerous studies over the past few decades have demonstrated that it is most helpful to teach comprehension strategies, text structures, and word-level strategies while students are engaged in reading challenging, content-rich texts. Such skills don't stick when practiced for their own sake."* (Heller & Greenleaf, 2007, p. 8)

But how about the majority of our students, those students who have not yet developed such a degree of independence as readers? How can we interweave proficient reader comprehension strategies into the daily instruction of our course content? In many classrooms, this question is quite frankly not addressed—if students are not yet proficient readers they will be left to figure out the adjustments they need to make on their own. At times, teachers do confront this issue but usually focus on a study tactic—taking notes, for example. Students may be shown how to take notes and then expected to use a note-taking format as a class requirement, but if the underlying comprehension strategy of determining importance is not directly emphasized during instruction then student note-taking may reflect little more than an arduous copying activity that does not facilitate comprehension.

The classroom strategies presented in Section 2 of this book depend on an apprentice learning model for comprehension instruction (Schoenbach, Greenleaf, Cziko, & Hurwitz, 1999). In their classic treatise on reading comprehension, Pearson and Gallagher (1983) coined the phrase *Gradual Release of Responsibility* to describe this apprenticeship dynamic in the classroom. Basing their model on the ideas of the great Russian educational theorist Lev Vygotsky, Pearson and Gallagher envisioned instruction that moved from explicit modeling and instruction, to guided practice, and then to activities that incrementally position students to become independent learners.

Consider times in your life when you were treated as an apprentice learner. For me, this model reflects the natural dynamic of growing up on a Wisconsin dairy farm, which meant a childhood where work and home were interchangeable. As a youngster, much of my time was spent alongside my parents as they engaged in the varied tasks of farming: bumping along on a dusty hay rack as bales of fragrant alfalfa were piled higher and higher, trailing pails of frothy milk being carried down the barn driveway to the milkhouse, tagging along on the daily circuit of chores, and managing the livestock. As a farm kid, I was expected to eventually assume responsibility for many of the tasks I had been witnessing from an early age. Gradually, I became trusted at the steering wheel of the Allis Chalmers tractor, first under the supervision of my father, then more and more out on my own, until I was regarded as a capable operator who could hitch up machinery and reliably accomplish fieldwork independent of my parents.

As an apprentice learner during those years, I was accorded ample opportunities to experience firsthand the work of the farm being properly executed. I was encouraged to ask questions—why things were done a certain way and what could happen if they weren't. I was granted the benefit of my parents' thinking, as they solved problems while they worked. I was given guidance and supervision as I began to try my hand at a range of important jobs. I was treated like someone who was capable of handling responsibility and doing the work, and it was also clear that I was transitioning into the role of peer, someone who would be expected to take over a slice of the daily farm routine, a person who could be "on my own."

This same apprentice learning model is necessary to mentor students progressively developing their comprehension abilities. In the classroom, Gradual Release of Responsibility (see Figure 1) begins with teacher modeling. Students need continued opportunities to see an expert—the teacher—at work, interacting with texts and showcasing thinking that undergirds doing a task well. The first stage of the Gradual Release

Figure 1
Gradual Release of Responsibility

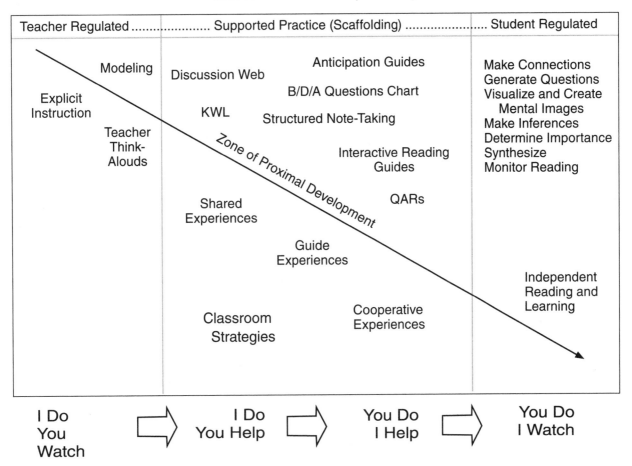

Teacher Regulated .... Supported Practice (Scaffolding) .... Student Regulated

Modeling

Explicit Instruction

Teacher Think-Alouds

Discussion Web

KWL

Anticipation Guides

B/D/A Questions Chart

Structured Note-Taking

Zone of Proximal Development

Interactive Reading Guides

QARs

Shared Experiences

Guide Experiences

Classroom Strategies

Cooperative Experiences

Make Connections
Generate Questions
Visualize and Create Mental Images
Make Inferences
Determine Importance
Synthesize
Monitor Reading

Independent Reading and Learning

I Do
You
Watch

I Do
You Help

You Do
I Help

You Do
I Watch

Note: Parts adapted from Wilhelm, J.D., Baker, T.N., & Dube, J. (2001). *Strategic reading: Guiding students to lifelong literacy, 6–12.* Portsmouth, NH: Heinemann.

model assumes that many students will at first not be able to handle the task that is the focus of the lesson. Students—novice learners in a topic area—may be confused about how to approach reading material in a particular content area or how to perform a specific activity. A "think-aloud" is a particularly powerful method for teachers to model their thinking as they make sense of a text. A think-aloud provides students with a window into the wisdom and strategy employed by an accomplished thinker during reading. These short sharing sessions become a means for modeling the thinking you will expect your students to try when they are confronted with a similar learning task.

Think-alouds need to underscore that the brain of an effective learner is constantly abuzz with mental activity, that thinking is not accidental but highly purposeful, and that thinking is always open to revision and reinterpretation. In addition, proficient readers sometimes encounter difficult texts, and, like many

students in your classroom, do not immediately "get it." But proficient readers know what to try to make sure that they can achieve a satisfactory level of comprehension. Short texts, or excerpts from assigned classroom material such as the textbook, make excellent sources for modeling your thinking.

Much of classroom instruction should take place in the central area of the Gradual Release model—the zone of proximal development (Vygotsky, 1978). During this stage students experiment with what you have modeled, as they converse with you and with other classmates to clarify their thinking and practice their new routines. "Teaching in the zone" relies on scaffolding, support that is integrated with a lesson to guide student learning and prompt effective thinking. A scaffold is a temporary structure that is constructed to help someone complete a task that would otherwise be very difficult. We use scaffolds frequently in life: scaffolds that are assembled to facilitate erecting or repairing a building, scaffolds used by painters to reach otherwise inaccessible areas; scaffolds dangling from high-rise offices that allow window washers to undertake a task unimaginable without such a device. But when the job is completed, scaffolds are dismantled; they are temporary structures.

Likewise, the classroom strategies in Section 2 of this book represent scaffolding, temporary lessons constructed to help students as they embark on unfamiliar thinking but designed to fade away as students become comfortable with learning and working without this type of teacher guidance. A critical aspect of scaffolding in the classroom is teacher feedback. Students need continual dialogue with a knowledgeable mentor to help focus their efforts and problem-solve through difficulties. Students will fail at times during scaffolded lessons, but they need to realize that failure during new learning is a normal phenomenon. Helping students digest what went wrong and why, and what needs to be done the next time, is an essential component of "teaching in the zone."

The Gradual Release model assumes that students will need considerable work that is scaffolded before they become independent. A number of educational observers argue that this dynamic of instruction—scaffolding—is not always adequately achieved in the classroom. Teachers may expect students to demonstrate independent thinking and learning before they have had sufficient practice and feedback to really get good at it. Struggling readers in particular need scaffolded lessons that remind them what effective thinkers do during learning and that guide them through challenging texts.

The rationale of the Gradual Release model is to cede increasing responsibility for directing their own learning to the students. Students need regular reminders that the focal point of instruction is to empower them to accomplish important and sophisticated tasks while phasing out the support of the teacher and their classmates. The Gradual Release model emphasizes comprehension instruction that mentors students into becoming capable thinkers and learners when handling the tasks with which they have not yet developed expertise.

> *"Vygotsky's ideas about actively assisting and instructing students to do complex cognitive tasks and for guiding them through the 'zone of proximal development'—the level at which they can do things with help that they cannot do alone—are apparent in highly successful programs for elementary students.... However, we rarely see these approaches used with older students." (Wilhelm, Baker, & Dube, 2001, p. 10)*

Metacognitive Conversations

Although classroom strategies like those presented in Section 2 of this book are becoming more commonplace in classrooms, researchers are concerned that students do not necessarily "own" them. If students are not privy to the insider thinking that made a particular strategy effective, they may not become more independent learners; instead, they will continue to depend on constant guidance from teachers in order to effectively learn course content.

"What were you thinking?" is the preeminent question that governs the learning in our classrooms. But if students are not accorded frequent opportunities to listen in on the thinking of successful learners, then how learning unfolds will remain a mystery. Their struggles and failures may lead many students to conclude that they lack the ability to learn the material. If students are regularly supplied with strong mental models for thinking as they read and learn across the curriculum, they can gradually emulate such effective thinking themselves. Therefore, making thinking public must assume a central role in classroom learning.

Researchers refer to these public discussions of thinking as *metacognitive conversations* (Schoenbach et al., 1999). Metacognition is a state of awareness about one's thinking; people who are metacognitive not only track *what* they are thinking but also monitor *how* they constructed their thoughts and *why* they decided upon the strategies to use to best achieve comprehension. Metacognitive learners are in personal control of their learning.

Metacognitive conversations invite students into the dialogue about thinking. The teacher's objective is ongoing classroom talk not only about what students are thinking but also about how they arrived at their thoughts. When students provide a response in your classroom, they should immediately expect a follow-up: "Talk about how you figured that out." "Tell us more about your thinking." These text-based discussions ask students to notice and then reconstruct their thinking as they read. Students who achieved comprehension fairly rapidly are not always cognizant of what it was that they did that served them well. Asking them to articulate their thinking reimmerses them into their thought processes, which may lead them to discover further ideas about a text.

Metacognitive conversations are especially critical for students who struggle with learning. Many of our students observe the people around them "getting it" on a daily basis, without truly knowing what they could do differently that would help them achieve a better understanding. As a result, many students question their intelligence and adopt a fatalistic approach to reading: "I probably won't be able to understand it, no matter what I try."

Metacognitive conversations involve all students in the inside game of learning—the *how* and *why* as well as the *what*. The more students are able to "eavesdrop" on the mental deliberations of others, and contribute their own versions of possible ways to think about a text, the more comfortable all students will become with tracking and adjusting their thinking during learning. Teachers should schedule regular debriefing sessions during classroom lessons that prompt metacognitive conversations. Students need to recognize how the structure of a lesson enhanced their learning and cued proficient reader behaviors such as making connections to background knowledge, posing questions to oneself and of the author, or determining what is most important in an author's message. Debriefing sessions focus discussion on how the classroom activities led to comprehension. Without a debriefing session, the students will leave the classroom still unduly dependent on a well-organized lesson to guide their learning. If students are to transition into increasingly independent learning, they need to regularly talk about their own thinking during the course of an effective lesson.

Metacognitive conversations can be categorized as *external* conversations: They take place in public, they are social in that multiple learners are included in the discussions, and students are not compelled to infer the direction of thought that led other students to their interpretations and conclusions. Ultimately, these metacognitive conversations need to become self-programmed as *internal* conversations—the mental dialogues we have with ourselves that shape our thinking as we read and learn. A variety of methods can be used with students to prompt the internal metacognitive conversation. Asking students to talk about their thinking in journal entries or learning logs is a popular strategy.

Metacognitive conversations are a natural fit for classroom discussions about learning. These critical discussions need to assume a permanent and organic role in classroom routines. Students become privileged to the inner workings of effective minds at work, allowing them to experiment with their own thinking as learners. In addition, students become increasingly comfortable using one another as learning resources, as discussions center less on "tell me the right answer" and more on "tell me how you decided that was the right answer."

Building Independent Learners

As teachers, we know that students will not learn everything they need to know in the 13 years leading up to graduation from high school. In daily work with students, we strive to encourage them to become life-long learners who will continue to deepen their understandings related to the various subject areas we teach. By using classroom strategies that scaffold comprehension, we foster the development of individuals who are purposeful thinkers and increasingly proficient readers.

It is perhaps easy for teachers to become discouraged with the ineffective reading behaviors they witness in their classrooms. When teachers believe their students are not capable of independently handling reading assignments, they frequently downplay the role of reading in their curriculum. Teacher presentations, hands-on activities, and other media replace written texts in classroom learning. Although all these methods of instruction have value, when students no longer read even average and above-average students fall behind in their development. Indeed, an extensive study by the American College Testing program (ACT, 2006) concluded that only 51% of today's college-bound students in the United States have developed the ability to read the complex texts central to college learning and the workplace. According the ACT, this alarming statistic is the result of years of teachers' neglecting to provide students with sufficient practice and instruction in reading appropriate texts in their subject areas.

Classroom strategies can play a significant role in developing proficient reader behaviors for all students. When teachers fully incorporate comprehension instruction into the fabric of their daily teaching, students not only learn more, but they also continue to develop their capacity as readers of increasingly more sophisticated texts. Table 2 indexes the 45 classroom strategies presented in Section 2 of this book according to the comprehension processes that receive instructional emphasis during application of each strategy. These comprehension processes are also provided in a Strategy Index that is displayed for each individual strategy in Section 2 of this book.

References

ACT. (2006). *Reading between the lines: What the ACT reveals about college readiness in reading.* Iowa City: Author. Available at www.act.org/research/policymakers/reports/reading.html

Adler, J., & Interlandi, J. (2007, October 29). Caution: Killing germs may be hazardous to your health. *Newsweek, CL*(18), 45–48.

Buehl, D. (2007). A professional development framework for embedding comprehension instruction into content classrooms. In J. Lewis & G. Moorman (Eds.), *Adolescent literacy instruction: Policies and promising practices* (pp. 192–211). Newark, DE: International Reading Association.

Duke, N.K., & Pearson, P.D. (2002). Effective practices for developing reading comprehension. In A. Farstrup & S.J. Samuels (Eds.), *What research has to say about reading instruction*

Table 2
Classroom Strategies Indexed by Comprehension Process

Comprehension Process	Classroom Strategies		
Making Connections to Prior Knowledge	Analogy Charting Anticipation Guide Author Says/I Say Brainstorming Prior Knowledge Concept/Definition Mapping Connect Two Different Perspectives Double-Entry Diaries Hands-On Reading History Change Frame Inquiry Charts Interactive Reading Guide	K-W-L Plus (Know/Want to Know/Learned) Math Reading Keys Mind Mapping Paired Reviews Problematic Situations Question–Answer Relationships Questioning the Author Quick Writes RAFT (Role/Audience/ Format/Topic) Role-Playing as Readers	Save the Last Word For Me Science Connection Overview Self-Questioning Taxonomy Story Impressions Student-Friendly Vocabulary Explanations Text Coding Vocabulary Overview Guide Word Family Trees Written Conversations
Generating Questions	Analogy Charting Anticipation Guide Author Says/I Say B/D/A Questioning Chart Brainstorming Prior Knowledge Chapter Tours Different Perspectives Double-Entry Diaries Follow the Characters Hands-On Reading History Change Frame	History Memory Bubbles Inquiry Charts Interactive Reading Guide K-W-L Plus (Know/Want to Know/Learned) Math Reading Keys Mind Mapping Paired Reviews Problematic Situations Role-Playing as Readers Question–Answer Relationships	Questioning the Author Save The Last Word For Me Science Connection Overview Self-Questioning Taxonomy Story Impressions Story Mapping Text Coding Written Conversations
Creating Mental Images	Analogy Charting Character Quotes Different Perspectives Double-Entry Diaries Follow the Characters First-Person Reading Guided Imagery	Hands-On Reading Interactive Reading Guides Mind Mapping Paired Reviews Problematic Situations RAFT (Role/Audience/ Format/Topic)	Role-Playing as Readers Self-Questioning Taxonomy Student-Friendly Vocabulary Explanations Text Coding

(continued)

Comprehension Process	Classroom Strategies		
Making Inferences	Analogy Charting Anticipation Guides Author Says/I Say Character Quotes Connect Two Different Perspectives Discussion Web Double-Entry Diaries First-Person Reading Follow the Characters Guided Imagery Hands-On Reading	Inquiry Charts Interactive Reading Guides K-W-L Plus (Know/Want to Know/Learned) Math Reading Keys Paired Reviews Question–Answer Relationships Questioning the Author RAFT (Role/Audience/Format/Topic) Role-Playing as Readers	Save the Last Word For Me Self-Questioning Taxonomy Story Mapping Student-Friendly Vocabulary Explanations Text Coding Vocabulary Overview Guide Word Family Trees Written Conversations
Determining Importance	Analogy Charting Anticipation Guide Author Says/I Say Chapter Tours Connect Two Discussion Web Double-Entry Diaries Follow the Characters Hands-On Reading History Change Frame History Memory Bubbles	Inquiry Charts Interactive Reading Guides K-W-L Plus (Know/Want to Know/Learned) Magnet Summaries Mind Mapping Paired Reviews Power Notes Pyramid Diagram Questioning the Author Quick Writes	Science Connection Overview Self-Questioning Taxonomy Story Mapping Structured Note-Taking Template Frames Text Coding Vocabulary Overview Guide Written Conversations
Synthesizing	Analogy Charting Author Says/I Say B/D/A Questioning Chart Character Quotes Concept/Definition Mapping Connect Two Different Perspectives Discussion Web Double-Entry Diaries First-Person Reading Follow the Characters	History Memory Bubbles Inquiry Charts Interactive Reading Guide K-W-L Plus (Know/Want to Know/Learned) Magnet Summaries Paired Reviews Point-of-View Guides Power Notes Pyramid Diagram Quick Writes RAFT (Role/Audience/Format/Topic)	Role-Playing as Readers Save The Last Word For Me Self-Questioning Taxonomy Story Mapping Student-Friendly Vocabulary Explanations Structured Note-Taking Template Frames Text Coding Written Conversations

(3rd ed., pp. 205–242). Newark, DE: International Reading Association.

Heller, R., & Greenleaf, C.L. (2007). *Literacy instruction in the content areas: Getting to the core of middle and high school improvement*. Washington, DC: Alliance for Excellent Education.

Keene, E.O., & Zimmermann, S. (2007). *Mosaic of thought: The power of comprehension strategy instruction* (2nd ed.). Portsmouth, NH: Heinemann.

Pearson, P.D., & Gallagher, M.C. (1983). The instruction of reading comprehension. *Contemporary Educational Psychology, 8*(3), 317–344. doi:10.1016/0361-476X(83)90019-X

RAND Reading Study Group. (2002). *Reading for understanding: Toward an R&D program in reading comprehension*. Santa Monica, CA: RAND.

Schoenbach, R., Greenleaf, C., Cziko, C., & Hurwitz, L. (1999). *Reading for understanding: A guide to improving reading in middle and high school classrooms*. San Francisco: Jossey-Bass.

Vygotsky, L.S. (1978). *Mind and society: The development of higher psychological processes*. Cambridge, MA: Harvard University Press.

Wilhelm, J.D., Baker, T.N., & Dube, J. (2001). *Strategic reading: Guiding students to lifelong literacy*, 6–12. Portsmouth, NH: Heinemann.

CHAPTER 2

Frontloading: The Key to Comprehension

*Z*oonosis—the word leaps out at you from a newspaper headline. This is a word you perhaps can't ever remember seeing before. Your curiosity thus piqued, you decide to see what this author has to say about this intriguing concept. You soon discover that Ebola, yellow fever, SARS, Lyme disease, and the West Nile virus are all examples of zoonosis. The author concedes that zoonosis is unfamiliar jargon to most of us, but warns that in the coming years we will increasingly encounter this phenomenon. Of course, you do know something about this uncommon term. You recognize the prefix *zoo-*, which means having to do with animals. You know that zoology is the branch of biology concerned with animals, and we all can connect to zoos, where animals are kept for exhibition. The author explains zoonosis as diseases that jump from animals to humans, and profiles scientific discoveries about these often fatal contagions, which are an ever-present reality in our lives. The author has a wealth of new insights on zoonosis to share with you.

In return, however, the author expects a great deal from you as a reader. The author assumes that you are already well-versed in the impact of past diseases such as rabies and smallpox, that you are geographically literate, and that you bring a degree of awareness of different cultures and conditions around the world. But in particular, the author posits readers who can tap into an extensive background in science. Terminology such as *pathogen, vectored, protozoan, prion, virulence, pandemic, ecosystem,* and *host species* predominate in this article, and the author especially focuses on standard research methods employed by scientists to investigate the world around us.

Your comprehension of such an article, then, is contingent on your ability to draw upon your previous knowledge base to meet this author's expectations, so that you can understand what the author assumes will be new knowledge to most readers. Perhaps the most fundamental question a reader must bring to any text is: "What does this author assume I already know?" Proficient readers become adept at sizing up their reading to determine the *match*. To what extent do the author's assumptions about what readers know match what they do indeed know? If the author and readers are "on the same page," then they "get" what

the author is telling them—there was an acceptable match between author demands and their knowledge. However, if the author assumes readers will know things that they do not know, a mismatch results. They are likely to be confused, frustrated, and confronted with a text that doesn't make sense. *Mismatches* undermine a reader's efforts to comprehend.

"Matching Up" With Authors: The Role of Hidden Knowledge

Daily classroom experiences with reading reveal frequent mismatches; many students capable of understanding fall short because an author assumes background knowledge that is lacking. Indeed, Alexander and Jetton (2000) conclude, "Of all the factors considered in this exploration, none exerts more influence on what students understand and remember than the knowledge they possess" (p. 291).

Imagine a student's background knowledge as a gray file cabinet standing in the corner of your classroom. The file cabinet represents a memory bank of everything a student knows about the world—personal experiences, perceptions, and definitions of reality. The contents of the cabinet provide the basis for the student's learning. The knowledge in the cabinet is divided into drawers, then into sections within the drawers, and finally into file folders within the sections. Sometimes new information is integrated with the mental file folders. If a folder is already bulging with knowledge about a particular topic, reading about that topic will add new pieces of information to an already well-understood topic. However, if a folder is empty or no folder exists for a topic, then reading comprehension will be imprecise, incomplete, and problematic. For example, consider your comprehension of the following sentence:

> There's a bear in a plain brown wrapper doing flip-flops on 78, taking pictures, and passing out green stamps.

> *"While reading, thoughtful readers use prior knowledge constantly to evaluate the adequacy of the model of meaning they have developed. This is true for readers of all ages or levels of sophistication." (Pearson, Roehler, Dole, & Duffy, 1992, p. 154)*

What does this sentence seem to be about? How confident are you of your interpretation? Is there anything particularly complicated about this text? Do you understand the vocabulary? On one level, this appears to be a deceptively simple statement—no hard words or intricate sentence structure. A readability score would place its difficulty at an elementary grade level. Therefore, if your comprehension falters, it is likely due to a mismatch between author assumptions and your knowledge. In fact, readers who "match-up" with the author of this sentence could confidently translate the sentence as follows:

> There's a law enforcement officer in an unmarked patrol car going back and forth across the median on highway 78, using radar and issuing speeding tickets.

Shaky initial comprehension of this sentence cannot be attributed to inadequate reading skills, difficult vocabulary, or complex writing style. Instead, the sentence will not make sense to many readers because of confusion about the author's message. You probably asked: "What do I know that can help me figure out this passage?" You were struggling to make a meaningful connection to the material. As readers, we are constantly evaluating the extent to which our knowledge base is a good match for what an author expects us to know. The more prior knowledge we have about what an author is telling us, the deeper and more reliable is our understanding of that text.

> *"Having knowledge is one thing; using it another. That readers often do not relate what they are reading to what they already know has prompted research about how to encourage more extensive use of prior knowledge...." (Pressley, 2002, p. 271)*

Many of our students do not necessarily realize that knowledge exists at two levels in written texts. One layer is the overt display of knowledge that is readily apparent: the author directly tells readers things they need to know to understand. But authors do not tell readers everything. In effect, authors establish a relationship with their readers—authors anticipate what they think their readers will already know and therefore do not need to be told. This creates a second layer of knowledge that can be explained to students as "hidden knowledge." Hidden knowledge is below the surface of a text, unstated but necessary for comprehension, and readers must assume the responsibility for filling in the rest of the message if the text is to make sense. There is much hidden knowledge in our speeding ticket example. The language is "trucker-talk"—Citizen Band (CB) radio lingo—popularized in the 1970s by a series of movies, television programs,

and songs. The vocabulary represents code words frequently used in CB communications. Although CB radios still exist, they have fallen into obscurity with the general public, and the language has become antiquated. As a result, an author's message that might have been a match with most readers 30 years ago is now a mismatch with large numbers of readers.

Students have similar problems when they launch into a reading assignment "cold," without an early alert on how to match their knowledge with a text. They may be unsure of what the material is about and may not have reviewed what they already might know about the topic. They glide along—reading words, noticing details, picking out pieces of information—but may be confounded by what they are attempting to read. The more teachers help students to understand concepts prior to reading about them, the better students will comprehend. By "frontloading" instruction—concentrating instruction before student reading—teachers can accomplish a number of important objectives. They can discover what students already know or do not know about a topic, build relevant background with students who are beginning a reading with insufficient knowledge, spotlight key vocabulary, and ignite student interest in a topic.

The importance of frontloading is underscored in many of the classroom strategies outlined in this book. By practicing frontloading techniques, teachers help students extract relevant information from "folders in their memories" and integrate new information into those folders.

The Importance of Academic Knowledge

Because authors write for a target audience, they assume they do not need to tell their readers everything and count on their readers to supply the necessary hidden knowledge to fill in the rest of the message. Therefore, frontloading activities should include frequent classroom conversations that make this assumed knowledge transparent. For example, consider how the following science passage can exemplify the concept of hidden knowledge:

> Does Pluto really have the qualifications to be considered a planet? Astronomers have long argued that its tiny size, less than one-fifth the diameter of Earth, and its strangely tilted orbit that propels it outside of Neptune every couple of hundred years, means that Pluto does not sufficiently behave like a true planet. The controversy became more pronounced in the summer of 2005 when astronomers discovered a new object larger than Pluto, also orbiting the sun in the Kuiper Belt region. Many astronomers maintained that either Pluto be demoted from its standing among the

nine planets of the solar system, or this new object, named Eris, which has a tiny moon, be added as our tenth planet. As a result, the International Astronomical Union reclassified Pluto as a dwarf planet in 2006.

As students examine what they need to know, but are not told by the author, they will discover much hidden knowledge. The author expects readers will have an understanding of the solar system and planets. The author expects knowledge of properties of planets, such as orbits and moons. The author expects recognition that astronomers are scientists who study the solar system and constantly discover new information about other bodies in outer space. The concept of diameter and the region of the Kuiper Belt are specific references the author assumes readers will grasp. Finally, the author expects readers to be literate about principles of science, and to be aware that scientists often disagree in their interpretations and conclusions and that varying explanations are an ongoing dynamic in science. Students will discover that the author expected a great deal from readers.

Frontloading instruction prompts students to intentionally connect their knowledge base to written texts. Three types of prior knowledge connections are possible (Harvey & Goudvis, 2007). First, readers may consider how personal experiences—events of their lives—can help them understand a passage (*text-to-self connection*). When a student connects to a planetarium visit or remembers gazing through a telescope at the skies, this student is accessing text-to-self connections that can contribute to comprehension. Second, readers may think about other texts they have previously read that can help them understand a passage (*text-to-text connection*). When a student remembers information learned about planets from a science textbook, a newspaper article about Pluto, or a pertinent scene in a science fiction short story, the student is employing a text-to-text connection to understand new material. And third, readers may rely on their overall conception of, and ideas about, a topic that they have gradually gleaned from an amalgam of sources, including other media, other people's talk, and so forth (*text-to-world connection*). When a reader brings to this passage a general sense of what the solar system is and how it works, or what astronomy is and how astronomers conduct their research, the reader is making a text-to-world connection.

Many of our students struggle with matching up what they know with texts they are asked to read in school. Certainly, direct firsthand experiences can provide readers with particularly powerful prior knowledge. When readers can relate their personal lives to a text, their connections tend to be deeper and more vivid. However, because students grow up in different circumstances, general knowledge and experiences vary widely among students. Although all students bring a personal core of general knowledge to the classroom, Marzano (2004) notes a wide disparity among students in useful *academic knowledge*. Academic knowledge parallels the background a person would develop when studying various academic disciplines, and it is narrower and more prescribed than general knowledge. In short, some students display a wealth of relevant academic knowledge while others are seriously deficient in what authors expect them to know. Their general knowledge will not be sufficient to compensate for the academic knowledge they are lacking.

> "The research literature supports one compelling fact: what students already know about the content is one of the strongest indicators of how well they will learn new information relative to the content." (Marzano, 2004, p. 1)

Marzano (2004) argued that much of academic knowledge is vocabulary driven; to a significant degree, teaching biology, history, music, art, math, and other disciplines is equivalent to teaching a language. Researchers refer to the language of an academic discipline as a *Discourse* (Gee, 2000). "Insiders" in an academic discourse, people like professionals in the field and teachers, are comfortable with this academic language, but "outsiders," people like our students, may feel overwhelmed or even alienated by all the jargon—an outsider's depiction of this specialized language—in a biology text, a math lesson, a history passage.

Readers familiar with the language of a discipline will have deeper and more precise academic knowledge to apply to written texts in content classrooms. Therefore it is likely that individual students may be more successful in some content environments and less successful in others. For example, they may be more proficient readers of short stories and novels in English class and less proficient readers of the science textbook in biology class. Students need to become increasingly comfortable with the "insider language" of academic texts; they have to develop the facility to "talk the talk" of an academic discipline.

But isn't academic knowledge essentially a product of schooling? Marzano (2004) cited a profusion of research that concluded that those students who gain the most academic knowledge from school are those who already have developed some of this academic knowledge on their own. To revisit our planets example, "Pluto" represents academic knowledge. Some readers will be able to recall personal experiences such as visits to museums that featured exhibits of the solar system and may also recall reading *National*

Geographic magazine articles that presented theories about the development of planets. They may have had conversations with knowledgeable adults on this topic, or could listen in as adults around them engaged in discussions—perhaps they overheard their parents debating whether Pluto should rightfully be considered a planet! These students had access to academic knowledge outside the classroom—access to personal experiences, rich texts, and knowledgeable others—that prepared them to match up well with the materials they subsequently encountered in classroom lessons. In particular, they probably have developed some familiarity with the "insider" terminology of a subject—in this case academic vocabulary words such as *astronomer, orbit, solar system, Pluto, Neptune, Kuiper Belt.* Thus, the students who can be expected to learn the most from their first encounter with planets in the classroom will be those students who already knew something about planets before the lesson.

> "The idea is not that content-area teachers should become reading and writing teachers, but rather than they should emphasize the reading and writing practices that are specific to their subjects, so students are encouraged to read and write like historians, scientists, mathematicians, and other subject-area experts." (Biancarosa & Snow, 2004, p. 15)

Students who arrive in the classroom with rich reservoirs of academic knowledge tend to have been privileged to a host of invaluable firsthand experiences—visits to museums, art galleries, plays, and concerts; travel opportunities outside their home area; interactions with knowledgeable adults who provide a foundation for text-to-world connections through conversation and mentoring; and ready access to print and other sources that can pique their interest and curiosity in the various domains of academic knowledge. Students who lack such direct experiences need frontloading activities that broaden their academic knowledge base as they prepare for reading and learning content information.

Teaching to the Match: Building New Background Knowledge

Teachers can have a significant impact on their students' comprehension of classroom materials by frontloading instruction—providing students with those missing pieces of assumed knowledge through a variety of classroom activities. With any text students will be reading, it is therefore necessary to evaluate the match. Some texts will clearly be a reach—the author's expectation of the background knowledge readers bring will prove to be out of sync with your students. In these cases, most of your readers do not know what they need to make sense of such texts. A text that is a mismatch for almost the entire class will be too difficult, unless substantial frontloading of background concepts is undertaken.

More typically, many texts will be a match for some of the students, but a mismatch for others. Two unsuccessful approaches are frequently taken for this condition. First, students may be sent into the reading relatively "cold," which means that those students lacking what the author assumes readers know will flounder during their reading. Some of these mismatched students will give up, others will plug along with only fleeting comprehension, and many will merely skim for answers that ultimately make little sense to them. This situation often plays out in classrooms as some students tend to "get it" and many others "have poor comprehension skills."

The second unsuccessful approach acknowledges student struggles with reading comprehension and overcompensates by generally eliminating reading tasks as central to learning new content. This practice is especially prevalent in classrooms where mismatches tend to outnumber matches. Because the material is "too hard" for many students to comprehend, instruction focuses on other methods to learn content—telling (lecture), visual media (such as video), and interactive activities. As a result, students do not develop the capacity to learn independently as readers, a potential that could have been realized if their deficiencies in background knowledge had been remedied.

A key factor in differentiating instruction is identifying potential mismatches and emphasizing proactive responses—activities that narrow the gap between what students know and what they need to know to access an author's message. Students can then be asked to read material that would have been otherwise too challenging had they been assigned to read it independently, without supporting instruction.

A basic classroom method of assessing "hidden knowledge"—what an author assumes readers already know—engages students in brainstorming prior knowledge. Frontloading instruction that includes brainstorming has several advantages:

- Students are provided with a social opportunity to revisit what they currently know about a topic; as others share, students are reminded of additional things they know.

- Students who would face a mismatch with a particular text are immersed in conversation about a topic that builds what they know before they read; some of what they will need to know emerges during the brainstorming activity as they listen to comments from classmates about the topic.

- Students are cued about the aspects of their knowledge most relevant for the specific expectations of the author; in essence, they prime themselves to actively bring their current knowledge to construct an understanding of an author's message.
- If students display few connections to the topic, the teacher will be alerted that a mismatch exists for most students, and the teacher will need to intervene with further instruction to ensure that comprehension will be possible.

Several classic brainstorming procedures can be employed by teachers. One of the most popular is the K-W-L Plus strategy (Carr & Ogle, 1987; see page 107), which begins by asking students to list what they know, or have heard, about a topic central to a text they will subsequently read. All students have an opportunity to tune in to the talk about the topic, which starts with immersion in students' current knowledge base. Students who otherwise would have confronted a mismatch receive a "heads-up" on the topic right before they are asked to read about it in more depth.

In cases where brainstorming will be insufficient (too many students exhibit mismatches), teachers must plan frontloading instruction that extends beyond tapping into current knowledge and focuses on building new background knowledge. Although teachers sometimes assume: "students should already know these things," clearly in our classrooms today many students do not, presenting us with a prime teachable moment. At this point, use of media such as video or highly visual resources such as illustrated texts, as well as teacher presentations, can be effective means to build missing academic knowledge. A common temptation is to substitute these activities for learning from text, as mentioned above. However, using such classroom methods to *prepare for* reading, rather than *replace* reading, will lead to students who can increasingly learn to comprehend content-rich texts.

Short clips from video can be especially effective for mediating classroom mismatches. Often video is shown after students read, but it can be a particularly powerful frontloading technique. Judicious use of video clips, rather than showing entire works, keeps the focus on building sufficient knowledge for a successful reading experience.

Finally, encouraging students to read broadly about a topic, in texts that are at appropriate individual difficulty levels, can reduce classroom mismatches. Much of the background knowledge we bring to texts is incidental—we read general works such as newspapers, magazines, and books and gradually accrue deeper understanding of various topics, even though

that is not necessarily our intention for reading. Taking the effort to incrementally grow classroom "text sets" (Harvey & Goudvis, 2007) can help students develop academic knowledge for content learning. Stockpiling materials on multiple reading levels related to significant curriculum topics can be resources for independent background reading. Although such materials may not specifically focus on the aspects emphasized in the curriculum, they can be immensely valuable in deepening academic knowledge on particular topics.

Teaching to the match is an often overlooked but essential factor in improving student comprehension of classroom texts. Frontloading prepares students to handle challenging texts, even though they may have otherwise experienced mismatches and insufficient comprehension. Students gain the necessary daily practice they need to develop as readers, as they are provided opportunities that make them more likely to succeed. And students begin to aggressively analyze the match between their knowledge and an author's assumptions as a regular habit of mind.

Embedding Strategies in Classroom Lessons: Identifying Instructional Focus

The classroom teaching strategies featured in this book are also categorized according to how they might be incorporated with the flow of a lesson. Each classroom strategy is introduced with a Strategy Index that is correlated with the three phases of instruction (see Table 3):

1. Frontloading learning (before-reading activities)
2. Guiding comprehension (during-reading activities)
3. Consolidating understanding (after-reading activities)

Frontloading learning strategies prepare students for successful reading. These strategies, in particular, address teaching to the match—matching what authors assume readers know with the knowledge students can bring to a text. Comprehension characteristics that receive primary emphasis are making connections and generating questions, and frontloading strategies also cue student purpose for reading, setting up determining importance.

Guiding comprehension strategies prompt student thinking during reading and learning. All seven comprehension characteristics are integrated into this phase of a lesson: making connections, generating questions, creating visual and sensory images, making inferences, determining importance, synthesizing, and monitoring reading.

Table 3
Classroom Strategies Indexed by Instructional Focus

Instructional Focus	Classroom Strategies		
Frontloading Learning	Analogy Charting Anticipation Guides B/D/A Questioning Chart Brainstorming Prior Knowledge Chapter Tours Character Quotes Concept/Definition Mapping	Connect Two Guided Imagery Hands-On Reading History Change Frame Inquiry Charts K-W-L Plus (Know/Want to Know/Learned) Math Reading Keys Mind Mapping	Problematic Situations Quick Writes Science Connection Overview Self-Questioning Taxonomy Story Impressions Student-Friendly Vocabulary Explanations
Guiding Comprehension	Analogy Charting Anticipation Guides Author Says/I Say B/D/A Questioning Chart Chapter Tours Character Quotes Concept/Definition Mapping Connect Two Double-Entry Diaries First Person Reading	Hands-On Reading History Change Frame History Memory Bubbles Inquiry Charts Interactive Reading Guides K-W-L Plus (Know/Want to Know/Learned) Math Reading Keys Mind Mapping Power Notes Problematic Situations	Pyramid Diagram Question-Answer Relationships Questioning the Author Role-Playing as Readers Science Connection Overview Self-Questioning Taxonomy Story Mapping Structured Note-Taking Text Coding
Consolidating Understanding	Analogy Charting Anticipation Guides Author Says/I Say B/D/A Questioning Chart Concept/Definition Mapping Connect Two Different Perspectives Discussion Web Double-Entry Diaries First Person Reading Follow the Characters Guided Imagery History Memory Bubbles	Inquiry Charts Written Conversations K-W-L Plus (Know/Want to Know/Learned) Magnet Summaries Paired Reviews Power Notes Pyramid Diagram Question-Answer Relationships Questioning the Author Quick Writes RAFT (Role/Audience/Format/Topic)	Role-Playing as Readers Save the Last Word for Me Story Impressions Story Mapping Student-Friendly Vocabulary Explanations Structured Note-Taking Template Frames Vocabulary Overview Guide Word Family Trees Written Conversations

Consolidating understanding strategies engage students in refining their comprehension and applying new learning to meaningful situations. While all seven comprehension characteristics continue to be integral to strategies in this phase of a lesson, synthesizing (summarizing understanding and personalizing new learning) is especially critical during this phase.

As you use the classroom strategies described in this book, notice how they might be embedded in various phases of lesson planning. For example, a frontloading strategy such as K-W-L Plus (page 107) is an excellent way to prepare students for new learning because it encourages them to activate what they know and focus their attention on questions for new learning. A guiding comprehension strategy such as the Interactive Reading Guide (see page 104) prompts students to selectively read and to meaningfully organize important information. A Role/Audience/Format/Topic (RAFT) writing exercise (see page 144) helps students integrate new concepts with their previous understandings by having them personalize their learning. A RAFT assignment also provides students with a creative way to apply what they have learned.

References

Alexander, P.A., & Jetton, T.L. (2000). Learning from text: A multidimensional and developmental perspective. In M.L. Kamil, P.B. Mosenthal, P.D. Pearson, & R. Barr (Eds.), *Handbook of reading research* (Vol. 3, pp. 285–310). Mahwah, NJ: Erlbaum.

Biancarosa, G., & Snow, C.E. (2004). *Reading next: A vision for action and research in middle and high school literacy.* Washington, DC: Alliance for Excellent Education.

Carr, E.M., & Ogle, D. (1987). K-W-L Plus: A strategy for comprehension and summarization. *Journal of Reading, 30*(7), 626–631.

Gee, J.P. (2000). Discourse and sociocultural studies in reading. In M.L. Kamil, P.B. Mosenthal, P.D. Pearson, & R. Barr (Eds.), *Handbook of reading research* (Vol. 3, pp. 195–207). Mahwah, NJ: Erlbaum.

Harvey, S., & Goudvis, A. (2007). *Strategies that work: Teaching comprehension for understanding and engagement* (2nd ed.). Portland, ME: Stenhouse.

Marzano, R. (2004). *Building background knowledge for academic achievement: Research on what works in schools.* Alexandria, VA: Association for Supervision and Curriculum Development.

Pearson, P.D., Roehler, L.R., Dole, J.A., & Duffy, G.G. (1992). Developing expertise in reading comprehension. In S.J. Samuels & A.E. Farstrup (Eds.), *What research has to say about reading instruction* (2nd ed., pp. 145–199). Newark, DE: International Reading Association.

Pressley, M. (2002). *Reading instruction that works* (2nd ed.). New York: Guilford.

CHAPTER 3

Guiding Comprehension Through Text Frames

I t is a quiet evening. You are settled in a comfortable chair, anticipating a few hours pleasantly lost in the latest J.D. Robb or Tony Hillerman mystery. As you initially open your book, what are you wondering? If you are a devoted fan, you are probably already wondering what predicament main characters Eve Dallas or Jim Chee will find themselves in. But you are also likely to automatically wonder a series of questions that will specifically guide your reading of this genre of literature. What mystery in this story will need to be solved? What steps might characters take to solve this mystery? What clues can be identified? What false leads must our detectives be wary of? Who are possible suspects? What might be their motives? How will the mystery eventually be resolved? In other words, you already know the "right" questions to ask yourself when engaged in reading a mystery.

Our minds tend to "wonder" when we are immersed as readers in the process of comprehension. As detailed in Chapter 1, question generation is a primary mental activity of readers striving to achieve understanding. The questions we pose to ourselves—and to authors—set our "frame of mind" for reading particular texts. So when we slip into our mystery frame of mind, we immediately begin to ask questions that a well-written mystery novel would be expected to answer. As you track these questions, you have assumed the perfect frame of mind to read this genre.

> *"Students who are knowledgeable about and/or follow the author's structure in their attempts to recall a text remember more than those who do not." (Pearson & Fielding, 1991, p. 827)*

Text Frames: Determining Importance Through Questioning

Of course, many students will tell us that their minds "wander," not wonder, as they attempt to read materials required in our curriculum. Students often feel as if they are being bombarded by details and factual information, and it is easy for them to become lost in the midst of all this "stuff." Reading may assume a random quality as students merely hunt for isolated snippets of fact, and as a result, no coherent understanding of an author's message can be constructed.

Comprehension is predicated on readers having an internal road map for determining what is important in texts packed with a wealth of background information. Proficient readers *use* reading—rather than *do* reading—as their questions provide a purpose for engaging with a text. Their questions establish why they are reading a particular selection and what they are looking for. In other words, proficient readers recognize an appropriate frame of mind that will structure their understanding of a particular text.

But what are the "right" questions to ask? Researchers use the term *text frame* to describe a set of questions that reflects how authors may organize their writing (Anderson & Armbruster, 1984). A frame provides a structure, outlines boundaries, delineates shape. Eyeglass frames, picture frames, and window frames all serve to hold things together in certain functional shapes or forms. Authors use text frames to structure interrelationships between specific details and facts. The "right" questions, then, focus on how an author chose to connect information to communicate ideas, concepts, themes, or conclusions.

Jones, Palincsar, Ogle, and Carr (1987) highlight six text frames typically used by authors to organize information: problem/solution, cause/effect, compare/contrast, goal/action/outcome, concept/definition, and proposition/support. Each text frame cues a reader to a different questioning frame of mind that best correlates to an author's message. Frame questions guide readers through a maze of details toward understanding the point of a piece of writing. A world history passage about colonialism might be best understood through posing problem/solution frame questions. A section in a chemistry textbook might be patterned around cause/effect frame questions. A newspaper editorial read during language arts instruction would likely elicit proposition/support frame questions. A geometry chapter about characteristics of different triangles might best correspond to compare/contrast frame questions. Table 4 highlights sample sets of text frame questions that help readers navigate details and information and guide their comprehension.

When we read a mystery we shift into posing problem/solution frame questions, which prompt us to search for clues, suspects, motives, and alibis. When we read about a sports competition in the daily

Table 4
Determining Text Frames

What Is the Point of the Material?	Sample Questions to Ask
That a problem needs solving? (Problem/Solution Frame)	• What is the problem? • Who has the problem? • What is causing the problem? • What are negative effects of the problem? • Who is trying to solve the problem? • What solutions are recommended or attempted? • What results from these solutions? • Is the problem solved? Do any new problems develop because of the solutions?
That certain conditions lead to certain results? (Cause/Effect Frame)	• What happens (or happened)? • What causes it to happen? • What are the important elements or factors that cause this effect? • How do these factors or elements interrelate? • Will this result always happen from these causes? Why or why not? • How would the result change if the elements or factors are different?
That certain things are similar or different? (Compare/Contrast Frame)	• What is being compared and contrasted? • What characteristics are compared and contrasted? • What makes them alike or similar? • What makes them not alike or different? • What are the most important qualities that make them similar? • What are the most important qualities that make them different? • In terms of what's most important, are they more alike or more different?
That someone is doing something for a specific reason? (Goal/Action/Outcome Frame)	• What is the goal? What is to be accomplished? • Who is trying to achieve this goal? • What actions/steps are taken to achieve this goal? • Is the sequence of actions/steps important? • What are the effects of these actions? What happens? • Were these actions successful for achieving the goal? • Are there unexpected outcomes from these actions? • Would other actions have been more effective? Could something else have been done?

(continued)

Table 4 (continued)
Determining Text Frames

What Is the Point of the Material?	Sample Questions to Ask
That a concept needs to be understood? (Concept/Definition Frame)	• What is the concept? • What category of things does this concept belong to? • What are its critical characteristics? • How does it work? • What does it do? • What are its functions? • What are examples of it? • What are examples of things that share some but not all of its characteristics?
That a viewpoint is being argued and supported? (Proposition/Support Frame)	• What is the general topic or issue? • What viewpoint, conclusion, theory, hypothesis, or thesis is being proposed? • How is this proposition supported? • Are examples provided to support the proposition? • Are data provided to support the proposition? • Is expert verification provided to support the proposition? • Is a logical argument provided to support the proposition? • Does the author make a convincing case for the proposition? • What are alternative perspectives to the author's proposition?

newspaper, we transition to cause/effect frame questions, as we wonder: Who won the game? What events contributed to the win? Were the results affected by notable individual performances? How did the game change team standings? Was the outcome affected by any special circumstances such as errors, injuries, or coaching decisions? Will the game influence future contests? In both cases, we are able to immediately figure out the right questions to pose to ourselves to understand what an author is telling us.

> "Strong early reading skills do not automatically develop into more complex skills that enable students to deal with the specialized and sophisticated reading of literature, science, history, and mathematics." (Shanahan & Shanahan, 2008, p. 43)

Students have developed the know-how to successfully read mystery stories and sports articles. Their experiences of learning and later reading these genres, as well as their years of watching movie and television mysteries and participating in sporting events, have prepared them to generate the appropriate frame questions. But what kind of writing do students encounter in our classrooms?

What frame of mind should they assume when reading a biology passage about microorganisms? Or a health article about smoking? Or a history chapter about the Roman Empire? Or a webpage on Beethoven? What should students be wondering as readers of each of these different texts? What text frames are represented in social studies, science, language arts, math, and other academic disciplines?

Metaphors for Text Frames

Posing questions within a text frame establishes a reader's frame of mind toward an assignment. Metaphors can help students assume an appropriate mind-set for reading. For example, a problem/solution text frame could prompt students to think like a doctor—a problem solver who determines what is wrong, why it is wrong, and how it can be fixed. A cause/effect text frame invites students to ponder like a scientist, asking what happens and why it happens. Students reading concept/definition material might imagine themselves a news reporter, asking who, what, where, when, why, and how questions. Students reading compare/contrast material might adopt a shopper's frame of mind, investigating how products are alike and different. Students might best approach a proposition/support text frame like a judge who analyzes arguments and weighs the strength of corroborating evidence. And with a goal/action/outcome text frame, students may strategize like a coach who thinks about goals, necessary actions to meet these goals, and evaluating results.

Figure 2 provides a framework for identifying text frames in classroom materials. For example, science texts frequently emphasize cause/effect relationships; students focus on how certain scientific phenomena lead to specific results, whether a chemical reaction, a law of physics, or a principle in earth science. Problem/solution relationships predominate in history texts, which tend to focus on stories about people who are confronted with problems and changes. Material that outlines a chronology, such as a short story of a

family immigrating to a new country; or a sequence of steps, such as the directions for operating woodworking equipment, a protocol for setting up a webpage, or a recipe for baking a spice cake, involve goal/action/outcome thinking. An article that presents a series of choices or options requires a compare/contrast frame of mind. A political speech, movie review, or a research article involves proposition/support thinking, by providing conclusions predicated on the author's basis for justification. Finally, highly descriptive texts, such as in biology, mandate a concept/definition frame of mind for reading.

In the discussion of comprehension in Chapter 1, determining importance was described as an essential characteristic of proficient reading. Text frames provide that "internal road map" that guides readers to discern the relationships that stitch together details and information to produce a message. Students learn

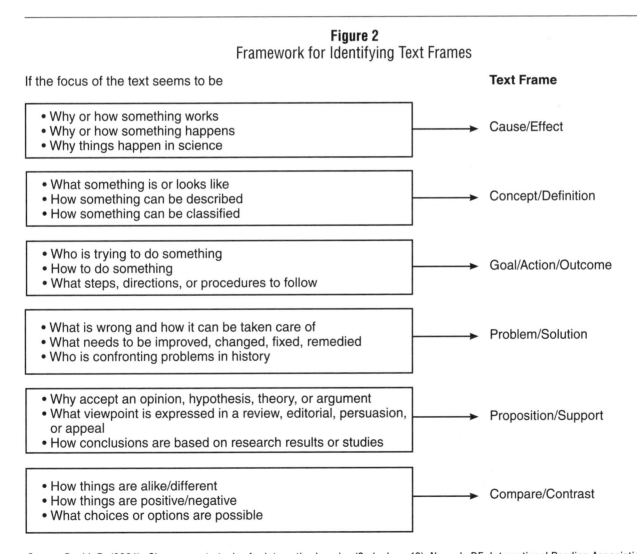

Figure 2
Framework for Identifying Text Frames

If the focus of the text seems to be   **Text Frame**

- Why or how something works
- Why or how something happens
- Why things happen in science   Cause/Effect

- What something is or looks like
- How something can be described
- How something can be classified   Concept/Definition

- Who is trying to do something
- How to do something
- What steps, directions, or procedures to follow   Goal/Action/Outcome

- What is wrong and how it can be taken care of
- What needs to be improved, changed, fixed, remedied
- Who is confronting problems in history   Problem/Solution

- Why accept an opinion, hypothesis, theory, or argument
- What viewpoint is expressed in a review, editorial, persuasion, or appeal
- How conclusions are based on research results or studies   Proposition/Support

- How things are alike/different
- How things are positive/negative
- What choices or options are possible   Compare/Contrast

Source: Buehl, D. (2001). *Classroom strategies for interactive learning* (2nd ed., p. 13). Newark, DE: International Reading Association.

to recognize these relationships as the foundation for what an author deems important in a text. Table 5 outlines these six text frames with materials that commonly are read in mathematics, social studies, science, and English language arts.

Classroom Strategies That Frame Instruction

A text frame organizes the most important arguments or information in a piece of writing so that the reader gets the point and can make sense of the material. So how can we encourage students to read with a questioning frame of mind when they tackle textbooks and other print material we use in our classrooms? The answer lies in the classroom strategies we use when involving students in reading assignments. We can employ strategies that tip off students to the appropriate frame for reading (see Table 6).

For example, if students are to read a passage about golden eagles, first determine which text frame

Table 5
Content Area Text Frames

Text Frame	Description
Text Frames in Mathematics	
Problem/Solution	Math texts that engage students in problem solving, including story problems and scenarios that challenge students to devise solutions
Cause/Effect	Logical reasoning: analyzing math principles and their applications (deductive), developing generalizations based on data (inductive)
Compare/Contrast	Examinations of critical differentiating characteristics, for example geometric shapes or measures of center (mean, median, mode)
Proposition/Support	Justifying decisions to apply specific math formulas or strategies in problem-solving situations
Goal/Action/Outcome	Specific algorithms that are followed to solve certain mathematical problems
Concept/Definition	Development of key math concepts, such as factor, prime number, square root, quadrilateral, circumference, or relative frequency
Text Frames in the Social Studies	
Problem/Solution	Historical texts that examine problems people encountered and how they addressed them
Cause/Effect	Factors which lead to certain results or conditions, such as in history or psychology
Compare/Contrast	Examinations of how things are alike or different, such as cultures, policies, philosophies, types of government
Proposition/Support	Articulation of points of view, position statements, and constructed arguments or theories
Goal/Action/Outcome	Steps taken by people, organizations, governments, or countries that are intended to achieve a certain aim or goal
Concept/Definition	Development of key social studies concepts, such as socialization, imperialism, nationalism, federalism, or democracy
Text Frames in Science	
Problem/Solution	Investigations of problems in the natural world and scientific explanations for possible actions to redress them, such as an avian flu epidemic, loss of swampland, disappearing habitats
Cause/Effect	Examinations of what happened and why it happened, or studies of what would happen if certain steps or processes were undertaken

(continued)

Table 5 (continued)
Content Area Text Frames

Text Frame	Description
Text Frames in Science (continued)	
Compare/Contrast	Analyses of how certain biological or physical phenomena are alike and how they are different
Proposition/Support	Hypotheses that are tested, and conclusions that are drawn from examinations of data and scientific evidence
Goal/Action/Outcome	Steps taken by scientists to investigate relationships and hypotheses, usually conducted as scientific experiments and research
Concept/Definition	Classification of biological and physical phenomena into categories according to defining characteristics and attributes
Text Frames in English Language Arts	
Problem/Solution	Literature that deals with characters attempting to resolve a problem, issue, dilemma, or conflict
Cause/Effect	Author's use of language and communication devices which influence interpretation of meaning, such as word choice, tone, or elements of speech
Compare/Contrast	Literature that presents contrasting characters which signal author's theme; alternative styles of writing or communication
Proposition/Support	Essays that present a point of view or line of argumentation with supporting evidence or logic; literature that provides a vehicle for expression of an author's ideas through plot, characterization, or theme
Goal/Action/Outcome	Literature that features characters who are striving to attain their dreams, desires, or personal fulfillment
Concept/Definition	Development of key literary concepts such as coming of age, social justice, metaphor, symbolism, protagonist, or haiku

Source: Buehl, D., & Stumpf, S. (2007). Literacy demands in content classrooms. In *Adolescent literacy toolkit* (pp. 33–51). Madison: Wisconsin Department of Public Instruction.

will best structure their thinking. If the passage emphasizes environmental hardships that the eagle encounters, devise your strategy around problem/solution questions. If the passage describes similarities and differences between the eagles and other predatory birds, structure the assignment around compare/contrast questions. If the passage discusses reasons why eagles are returning to some geographical regions, work within a cause/effect frame. If the passage presents theories why golden eagles have survived but other species have not, stress proposition/support relationships. If the article focuses on environmental groups' efforts to protect eagles, then structure a goal/action/outcome assignment. If the passage is a general informational segment about eagles, then concept/definition questions should guide comprehension.

Of course, authors may employ multiple text frames to organize information in a piece of writing.

For example, an author might *argue* that if we *compare* various proposals to combat global warming, certain *solutions* should be adopted as our best response. In effect, that author has combined three text frames—proposition/support, compare/contrast, and problem/solution—to structure thinking about this issue.

The classroom strategies presented in this book can be used effectively to signal text frames to students and to provide the support they need to read in the right frame of mind. In addition, strategies that direct student thinking toward a specific text frame can help them overcome text that is poorly written, confusing, or challenging. Struggling readers, in particular, benefit from strategies that provide them with an organized way of thinking about information that otherwise may be overwhelming.

Table 6
Text Frames and Corresponding Classroom Strategies

Text Frame	Classroom Strategies		
Cause/Effect	Anticipation Guides Author Says/I Say B/D/A Questioning Chart Double-Entry Diaries First-Person Reading Follow the Characters Hands-On Reading History Change Frame	Interactive Reading Guides Problematic Situations Question–Answer Relationships Questioning the Author Quick Writes RAFT (Role/Audience/Format/Topic)	Science Connection Overview Self-Questioning Taxonomy Story Impressions Structured Note-Taking Template Frames Text Coding Written Conversations
Concept/Definition	Analogy Charting Brainstorming Prior Knowledge Chapter Tours Concept/Definition Mapping Connect Two Double-Entry Diaries Guided Imagery History Memory Bubbles Interactive Reading Guides	Magnet Summaries Math Reading Keys Mind Mapping Paired Reviews Power Notes Pyramid Diagram Quick Writes RAFT (Role/Audience/Format/Topic) Science Connection Overview	Self-Questioning Taxonomy Story Impressions Structured Note-Taking Student-Friendly Vocabulary Explanations Template Frames Text Coding Vocabulary Overview Guide Word Family Trees
Problem/Solution	Anticipation Guides Double-Entry Diaries Hands-On Reading History Change Frame History Memory Bubbles Interactive Reading Guides	Math Reading Keys Paired Reviews Problematic Situations Quick Writes RAFT (Role/Audience/Format/Topic) Self-Questioning Taxonomy	Structured Note-Taking Template Frames Text Coding Written Conversations
Compare/Contrast	Analogy Charting Author Says/I Say B/D/A Questioning Chart Different Perspectives Discussion Web Double-Entry Diaries History Change Frame	Inquiry Charts Interactive Reading Guides Paired Reviews Pyramid Diagram Quick Writes RAFT (Role/Audience/Format/Topic)	Self-Questioning Taxonomy Student-Friendly Vocabulary Explanations Structured Note-Taking Template Frames Text Coding Written Conversations

(continued)

Table 6 (continued)
Text Frames and Corresponding Classroom Strategies

Text Frame	Classroom Strategies		
Proposition/Support	Anticipation Guides Author Says/I Say Character Quotes Discussion Web Double-Entry Diaries First-Person Reading Follow the Characters	Inquiry Charts Interactive Reading Guides Paired Reviews Quick Writes RAFT (Role/Audience/Format/Topic) Role-Playing as Readers	Save the Last Word for Me Self-Questioning Taxonomy Structured Note-Taking Template Frames Text Coding Written Conversations
Goal/Action/Outcome	Chapter Tours Hands-On Reading History Change Frame Inquiry Charts Interactive Reading Guides	K-W-L Plus Math Reading Keys Question–Answer Relationships Questioning the Author Quick Writes	RAFT (Role/Audience/Format/Topic) Read-Alouds Story Mapping Structured Note-Taking Template Frames Text Coding

References

Anderson, T.H., & Armbruster, B.B. (1984). Studying. In P.D. Pearson, R. Barr, M.L. Kamil, & P.B. Mosenthal (Eds.), *Handbook of reading research* (Vol. 1, pp. 657–679). New York: Longman.

Buehl, D., & Stumpf, S. (2007). Literacy demands in content classrooms. In *Adolescent literacy toolkit* (pp. 33–51). Madison: Wisconsin Department of Public Instruction.

Jones, B.F., Palincsar, A.S., Ogle, D.S., & Carr, E.G. (1987). *Strategic teaching and learning: Cognitive instruction in the content areas.* Alexandria, VA: Association for Supervision and Curriculum Development.

Pearson, P.D., & Fielding, L. (1991). Comprehension instruction. In R. Barr, M.L. Kamil, P. Mosenthal, & P.D. Pearson (Eds.), *Handbook of reading research* (Vol. 2, pp. 815–860). New York: Longman.

Shanahan, T., & Shanahan, C. (2008). Teaching disciplinary literacy to adolescents: Rethinking content-area literacy. *Harvard Educational Review, 78*(1), 40–59.

Suggested Reading

Buehl, D. (1991). Frames of mind. *The Exchange: Newsletter of the IRA Secondary Reading Special Interest Group, 4*(2), 4–5.

CHAPTER 4

Consolidating Understanding With Fact Pyramids

" If you remember only one thing about this, it ought to be...." For many students, remembering a single thing about a unit, chapter, or lesson days after the fact would be a tall order. Unfortunately, many students conceptualize learning in school as a short-term process. Students steel themselves each day for a steady barrage of information, and they cope by trying to remember only long enough to pass a test. Then it is on to the next material. Teachers find it discouraging that so many students seem to retain little of what they supposedly "learned" in school.

Of course, we realize that losing some of what is learned is a natural phenomenon. Each of us can think of personal instances of selective forgetting. We all have experienced moments when we have to admit to a student (or a son or daughter) that we cannot recall enough to help him or her with the homework for another teacher's class. Ideally, we have retained central concepts of the material, but like most people we have forgotten the specific details.

The Forest and Acres and Acres of Trees

One reason students seem so readily disposed to quickly forget what they encounter in school is the nature of the classroom texts they read. Proficient readers differentiate and prioritize as they process material—they determine what is most important and worthy of knowing over time. But textbooks in particular make these comprehension processes a demanding task for students. In a critical analysis, Daniels and Zemelman (2004) fault textbooks for burying "big ideas"—those most worthy of being remembered—underneath a tremendous array of superficial details. Textbooks are often poorly organized and do not satisfactorily cue students as to how to maneuver through all the factual information and visual displays so that they can make sense of the material. Textbooks tend to be written to *expose* students to information rather than to help them truly understand it.

Figure 3 is a visual representation of the challenges facing students when they attempt to read classroom texts. Comprehension is achieved when readers can organize their learning (see the center of the diagram in Figure 3) so that they are able to articulate a personal understanding (see the top of the diagram). But many students become mired in the details—isolated "factlets" of information (see the bottom of the diagram). Rather than actively connecting material to previous knowledge, raising questions, creating mental images, and drawing inferences, their minds instead are merely ticking off factlets one by one, as follows:

> Here's a fact. Here's another fact. Here's a fact in bold print (I'll have to copy something down about that one!). Here's another fact. Another one. Another fact in bold.

And so on through the remainder of a passage. But what do all these facts and details mean? At the end of a passage students may have accumulated a mass of disorganized information for which they have little use. They have not engaged in the critical comprehension processes of determining importance and synthesizing understanding.

Understanding occurs when students are able to interconnect facts and details, to organize information into a coherent message to make sense of it. *Text frames* are discussed in Chapter 3 as the mental frameworks authors use for meaningfully organizing information. When students are able to perceive how background details fit together—that the point of a passage is a cause/effect relationship, for example, which binds together all those facts—they are able to think about the implications of what they are reading. They can synthesize understanding—draw conclusions, make generalizations, and develop broad conceptual insights about important content. Without this synthesis of understanding, learning does not occur, and inevitably another round of forgetting results.

The reality of school for many students is that of an overwhelming onslaught of factual information that is never sorted into anything useful or worth remembering. The old adage that they "can't see the forest for the trees" becomes a daily occurrence for students immersed in the factual detail of classroom reading. Furthermore, the primary method of directing students through classroom materials—asking them to respond to questions—often does little to promote comprehension. A litany of concerns about classroom questioning stretches back to Durkin's (1978/1979) landmark

Figure 3
Hierarchy of Knowledge

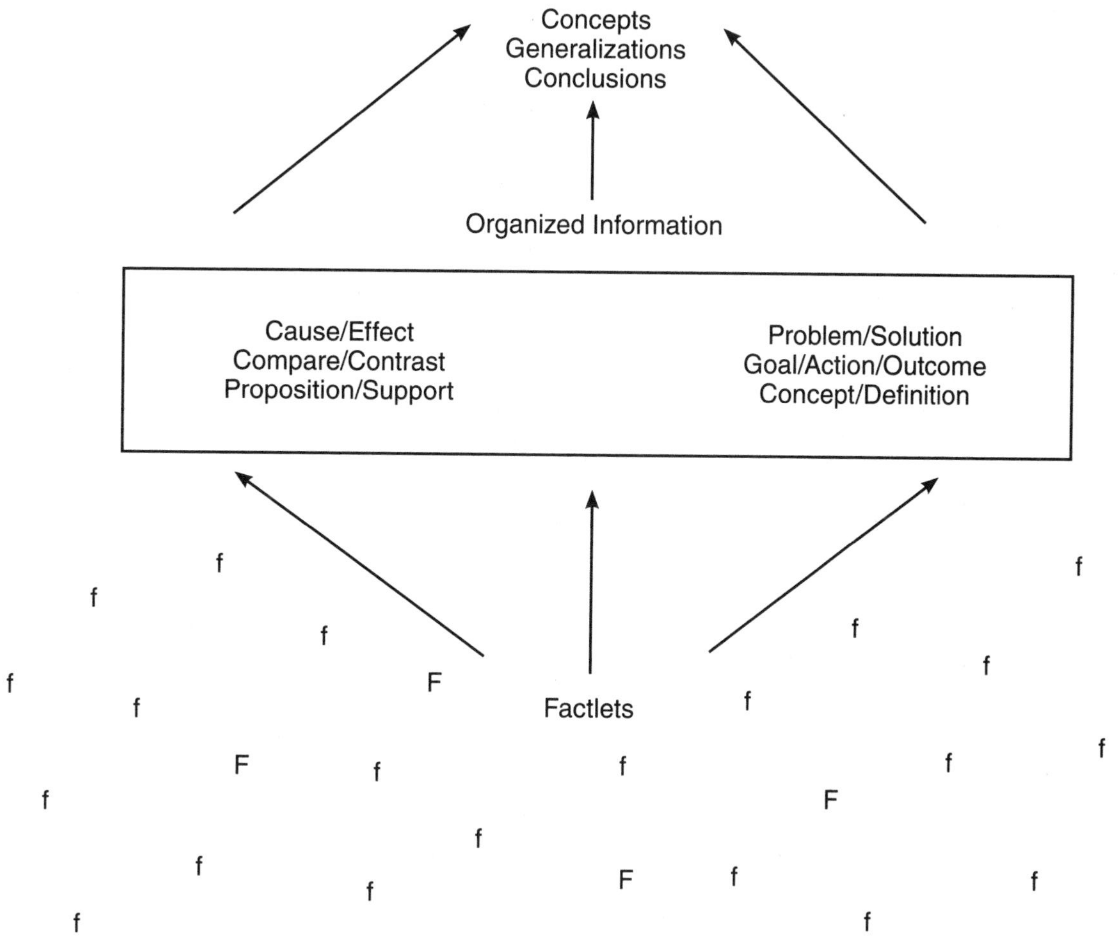

Concepts
Generalizations
Conclusions

Organized Information

Cause/Effect Compare/Contrast Proposition/Support	Problem/Solution Goal/Action/Outcome Concept/Definition

f f f f f F
f f f f
F f f
f f f f
f f F f
f f F f f
f f F f f f
f f f

Factlets

---

research which revealed that few questions are actually designed to guide comprehension. Most questioning doesn't help students understand but merely assesses whether or not they could arrive at certain "answers." Other criticisms fault questioning that predominately targets "getting the facts" or that asks students to locate details. As a result, too many questions can be answered with a rote, paraphrase level of processing and often with only a single word or short phrase. Finally, most classroom questioning, especially in textbooks, has no clear and coherent focus. In contrast to text frame questions—natural sets of questions that readers pose to guide their thinking (see Chapter 3)—classroom questions disproportionately target isolated facts, making it unlikely that readers will perceive central relationships. Students resignedly assume that anything that appears on a page of print is fair game for a question, whether it is truly important or not. In many

assignments, students may answer every question correctly and be no closer to understanding than when they started.

World Brains and School Brains

When they are in school, many students operate as if they possessed not one, but two brains. Imagine that their minds were split into a *world brain* and a *school brain*. The *world brain* can be visualized as taking up most of the room in a student's head. The world brain stores all of what this student knows and understands about the world, all of life's experiences and personal explanations of *what is*, *why*, and *how*. The student relies on this world brain to make sense of the world (in Chapter 2 we extensively describe the world brain as "prior knowledge").

Now imagine the *school brain*, located in an out-of-the-way corner of the mind and occupying only a small space. Think of the school brain as carefully insulated from the world brain—very little that enters it ever gets transferred into the brain that makes sense of things. The school brain has a minuscule storage capacity; information does not stay there very long. The most distinctive feature of the school brain is an ever-open chute, ready to dump yesterday's lesson quickly and irrevocably into oblivion. Students use the school brain for short-term "warehousing" of the daily stuff of school—some brain researchers refer to this temporary destination as *working memory* (Sousa, 2005). As soon as the test is over or a new chapter started, they flush out the backlog of old facts and stray information and ready themselves for another cycle of short-term learning.

Certainly some of our students are adept at perceiving the connections between what they already know and what they are learning in the classroom, of transferring classroom learning from working memory into long-term storage. They are able to synthesize their understandings with their existing knowledge, and they find that new learning does indeed help them make more sense of their world. But for many students, school has little to do with the real world, and their failure to make connections and synthesize understandings virtually ensures that much of what they learn in school will be lost—relegated to the dead-end depot of the school brain.

> *"To put it in an odd way, too many teachers focus on the teaching and not the learning. They spend most of their time thinking, first, about what they will do, what materials they will use, and what they will ask students to do rather than first considering what the learner will need in order to accomplish the learning goals." (Wiggins & McTighe, 2005, p. 15)*

How can teachers plan instruction so that real learning takes place, so that true conceptual changes occur in the mind, and so that understandings are retained over time and not merely long enough to pass tests? Classroom strategies that guide students into making connections between their background knowledge (world brain) and what they are studying in class (school brain) will significantly increase the probability that the new information will find its niche in long-term memory.

Imagine the following scenario: Five years from now as you stroll down the street, you chance upon a student you taught this year. What will this person still remember from your class? You realize that much of the specific information the student had encountered will be forgotten. But what learning should still be retained (lest you be bitterly disappointed)? What

should this former student remember about the Cold War, or cell division, or congruent triangles, or George Orwell's *Animal Farm*? Did this former student "get the point" from these various units of our curricula?

It is unlikely you would be crestfallen if your former student could not recite all the member countries of the Warsaw Pact or identify former communist leader Marshall Tito, likely items on some long-ago exam. But the *Cold War*—a period of intense confrontation between the antagonistic ideologies of communism and western democracy that resulted in regional conflicts and fears of nuclear destruction—should have significant associations for this individual. Likewise, you probably would not expect your former student to name the various stages of mitosis or recall specific mathematic theorems. You would, however, expect a general understanding of the implications of cell division and a sense of the basic principles of triangles. You would accept that your student has forgotten most of the characters and plot details of *Animal Farm*, but you would hope that Orwell's basic premises of the oppressed becoming the oppressors and the corruption of power would be remembered. Essentially, you would concede that most factual information is forgotten over time, but that more transcendent understandings must be remembered if one is to be regarded as a literate individual.

Essential Questions and Comprehension

Consider for a moment: What makes a work of art great? Why do people find the painting *Guernica* by Pablo Picasso so compelling? What makes a Frank Lloyd Wright building so remarkable? Why is Edward Elgar's lyrical *Enigma Variations* such a heralded piece of music? What was it about Dorothea Lange's photographs that render her images so memorable? Why do generations keep discovering magic in a novel such as Harper Lee's *To Kill A Mockingbird*? How do we explain the appeal of a Wolfgang Amadeus Mozart opera, an Emily Dickinson poem, a Henry Moore sculpture, a Sergei Eisenstein motion picture, a Billie Holiday recording? How do we account for what makes some artistic works great?

Certainly, this is an essential question, a question that cuts right to the core of understanding art and what makes some art meaningful, powerful, and enduring. And it's a question that would undoubtedly elicit a variety of possible answers, probably some disagreement, and perhaps even heated passions. In their influential guide to curriculum planning, *Understanding by Design*, Wiggins and McTighe (2005) propose organizing instruction around "big ideas," the central and focusing ideas within a topic that make it worthy of study, the gist of a unit that provides students with important insights on their world, the essence of learning that students retain long after their days in the classroom are over. The way to get at big ideas, Wiggins and McTighe suggest, is through essential questions.

Most of the questions that confront students in our curriculum are leading questions. Leading questions direct students toward a set answer and are helpful for clarifying key information. However, essential questions help students dig deeper into a topic. Instruction organized around essential questions considers the transcendent, overarching ideas that position students to examine critical connections or relationships within a topic area: Why exactly are we studying this? How can this be applied in the larger world? What couldn't we do if we didn't understand this? What ideas is the author exploring in this story? What is worth remembering, after time has passed, about this topic, unit, novel, or experiment?

For example, why should students read William Golding's novel *Lord of the Flies*? Why read this book and not another? What will they gain from this experience that will make a difference to them? What are the big ideas in this work? What makes this book a classic? Questions like these help teachers focus on the "point" of instruction. Unlike leading questions, which could help students follow key events of the plot, spot the author's use of symbolism, or clarify characterization, these overarching questions tap into larger ideas that can be accessed during a unit such as a novel study of *Lord of the Flies*.

Essential questions have a number of critical attributes. First, they are arguable; there is no single obvious right answer. Such questions ask students to "uncover" ideas, problems, controversies, philosophical positions, or perspectives. Second, essential questions often reach across subject boundaries and engender a series of ensuing and related questions that help us reach an understanding. Third, these questions often strike right at the heart of a discipline, such as what novels can tell us, whose version of history is being told, what we ultimately can prove in science, and how we know what we think we know. For example, essential questions germane to *Lord of the Flies* might include: What does it mean to be civilized? Are modern civilizations more civilized than ancient ones? What is necessary to ensure civilized behavior? Do children need to be taught to be civilized? What causes us to stop behaving in a civilized manner?

Essential questions are also recursive; that is, they naturally reoccur, often many times, during the study of a discipline. First graders as well as college students can offer valid aesthetic judgments about what makes a book great. Finally, essential questions provide a focus for sifting through the information and details of a unit of study, and they especially encourage student inquiry, discussion, and research. They involve students in personalizing their learning and developing individual insights on a topic. Students frequently complain that they do not see the point of studying a certain topic or that they won't use any of this stuff in their lives. Essential questions guide students through the curriculum and help them understand the intent behind a unit of study so they can perceive lasting value.

For example, essential questions for a history unit on manifest destiny and the movement of settlers west in the United States could include: Why do people move? Do people migrate for the same reasons today that they did in the 19th century? Who has the right to a particular territory? Who wins and who loses during major population shifts? Questions such as these can help students focus on big ideas as they study a panorama of events in United States history: the Oregon Trail, the Mexican War, the California Gold Rush, the conflicts between settlers and American Indian nations in the Great Plains, and the waves of immigration to North America.

Much of our curriculum is geared to telling students *what*. Essential questions engage students in asking *why*. As critical thinkers about big ideas, students begin to expect more than factual information from their learning and they become accustomed to examining topics and issues in depth. Students are encouraged to adopt an inquiring approach to the curriculum, to develop answers that personalize their learning, and to constantly focus on determining importance in their studies. And ultimately, learning centered around essential questions is likely to be remembered over time rather than forgotten after a test has been taken.

"As these (highly effective) teachers encouraged literate discussion, they also made overt connections between knowledge, skills, and ideas and across lessons, days, units, classes, and grades.... Almost 90 percent of the effective teachers made three types of connections constantly: within lessons, across lessons, and with both in- and out-of-school applications and activities." (Allington, 2007, p. 284)

Integrating Fact Pyramids With Teaching

Fact Pyramids (Buehl, 1991) provide teachers with a procedure for analyzing their curriculum so that instruction guides comprehension toward big ideas—the understandings that we truly want students to remember over time. Teachers use Fact Pyramids as a planning tool to graphically categorize text information into three levels: (1) essential knowledge, (2) short-term information, and (3) background detail (see Figure 4).

Essential knowledge is what one would expect a literate person to know or be able to do over time: If you remember only one thing about a lesson or unit, this is it. Essential knowledge is still with us years later. It represents the "point" of the lesson, which resides in the point of the fact pyramid. Curriculum standards to be met by a unit of study are reflected in these "tip of the pyramid" priorities. Essential knowledge represents the heart of the comprehension processes of determining importance and synthesizing understanding.

Short-term information comprises the necessary facts and details we use to deepen our understandings, but these are generally forgotten over time. This information occupies much of the language of class discussion and instruction—the key vocabulary and major details—but ultimately is not important as an end in itself. We *use* short-term information to make generalizations and draw conclusions that become memorable, but the factual baseline gradually drifts away. Often we tell students, "you need to know this," but what we are really saying is that this short-term information will be on the test. We would be hard-pressed to locate many literate adults who know this short-term information. Only individuals who make repeated trips through the material—such as professionals in a particular field, or teachers for that matter—tend to remember short-term information over time.

Background detail is the supporting information that provides the depth for fleshing out an understanding but certainly does not need to be learned for its own sake. A rich text supplies readers with more than headlines and boldface vocabulary. Background detail

comprises the "semantic glue" for a text, the elaborations and examples that help to illuminate understanding. Background detail can be an asset in classroom materials, but such information should not be emphasized as "factlets" that draw students' attention away from central ideas. Classroom questions, activities, and assessments should not ask students to be responsible for background detail. Instead, students should be expected to generalize and summarize: "Basically, what the author is telling me in these three paragraphs is...."

Using Fact Pyramids as a planning tool can help teachers make decisions about which classroom strategies best differentiate among the levels of information delivered in a chapter. By categorizing information in terms of the three levels, teachers can identify shortcomings in a text's organization and presentation of ideas. Is essential knowledge readily apparent, or will students become overwhelmed by factual information and not realize the point of the material? Will students be able to synthesize understandings, or will they stumble, lost, through forests of details?

Unfortunately, as previously discussed, classroom questioning frequently diverts attention away from essential knowledge. For example, the following question—typical in world history textbooks—asks students to process background detail to complete an assignment about the crusades:

Identify the following:
(a) Urban II
(b) Saladin
(c) Richard I
(d) Seljuq Turks
(e) Children's Crusade

Such a question sends a faulty message to students. First, they are led to believe that all historical facts mentioned in a text are equally important. A few of us might recognize Richard I as the famous Richard the Lionheart, but most literate adults would have scant notion of the other items. Such assignments give students no direction for evaluating which information is most deserving of emphasis. In addition, students know they will forget whatever they write down about these facts within a short period of time, so they begin to cynically regard all information encountered in history as equally forgettable. A Fact Pyramid would help clarify important text information for students to write about and remember (see Figure 5). A history teacher might decide that the primary focus for a unit on the crusades—what literate people should remember over time—should center on three big ideas:

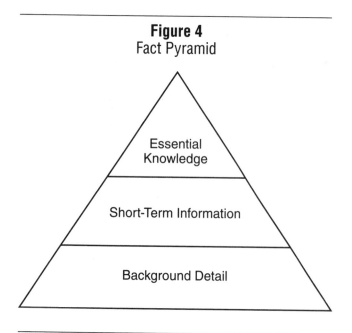

Figure 4
Fact Pyramid

Essential Knowledge

Short-Term Information

Background Detail

- Causes of the Crusades: European Christians regarded it a moral imperative to contest Muslim control of territory in the Middle East regarded as holy lands.
- Effects of the Crusades: Years of contact between Christian and Muslim worlds led to profound changes in trade, political structures, warfare, economics, scientific knowledge, and spread of ideas.
- Impact on Today: Attitudes and issues created by the Crusades provide insight on understanding current tensions and conflict in the Middle East.

Short-term information for the crusades unit might include the First, Second, Third, and Fourth Crusades. Details regarding major defining events, such as the massacre of Jerusalem, the plunder of Constantinople, the creation of crusader states, and the Children's Crusade will become hazy for most people over time, but an awareness of the controversies engendered by the crusades should remain. Class discussions might also include the decline of feudalism, new technologies like gunpowder, siege warfare tactics, and rise of nation-states.

Background information about historical figures such as Pope Urban II, Saladin, Louis VII of France, or Frederick Barbarossa, or facts like the establishment of the Principality of Antioch, *cruciata* means "marked with a cross," and details about the Byzantine and Holy Roman Empires represent supportive information

useful in broadening and enriching an understanding of this unit's big ideas. Few literate adults could successfully identify most of this information. Students should *not* be asked to identify and respond to such background detail.

A Fact Pyramid created by a teacher for an earth science unit on movements of the earth's surface features can be seen in Figure 6. The textbook contains a great deal of detailed information and terminology on plate tectonics that would be difficult for students. What would a science teacher expect a former student to remember about this material five years from now? Three big ideas could emerge as essential knowledge.

- Scientists believe that the earth's crust is broken into sections, called plates, which move, and sometimes impact each other.
- Plates on the earth's crust can move into or away from one another, can collide, or can slide past one another.
- Plate movements explain a number of important features on the earth's surface: faults, rift valleys, mountains, earthquakes, and volcanoes.

> *"Along with making thoughtful decisions about what information to stress, teachers must orchestrate learning opportunities that permit students to explore these concepts more deeply and fully." (Alexander & Jetton, 2000, p. 287)*

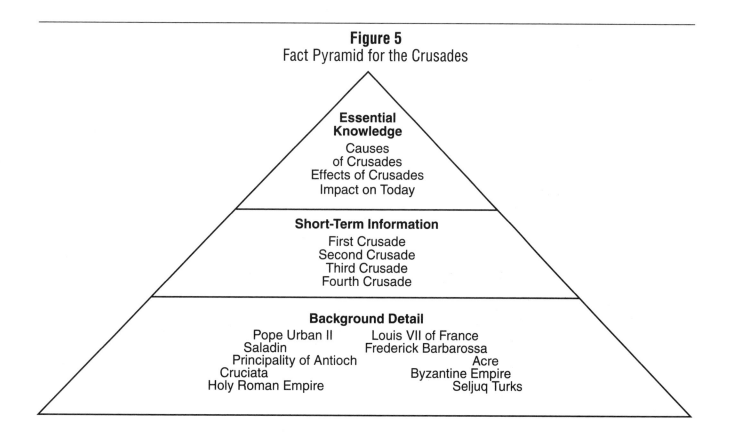

Figure 5
Fact Pyramid for the Crusades

Essential Knowledge
Causes of Crusades
Effects of Crusades
Impact on Today

Short-Term Information
First Crusade
Second Crusade
Third Crusade
Fourth Crusade

Background Detail
Pope Urban II   Louis VII of France
Saladin   Frederick Barbarossa
Principality of Antioch   Acre
Cruciata   Byzantine Empire
Holy Roman Empire   Seljuq Turks

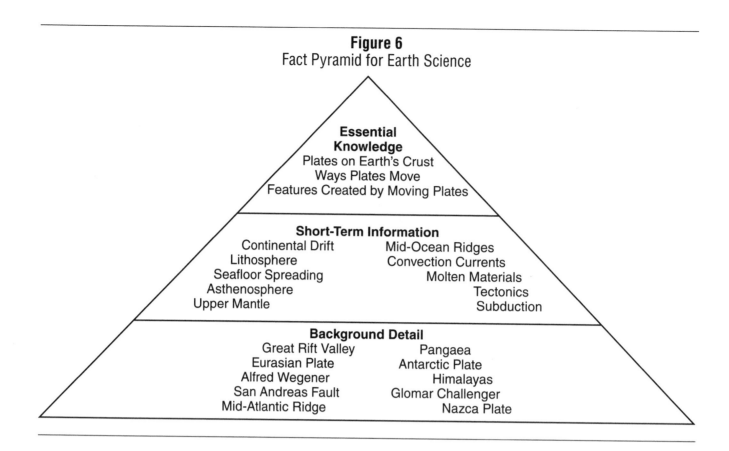

Figure 6
Fact Pyramid for Earth Science

Essential Knowledge
Plates on Earth's Crust
Ways Plates Move
Features Created by Moving Plates

Short-Term Information
Continental Drift — Mid-Ocean Ridges
Lithosphere — Convection Currents
Seafloor Spreading — Molten Materials
Asthenosphere — Tectonics
Upper Mantle — Subduction

Background Detail
Great Rift Valley — Pangaea
Eurasian Plate — Antarctic Plate
Alfred Wegener — Himalayas
San Andreas Fault — Glomar Challenger
Mid-Atlantic Ridge — Nazca Plate

Short-term information students will use to construct comprehension includes continental drift, mid-ocean ridges, the lithosphere, convection currents, seafloor spreading, molten materials in the asthenosphere, and terms like *tectonics*, *upper mantle*, and *subduction*. Students develop their understandings of the big ideas of this unit by interacting with this information, but over time much of these specifics will become blurred in memory.

Most of the earth science chapter is jam-packed with background material, details about the Great Rift Valley, Pangaea, Eurasian Plate, Antarctic Plate, Alfred Wegener, the Himalayas, San Andreas Fault, and so forth. Assignments and assessments that ask students to respond to these details distract them from the overall point of the material.

Fact Pyramids provide teachers with a planning tool to spotlight what is important and worthy of being remembered over time. Fact Pyramids emphasize instruction that helps students determine what is important and to synthesize understandings to get the point—the "tip of the pyramid."

References

Alexander, P.A., & Jetton, T.L. (2000). Learning from text: A multidimensional and developmental perspective. In M.L. Kamil, P.B. Mosenthal, P.D. Pearson, & R. Barr (Eds.), *Handbook of reading research* (Vol. 3, pp. 285–310). Mahwah, NJ: Erlbaum.

Allington, R.L. (2007). Effective teachers, effective instruction. In K. Beers, R.E. Probst, & L. Rief (Eds.), *Adolescent literacy: Turning promise into practice* (pp. 273–288). Portsmouth, NH: Heinemann.

Buehl, D. (1991). Fact pyramids. *New Perspectives: Reading Across the Curriculum, 7*(6), 1–2.

Daniels, H., & Zemelman, S. (2004). *Subjects matter: Every teacher's guide to content-area reading.* Portsmouth, NH: Heinemann.

Durkin, D. (1978/1979). What classroom observations reveal about reading comprehension instruction. *Reading Research Quarterly, 14*(4), 481–533. doi:10.1598/RRQ.14.4.2

Sousa, D.A. (2005). *How the brain learns to read.* Thousand Oaks, CA: Corwin.

Wiggins, G., & McTighe, J. (2005). *Understanding by design* (2nd ed.). Alexandra, VA: Association for Supervision and Curriculum Development.

Classroom Strategies for Teaching and Learning

Integrating Strategies and Instruction

What are promising literacy practices that embed comprehension instruction into the daily routines of teaching and learning? Section 2 features 45 strategies that integrate proficient reader characteristics with the rhythm of learning experienced by students in our classrooms. Each of these strategies can be considered a prototype—a blueprint for scaffolding learning that can be adapted for application in any academic discipline, from elementary school through high school. These classroom strategies represent innovative ideas for supporting learning in diverse classrooms with students who exhibit a variety of learning needs.

Three guidelines will help teachers make effective decisions regarding the use of these strategies with their students. First, remember that student learning drives strategy selection. Once you decide what students need to know and to be able to do, consider which strategies would be appropriate to frontload learning, guide comprehension, and consolidate understanding. A classroom strategy may work well with some lessons, but be a poor fit with others. Make sure the teaching strategy is aligned with student goals for learning.

Second, it is the students' thinking that counts, not the specific classroom strategy. The strategies are designed to prompt the thinking characteristic of proficient readers and learners, but merely following the steps of a strategy does not guarantee that students will automatically engage in this thinking. The classroom strategies in this book do not lead magically or inevitably to success. It is easy for students to fall into a routine of "going through the motions." Be alert for students just "doing" rather than thinking, and schedule frequent metacognitive debriefing sessions that focus students on evaluating their own understandings.

Third, tailor the classroom strategy to match your students and your academic discipline. Although these classroom strategies are conveniently described as a series of steps, be aggressive in adapting these ideas so that the specific needs of your students and demands of your curriculum are factored in. Again, these strategies are prototypes that will look somewhat different in their application depending on the nature of the content. How can a strategy be customized to support learning in a world language classroom? How might the same strategy be tweaked to support learning in

math? Although the comprehension processes are universal, specific instructional applications will vary.

To assist teachers in their instructional planning, each classroom strategy is identified by a Strategy Index, which is found in the lower outside corner of the page on which the strategy is introduced. The Strategy Index highlights the strengths of each strategy in terms of instructional focus, text frames, and comprehension processes.

Instructional focus refers to how the strategy might be integrated with a lesson: frontloading learning (before-reading activities), guiding comprehension (during-reading activities), and consolidating understanding (after-reading activities) (see Chapter 2).

Text frames refer to the way thinking is organized during reading and learning activities. Chapter 3 outlined six basic text frames that condition a student's frame of mind during the lesson: cause/effect, concept/definition, problem/solution, compare/contrast, proposition/support, and goal/action/outcome. Text frames help students ask themselves the right questions about the material as they learn.

Comprehension processes refer to characteristics of proficient reading that were outlined in Chapter 1: making connections, generating questions, creating mental images, making inferences, determining importance, and synthesizing.

Notice that most classroom strategies emphasize more than one comprehension process, text frame, or instructional focus. For example, the second classroom strategy in this section is Anticipation Guides (see page 45). As shown on the lower outside corner of this page, in the Strategy Index under Instructional Focus, all three are highlighted because this strategy can be used to frontload

Strategy Index
Instructional Focus
Frontloading Learning
Guiding Comprehension
Consolidating Understanding
Text Frames
Cause/Effect
Concept/Definition
Problem/Solution
Compare/Contrast
Proposition/Support
Goal/Action/Outcome
Comprehension Processess
Making Connections
Generating Questions
Creating Mental Images
Making Inferences
Determining Importance
Synthesizing

instruction, to guide student comprehension as they read, and to synthesize their understandings after reading. The three highlighted boxes under Text Frames—cause/effect, problem/solution, and proposition/support—indicate that Anticipation Guides are especially effective for exploring these relationships during a lesson. Four Comprehension Processes are highlighted because phases of Anticipation Guides engage students in making connections, generating questions, inferring, and determining importance.

Effective classroom strategies engage students in a wide variety of interactive practices, as shown in the Strategy Index included in each strategy discussion. In addition, Table 7 categorizes the 45 strategies presented in this section in terms of particular student activities emphasized by each. If you are looking for a strategy that emphasizes vocabulary building, for example, you can use Table 7 to quickly evaluate which of those listed under "Developing Vocabulary" would be most appropriate to your needs. Other strategies are particularly rich in providing discussion formats, structures for student collaboration, and class brainstorming opportunities. Two categories focus on ways students can be asked to express their understandings: through personal response and by encouraging writing. Some strategies include visual representations of learning and several are particularly well suited for developing student study skills. Table 7 can provide teachers with more in-depth knowledge of how to use these strategies.

Table 7
Classroom Teaching Strategies Outlined by Student Activity

Student Activity	Classroom Strategy	
Developing Vocabulary	Analogy Charting Concept/Definition Mapping Connect Two History Memory Bubbles Magnet Summaries Math Reading Keys Mind Mapping	Science Connection Overview Story Impressions Student-Friendly Vocabulary Explanations Vocabulary Overview Guide Word Family Trees
Brainstorming Ideas	Analogy Charting Anticipation Guides B/D/A Questioning Chart Brainstorming Prior Knowledge Character Quotes Different Perspectives Inquiry Charts	K-W-L Plus (Know/Want to Know/ Learned) Mind Mapping Possible Sentences Problematic Situations Self-Questioning Taxonomy Story Impressions Vocabulary Overview Guide
Learning Collaboratively	Anticipation Guides Character Quotes Connect Two Different Perspectives Discussion Web Follow the Characters Hands-On Reading Inquiry Charts Interactive Reading Guides	K-W-L Plus (Know/Want to Know/ Learned) Math Reading Keys Paired Reviews Problematic Situations Role-Playing as Readers Save the Last Word for Me Story Impressions Written Conversations

(continued)

Student Activity	Classroom Strategy	
Promoting Discussion	Analogy Charting Anticipation Guides B/D/A Questioning Charts Brainstorming Prior Knowledge Character Quotes Different Perspectives Discussion Web Follow the Characters	Interactive Reading Guides K-W-L Plus (Know/Want to Know/ Learned) Paired Reviews Problematic Situations Pyramid Diagram Save the Last Word for Me Written Conversations
Responding Personally	Author Says/I Say B/D/A Questioning Chart Different Perspectives Discussion Web Double-Entry Diaries First-Person Reading Inquiry Charts	Interactive Reading Guides Paired Reviews Quick Writes RAFT (Role/Audience/Format/Topic) Role-Playing as Readers Save the Last Word for Me Written Conversations
Encouraging Writing	Author Says/I Say Connect Two Discussion Web First-Person Reading Inquiry Charts K-W-L Plus (Know/Want to Know/ Learned) Learning Logs Magnet Summaries	Power Notes Proposition/Support Outlines Pyramid Diagram Quick Writes RAFT (Role/Audience/Format/Topic) Role-Playing as Readers Story Impressions Template Frames Written Conversations
Representing Graphically	Analogy Charting Author Says/I Say Concept/Definition Maps Different Perspectives Discussion Web First-Person Reading Follow the Characters History Change Frame History Memory Bubbles Inquiry Charts	K-W-L Plus (Know/Want to Know/ Learned) Mind Mapping Power Notes Pyramid Diagram Science Connection Overview Story Mapping Structured Note-Taking Vocabulary Overview Guide Word Family Trees
Building Study Skills	B/D/A Questioning Chart Chapter Tours Double-Entry Diaries Follow the Characters Guided Imagery Hands-On Reading History Change Frame History Memory Bubbles Inquiry Charts Interactive Reading Guides Magnet Summaries Math Reading Keys	Paired Reviews Power Notes Question–Answer Relationships Question the Author Science Connection Overview Self-Questioning Taxonomy Story Mapping Student-Friendly Vocabulary Explanations Structured Note-Taking Template Frames Text Coding

Analogy Charting

"You mean it's like...?" Their eyes light up. The concept you are teaching comes alive. An analogy that relates to your students' lives has helped them make a connection. Teachers know that analogies are a powerful way to help students understand new information or concepts.

> Cells are the building blocks of your body like bricks are the building blocks of this school.
>
> The judicial branch of government functions like umpires in baseball.
>
> Punctuation marks in a sentence are like traffic signs.

Analogies help students link new learning to familiar concepts. Chapter 2 outlined three types of connections students bring to their comprehension of written texts: text-to-self, text-to-text, and text-to-world. Text-to-self connections are especially powerful; students can see how their personal lives intersect with what an author tells them. Analogies take advantage of text-to-self connections by suggesting ways students may draw upon personal experiences as a bridge to understanding new and unfamiliar territory.

Analogy Charting (Buehl & Hein, 1990; Buehl, 1995) is a classroom strategy that provides a visual framework for students to analyze key relationships in an analogy in depth. Analogies are based on the compare/contrast text frame, and as students explore relationships by connecting to already known ideas, they broaden their understanding of important concepts or vocabulary. Analogy Charting (see the Analogy Chart example) can be used with students to introduce a topic, to guide comprehension while reading, or synthesize understanding after reading.

Using the Strategy

Analogy Charting uses analogy to help students perceive similarities and differences between a new concept and something familiar in their lives. Using this strategy involves the following steps:

1 Determine what students already know to establish an analogous relationship to the new concept to be introduced. Selecting a familiar concept can provide a foundation for understanding the new concept. For example, students studying the concept of *colony* in history class can relate it to a highly familiar situation—being a dependent child in a family.

2 Introduce the Analogy Chart on an overhead transparency (see the Appendix for a reproducible version of the Analogy Chart) and provide copies for students to complete as you examine the analogy. Start brainstorming with students to generate ideas about specific characteristics or properties common to both concepts. Enter these in the *Similarities* column. Students might offer that a colony and a dependent child share the following characteristics: they rely on a parent figure for their needs, they must follow rules or laws set by others, they are related or somehow connected to the parent figure, and they sometimes have feelings of resentment and a desire to be independent and on their own.

3 Ask students to next brainstorm how the two concepts are different and enter these in the *Differences* column. This is a vital step, as it will ensure that students do not overgeneralize how the two concepts are alike, and it will reinforce that analogous relationships are not *identical* relationships. Initially, Steps 2 and 3 need to be modeled extensively by the teacher, but after students develop more independence, have them complete individual copies of a blank Analogy Chart in cooperative groups.

Students may note the following in our history example: (a) a colony usually is separated geographically from the parent figure, while a child usually lives with the parent figure in a family group, (b) a colony is regarded as a negative system, while families are not, and (c) a colony's independence has historically been associated with

Strategy Index
Instructional Focus
Frontloading Learning
Guiding Comprehension
Consolidating Understanding
Text Frames
Cause/Effect
Concept/Definition
Problem/Solution
Compare/Contrast
Proposition/Support
Goal/Action/Outcome
Comprehension Processess
Making Connections
Generating Questions
Creating Mental Images
Making Inferences
Determining Importance
Synthesizing

Analogy Chart

New Concept

Colony

Familiar Concept

A child in a family

Similarities

Mother country/parents set the rules
Are dependent for protection, support, and other things
Are related to parents or mother country (Settlers)
Are at early stage of development
Sometimes feel resentment about status
Eventually want to be independent

Differences

Child lives with family; colony is in a separate area
Colony is now regarded as a negative system; family is positive
Colony often includes many different peoples (natives); family is usually related
Colony tends to be exploited by mother country; child is nurtured
Colony's independence often connected with violence

Relationship Categories

Dependence on others Kinship/family background Control/self-determination

What do you understand now about <u>colonies</u>**?**
I can see why people in a colony would feel resentful, because in a way they were treated like a child. They don't get to set their own rules and laws and they had to rely on "the mother country" for practically everything, like money and protection. Children get to grow up and live their own lives, but colonies were expected to be "children" forever, so no wonder they often had to fight to get their freedom.

Source: Buehl, D. (1995). *Classroom strategies for interactive learning* (p. 26). Madison: Wisconsin State Reading Association.

violence, which is not characteristic of children coming of age in most families.

4 Discuss with students categories that make up the basis for the comparison. For example, some relationships (both rely on the parent for protection and other basic needs, and both represent an early stage of "development") might be labeled as *Dependence on others*, while other similarities might be labeled as *Kinship or Family background*, and *Control/self-determination*.

5 Have students write a summary statement about the similarities of the new concept and the familiar concept using their Analogy Charts. Students may write about how children and colonies often depend a great deal on the parent, how they eventually grow up or mature and want to assume control over themselves, how they may feel exploited, or how resentments lead to arguments or violence in the process of gaining independence.

Advantages

- Students enhance their understanding of new concepts or vocabulary through the analysis of familiar analogous concepts.

- Students make connections to new material by activating related experiences and background.

- Students gain practice in writing well-organized summaries that follow a compare/contrast text frame.

References

Buehl, D. (1995). *Classroom strategies for interactive learning.* Schofield: Wisconsin State Reading Association.

Buehl, D., & Hein, D. (1990). Analogy graphic organizer. *The Exchange. Newsletter of the International Reading Association Secondary Reading Special Interest Group, 3*(2), 6.

Suggested Readings

Bean, T., Singer, H., & Cowan, S. (1985). Analogical study guides: Improving comprehension in science. *Journal of Reading, 29*(3), 246–250.

Cook, D. (Ed.). (1989). *Strategic learning in the content areas.* Madison, WI: Department of Public Instruction.

Anticipation Guides

Suppose you are invited out for dinner at a gourmet restaurant. As you anticipate the meal, which of the following statements reflect your expectations?

- Gourmet meals are very expensive.

- Gourmet meals feature elaborate recipes difficult to prepare at home.

- Gourmet dining is a relaxed and very pleasurable experience.

- Gourmet meals feature small portions.

- Gourmet foods are delicious but fattening.

After dinner as you drive home from the restaurant, you will likely reflect whether your actual experience was consistent with your expectations.

The Anticipation Guide (Herber, 1978) is a frontloading strategy that forecasts major ideas in a passage with statements that activate students' thoughts and prior understandings. Before reading a selection, students respond to statements that challenge or support their preconceived ideas about key concepts in the passage. Students then explain or elaborate on their responses in small-group or class discussion. This process arouses interest, sets purposes for reading, and encourages raising questions—all important facets of comprehension. When students have completed their reading, they return to the Anticipation Guide to evaluate their understandings of the material and to correct misconceptions that surfaced during their initial deliberations.

Using the Strategies

Anticipation Guides are a good fit for instruction in all content disciplines and are equally effective with print and nonprint media. The Prediction Guide, a closely related strategy, is also presented.

An Anticipation Guide engages students in examining their knowledge and beliefs about a topic and then prompts them to reassess their thinking after reading a text. Using this strategy involves the following steps:

1 Identify the major ideas and concepts in a text that the students will be reading. For example, a science teacher may decide that students studying acid rain should focus attention on the following ideas as they read:

- Acid rain has a harmful effect on aquatic life.

- Acid rain destroys bridges, buildings, and statues.

- Acid rain has multiple causes including auto and factory emissions.

- Acid rain prevention involves economic trade-offs.

- Acid rain problems are increasing in many regions of the world.

2 Consider what students might already know about the topic to ensure that they are able to respond to items on an Anticipation Guide. Otherwise, they may adopt an "I don't know" posture as they go through the statements on the guide. In addition, factor in students' experiences and beliefs that will be either supported or challenged by the reading. Most students will have heard of acid rain and its negative effect on rivers and lakes. Some may have opinions about its impact in different parts of the world, including their own region. Some students will know that acid rain is connected to the burning of fossil fuels, and that the control of fossil fuel consumption is controversial.

3 Create an Anticipation Guide with four to six statements that challenge or modify students' preexisting understandings of the material. Include statements that will elicit agreement between students and the author. The most effective statements are those about which students have some knowledge but not necessarily a complete understanding. If possible, include a statement that taps into possible misconceptions about the topic (see Anticipation Guide for Science). As a second example, to prepare students in

Strategy Index
Instructional Focus
Frontloading Learning
Guiding Comprehension
Consolidating Understanding
Text Frames
Cause/Effect
Concept/Definition
Problem/Solution
Compare/Contrast
Proposition/Support
Goal/Action/Outcome
Comprehension Processess
Making Connections
Generating Questions
Creating Mental Images
Making Inferences
Determining Importance
Synthesizing

a literature class for the major themes of Jack London's novel *The Call of the Wild*, an English language arts teacher can create an Anticipation Guide that elicits student perspectives on ideas and themes explored by the author (see Anticipation Guide for Literature).

4 Present the Anticipation Guide on an overhead projector or as individual student handouts. Leave space for individual or small-group responses. As each statement is discussed, have students provide justification for their ideas; ask them to talk about their thinking on the statements. You may wish to have students first complete the guide individually and then share their thinking in small-group or class discussions. Another variation is to have students rank statements, starting with 1 for the statement that they agree with most and so forth, until the highest number is given to the statement with which they agree least.

Anticipation Guide for Science

Acid Rain

Directions:

- Read the following statements concerning problems associated with acid rain.
- Put a check next to each statement with which you agree.
- Be prepared to support your views on each statement by thinking what you know about acid rain and its effects. Share this information with other members of your group as you discuss the following six statements:

_____ 1. Acid rain kills fish.

_____ 2. The major cause of acid rain is fuel emissions from automobiles.

_____ 3. Stopping acid rain will cause some people to lose their jobs.

_____ 4. Acid rain problems are not yet serious in our region.

_____ 5. Acid rain is made up of sulfur oxides.

_____ 6. If acid rain is not controlled, we will experience a major environmental disaster.

Source: Buehl, D. (1995). *Classroom strategies for interactive learning* (p. 29). Madison: Wisconsin State Reading Association.

Anticipation Guide for Literature

Call of the Wild

Directions:

- Read the following statements about the book *Call of the Wild*.
- Compare your opinions about these statements with those of the author, Jack London.
- Check the column labeled *You* for those statements with which you agree. Be prepared to support your opinions with examples.
- Check the column labeled *Jack London* for those statements with which you feel he would agree.

	You	Jack London
1. Only the strong survive in this world.	_____	_____
2. People must live in harmony with their environment.	_____	_____
3. Greed makes people cruel.	_____	_____
4. The primitive instinct exists in all people.	_____	_____
5. Much of what happens to people is the result of fate.	_____	_____
6. People will adapt to their surroundings and survive.	_____	_____

Source: Buehl, D. (1995). *Classroom strategies for interactive learning* (p. 30). Madison: Wisconsin State Reading Association. Developed by Sarah Conroy, 1993, Madison East High School, Madison, WI, USA.

5 Students read the selection. Ask them to focus on information in the text that confirms, elaborates, or rejects each of the statements in the Anticipation Guide. If students are reading material that can be marked, instruct them to underline or highlight sections that are germane to each statement and annotate with the number of the item this section concerns. Or they can affix sticky notes to textbook pages alongside information that supports or rebuts each statement.

6 After students complete the reading, have them return to the statements in the Anticipation Guide to determine how they have changed their thinking regarding any of them. In cooperative groups, have them locate the information from the text that supports or rejects each statement. Students then "correct" the Anticipation Guide by rewriting any statement to make it consistent with the selection they have read.

Another option is to include two columns in the Anticipation Guide for responses—one for students and one for the author. After reading the passage, students then compare their thoughts on each statement with those of the author. This is especially effective when responding to ideas presented in literature (see Anticipation Guide for Literature). In this case, students determine the extent to which they accept Jack London's basic premises on human nature as he illustrates them in his novel.

Prediction Guides

Prediction Guides are a variation of this strategy. Predictions are a natural human response to the avalanche of phenomena that we encounter in our lives. Our hours hum with predictions: How long will it take to prepare this meal? How will students respond to this particular lesson? How will my father like the gift I selected? How much longer will it be before we have to trade in this increasingly unreliable second car?

Making predictions is also a core strategy for reading comprehension. Proficient readers constantly attempt to read ahead of an author—picking up clues and predicting what might unfold. Predictions are a category of inference: when we predict, we are going beyond what is explicitly stated to anticipate what, where, why, how, who, if. Using this strategy involves the following steps:

1 Establish with students the characteristics of solid predictions. Predictions are not haphazard "shots in the dark," nor are they merely opinions. Instead, a good prediction is grounded in two ways. First, the prediction must be consistent with the available evidence. Students making a prediction must be able to cite relevant information from a text that lends support to the reasonableness of their hunch. Second, the prediction

must be consistent with previous experiences. What we already know about a situation, or what has happened previously in similar circumstances, allow us to conjecture about this particular instance.

As students explore various predictions, introduce a critical proviso: although a prediction may be thoughtful and well-founded, it still may turn out to be incorrect. Many excellent predictions fail to be realized. Emphasize that predicting is sophisticated thinking that draws upon incomplete information. The process of confirming and rejecting predictions is an essential dynamic of comprehension and the essence of active reading.

2 Model predicting as a think-aloud. Select a short text that can be displayed on the overhead projector or provide students with a copy. As you think aloud, speculate what you think the author might say next, where you think a story might be heading, or other aspects you might be wondering about. Show how various statements or hints in the text prompt your predictions, and also how your personal knowledge and experience guides and shapes your predictions.

3 Create a Prediction Guide that features a series of statements about the topic that may or may not be validated in the text. For example, a newspaper article entitled "In an Obese World, Sweet Nothings Add Up" (Brody, 2004), could elicit predictions regarding the consumption of sugar in our diet (see Prediction Guide for Health). Students complete the guide individually or with partners, and talk about their predictions in cooperative groups, before sharing with the entire class. The first stage involves making predictions about whether the article will confirm each statement. This stage engages students in searching their personal knowledge and experience base to justify their predictions.

4 Students read the assigned material to discover which of their predictions will be supported by the author. Students need to search for textual evidence that can back up a prediction or contradict it. The Prediction Guide gives students a clear purpose for reading, which parallels what proficient readers do as a matter of habit—reading to substantiate predictions.

5 Students rejoin their groups or partners to complete the second stage of the Prediction Guide: checking those statements confirmed by the author. Because Guide statements should not be merely "lifted" from the text verbatim, students will need to summarize and make inferences to ascertain whether the author did indeed confirm or reject some of the statements.

6 Ask students to generate their own predictions from a text by examining the title, headings and

Prediction Guide for Health

You will be reading an article from the *New York Times* that is entitled "In an Obese World, Sweet Nothings Add Up." Check each of the statements below that you predict the article will say. Share your predictions with a partner. Then read the article to confirm or reject your predictions.

	Your Prediction	Confirmed by Author
1. Sugar has a beneficial effect on your body.	_____	_____
2. Americans eat too many foods that contain high amounts of sugar.	_____	_____
3. Fruit drinks are better for you than soft drinks.	_____	_____
4. Artificial sweeteners are better for your body than sugar.	_____	_____
5. Because of the popularity of organic foods, sugar consumption for Americans has actually gone down in recent years.	_____	_____
6. Sugar is not related to hyperactivity in children.	_____	_____

Source: Buehl, D. (2004). Predicting what lies ahead. *OnWEAC In Print, 4*(7), 13.

---

subheadings, pictures, and other visual information. They can also be asked to pause at the end of prescribed paragraphs or sections, or at the end of chapters, to consider possible predictions that they feel are justified by their reading so far. Model appropriate predicting language, as in the following examples:

- From the title/paragraph, I predict this chapter will be about....
- The reason I believe this is....
- Based on...I predict this story will....
- I think this because....
- My prediction was confirmed because....
- My prediction was not confirmed because....

Advantages

- Students are cued into the major ideas of a selection before they start reading.
- Students activate their background knowledge about a topic before they read, which they can share with classmates.
- Students are motivated to read to determine whether the text will confirm or contradict their conjectures.

- Students' misconceptions about a topic are addressed openly and are more likely to be changed after reading and discussing the new material.
- Students learn to risk airing their ideas, as they come to understand that many reasonable predictions will not be confirmed by a text.

References

Brody, J. (2004, March 9). In an obese world, sweet nothings add up. *The New York Times*, D7.

Buehl, D. (1995). *Classroom strategies for interactive learning.* Madison: Wisconsin State Reading Association.

Buehl, D. (2004). Predicting what lies ahead. *OnWEAC In Print, 4*(7), 13.

Herber, H. (1978). *Teaching reading in content areas* (2nd ed.). Englewood Cliffs, NJ: Prentice Hall.

Suggested Readings

Nichols, J.N. (1983). Using prediction to increase content area interest and understanding. *Journal of Reading, 27*(3), 225–228.

Readence, J.E., Bean, T.W., & Baldwin, R.S. (2004). *Content area literacy: An integrated approach* (8th ed.). Dubuque, IA: Kendall/Hunt.

Author Says/I Say

Hmmm.... Jet lag.... The author of this article says that sleep cycles are not the only body system disrupted by jet lag. Traveling across several time zones also impacts the body's digestive system, temperature, and hormone secretions. I certainly noticed this phenomenon personally. I not only felt sleep deprived, but I had an unsettled stomach for several days after that first flight to England. I was fatigued and generally "under the weather" until I was able to adjust to London time. This information underscores that jet lag is more than merely not getting enough sleep one evening. Jet lag disrupts the way your body is used to functioning. The author goes on to criticize a jet lag diet for being nutritionally problematic as well as highly inconvenient. But I tried such a diet the second time I flew to England and it seemed to work remarkably well.

Imagine eavesdropping into the thinking of a reader immersed in the flow of comprehension of a newspaper article offering advice on jet lag. On one level, the reader attends to the words of the author, who dedicated time to compose this message. But invariably, as readers, we can't help but personalize what an author tells us. We find ourselves talking through an author's message, interjecting our own thoughts and experiences, as we customize our understanding of what a text means.

We recognize these internal dialogues with ourselves as a familiar daily mental routine. Reading is, in many respects, a conversation with another person. Although the author is not physically present, this individual is definitely talking to us—the reader—to tell a story, to inform and enlighten, or even to influence. As we track what an author has to say to us, we can't help but talk back. We remind ourselves of how our lives connect to the author's words. We factor in something from our personal knowledge banks. In some cases we may even want to argue or disagree. And as this exchange between author and reader unfolds, we periodically take stock of our thinking. We register what we understand, we sum up key thoughts and ideas, and we periodically draw conclusions and make judgments.

Using the Strategies

The Author Says/I Say strategy is a variation of a strategy developed by Beers (2003), which uses a chart to guide students in constructing meaning from a written text. The Say Something Read-Aloud, a related strategy, is also presented here.

Using the Author Says/I Say strategy involves the following steps:

1 Introduce the Author Says/I Say Chart (see the Appendix for a reproducible version of the Author Says/I Say chart). The chart is devised so that readers connect what the text makes them wonder about with what an author says. In addition, readers are prompted to "weigh in" with what they are thinking. The final column returns students to what they were wondering, as they sum up what they now understand. In effect, five key comprehension processes are elicited: questioning ("I Wonder"), determining importance ("The Author Says"), making connections to prior knowledge and inferring ("I Say"), and finally, synthesizing new understandings ("And So").

2 Model this strategy with a think-aloud. For example, an article on food safety (Shute, 2007) provides an excellent opportunity to demonstrate all these phases of thinking using the Author Says/I Say strategy (see Author Says/I Say Chart example).

This article focuses on what people can do to avoid becoming ill from the food they eat. I wonder how serious a problem this is. The author says that 76 million Americans become sick from food related illnesses each year, and 5000 die. I had no idea "bad" food was this extensive, although I remember reading about deaths from spinach and pet food that

Strategy Index
Instructional Focus
Frontloading Learning
Guiding Comprehension
Consolidating Understanding
Text Frames
Cause/Effect
Concept/Definition
Problem/Solution
Compare/Contrast
Proposition/Support
Goal/Action/Outcome
Comprehension Processess
Making Connections
Generating Questions
Creating Mental Images
Making Inferences
Determining Importance
Synthesizing

Author Says/I Say Chart for Food Safety Article

I Wonder	The Author Says	I Say	And So
How widespread is unsafe food?	Each year 76 million Americans get sick from food causes, 300,000 are hospitalized, and 5000 die.	I remember tainted spinach killing some people, and I also recall pet food that was contaminated.	It seems we are taking food safety for granted, when we really shouldn't be!
How can we prevent getting sick from food?	The only way to be sure you don't get sick from food is to not eat.	I don't think the author is really serious about this.	I think the author is really saying that we will always face a danger of getting sick from food.
	The best defense is in the kitchen—we should wash all foods, even organic foods.	I don't always wash fruits and vegetables, and I've heard that kitchen counters and cutting boards harbor lots of germs.	I need to change my habits preparing foods, wash everything more thoroughly, and wash my hands more around food.
	Cooking foods is safer than eating foods that are uncooked.	I know you have to thoroughly cook meats like hamburger, but I thought uncooked vegetables have more vitamins than if cooked.	I need to be extra careful with raw foods, especially fruits and vegetables that are eaten uncooked.
Is organic food safer?	Organic food is freer of pesticides, herbicides, and antibiotics, but still can be contaminated by bacteria, metals, and other dangerous substances.	People assume that organic food is safe, and organic farmers try to use natural and nontoxic growing methods.	We can't assume any food is free of problems, although organic food might present fewer problems.
Is buying locally grown food safer?	Many foods produced in other countries are grown in poor sanitation conditions & could contain pesticides banned in the U.S.	I know DDT has long been banned in the U.S. but is still sold to countries that sell us food.	It is a good idea to know where the food you eat is produced.

Source: Buehl, D. (2007, June). The author says/I say. *OnWEAC*. Retrieved from www.weac.org/News/2006-07/june07/readingroom.htm

was contaminated. It seems that we take our food supply for granted and we need to be much more careful about checking what we eat....

As you talk your way through the text, emphasize how statements by the author sparks your thinking about food safety. Reading becomes an interchange between the author and reader, as both have something to say about the topic. The key is the "And So" column, which registers how you have pulled your thinking together into ideas that you have learned from this text. This column for summarizing prompts students to verbalize what they will take away from the text.

3 Provide ample opportunities for students to practice using this strategy to enhance comprehension of potentially problematic texts. One method involves asking students to use sticky notes to record those questions they notice themselves wondering about— before, during, and after reading. Then instruct them to focus on five questions that seem to be the most significant. These five questions are then charted on the Author Says/I Say Chart.

Say Something Read-Aloud

The Say Something strategy (Gaither, 1997) is another variation that allows students to "talk back" to an author.

1 Partners switch off with oral reading of paragraphs from classroom materials. For example, history students read a history textbook passage about life during the Depression. One student reads aloud the first paragraph while the partner follows along and listens. When the reader finishes, the listener must *say something* about what was read: comment on interesting material, make a prediction, wonder about something stated, identify confusing information, or relate information from the paragraph to personal background experiences or knowledge.

2 Ask partners to switch roles and continue with the next paragraph. Unlike round robin reading—one student reading and the entire class listening—paired reading involves half the class reading while partners listen. Because all students are either reading aloud or listening and commenting, the sound level in the classroom accords a measure of privacy to individual readers, which is especially helpful to struggling readers who may need assistance from their partners as they read. The Say Something strategy provides a more interactive format for classroom read-alouds and allocates students more opportunity to practice oral reading fluency. The strategy stimulates conversation about a passage and encourages students to make connections as they read, and to work at clarifying information that is difficult or confusing.

Advantages

- Students are continually reminded that reading involves a mental conversation between an author and a reader; both need to contribute to the conversation if comprehension is to occur.

- Students are provided with cues that guide them into accessing implicit layers of meaning that necessitate inferential thinking.

- Students verbalize their understandings as they sum up what they have gained from their reading.

References

Beers, K. (2003). *When kids can't read: What teachers can do: A guide for teachers 6–12*. Portsmouth, NH: Heinemann.

Buehl, D. (2007, June). The author says/I say. *OnWEAC*. Retrieved from www.weac.org/News/2006-07/june07/reading room.htm

Gaither, P. (1997, May). *Caught in the act: Strategies to engage readers with informational text*. Paper presented at the 42nd annual convention of the International Reading Association, Atlanta, GA.

Shute, N. (2007, May 28). Better safe than sorry. *U.S. News & World Report, 142*(19), 67–72.

B/D/A Questioning Charts

Any questions?

Questioning is an integral part of our daily routines, and sometimes it seems we are constantly invited to pose our questions. We outline instructions for the babysitter—any questions? Our doctor describes procedures for taking a new medication—any questions? We purchase a new product and scan through the explanations for use—any questions? We are assigned a project to complete from our supervisor at work—any questions? We leave our spouse directions for assembling the evening meal—any questions? The questioning goes on and on.

Consider how your mind literally buzzes with questions as you contemplate the reading of a long-awaited new novel. Even before you open the volume and dig in, you are wondering about a host of things. Some of your inquisitiveness concerns the content of the book—what is the plot, how will the storyline unfold, and what might I expect will happen as I read along? But you will also be wondering about the actual experience of reading this book—will I enjoy it as much as I anticipate, will I find events and characters predictable or refreshing, will I admire how this author uses language or crafts the suspense, and will I find that I can't put the book down or that I'm disappointed? If you have sampled this author before, you are also probably wondering how this book will "stack up" compared with the others you have read.

Of course, the questions keep coming once you slip into the pages. And our questions don't end when we reach that last page and set the book aside. Likely, we are still wondering. Could this story really be plausible? Did the author base this book on actual people or historical events? And on a more personal level, we might savor where our imaginations transported us. Would I have made the same decisions as the protagonists in the novel? What would it have been like if I had been a character in this story myself? What has this author got me thinking?

Asking questions is our particularly human way of narrowing our understanding, of making sense. Asking questions is how we zig-zag our way between knowing and not knowing—questions are how we navigate our personal learning. But our students would probably offer a dramatically different take on questions. For the most part, students perceive questioning as an "interrogation" by others; they are regularly confronted in school with the task of answering the queries of somebody else: a teacher, a textbook editor, an exam developer. In many classrooms, the balance between question-posing and question-responding is badly askew. As a result, students receive inadequate practice in generating their own questions about new learning, and instead they relegate their thinking to a superficial "looking for answers."

Using the Strategy

The B/D/A (Before/During/After Reading) Questioning Chart (adapted from Laverick, 2002) prompts students to ask their own questions before, during, and after reading. Using this strategy involves the following steps:

1 Introduce the concepts of *thick* and *thin* questions (Buehl, 2005). We ask ourselves "thin" questions to clarify what an author tells us. We ask ourselves "thick" questions to ponder deeper ideas, which may take us far beyond the text that started our thinking. Model thick and thin questions that guide your understanding of a short text.

For example, while reading aloud a newspaper article on a topic such as the avian flu, note students' thin questions that occur to you: What does the author say causes avian flu? How can it infect humans? What is worrying public health officials? Questions such as these are specific to the text and help guide you in clarifying the author's message.

Thin questions may target clarification of key vocabulary (What exactly is a "pandemic"?) or clarification of an important fact (What was the Spanish flu outbreak in 1918?). The author may provide a direct answer to some of your

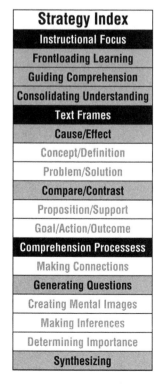

Strategy Index
Instructional Focus
Frontloading Learning
Guiding Comprehension
Consolidating Understanding
Text Frames
Cause/Effect
Concept/Definition
Problem/Solution
Compare/Contrast
Proposition/Support
Goal/Action/Outcome
Comprehension Processess
Making Connections
Generating Questions
Creating Mental Images
Making Inferences
Determining Importance
Synthesizing

thin questions, you may have to infer the answers to other of your thin questions, or some thin questions may be unanswered because the author is depending on the reader to access background knowledge to fill in the missing information. Underscore these different varieties of thin questions as you talk with students; some excellent thin questions will be unanswerable using the text alone, necessitating that other sources (such as a dictionary) be consulted.

Also demonstrate thick questions related to this topic that expand your thinking beyond the text: Why are governments apparently not very well prepared to meet epidemic threats like the avian flu? Are there really effective ways to protect ourselves? Will we some-day experience a pandemic like the Spanish flu of 1918 when millions died? When are these public health warnings real, and when are they exaggerated? Will I, or someone close to me, be struck with a disease like the avian flu?

Thick questions are often the ones we care most about as we personalize our understandings and learning. Thick questions represent the upper layers of Bloom's Taxonomy (Bloom, Englehart, Furst, Hill, & Krathwohl, 1956), such as application, analysis, evaluation, and synthesis (see Self-Questioning Taxonomy, page 157), when we truly engage with new ideas. Thick questions lead to rich conversation, divergent viewpoints, and further exploration of ideas. Are people today becoming more at risk for dangerous diseases

like the avian flu? Why might this be so? What can be done to diminish such risks? Are we likely to under-take these necessary steps? Why or why not? What can I personally do?

2 Select a short text related to the curriculum, and model how generating questions is a natural component of our thinking when we read. Explain that before we begin a text, we pose a range of generic questions, such as, What will this text be about? How much do I already know about this topic? How challenging will this be to read? and so forth. Ask students to examine textual features that can elicit specific questions. The title of a newspaper article, "In Adolescents, Addiction to Tobacco Comes Easy" (Brody, 2008), might lead a reader to wonder, Why would adolescents be more vulnerable to tobacco addiction? How easy is it for adolescents to become addicted? Headings, photos, visual displays, and features such as "pull-quotes" also provide grist for questions before reading. For example, a heading that states "New Strategies Needed" leads easily to the question, What are the new strategies advocated by this author?

Have students record these questions in the "Before Reading" column on a B/D/A Questioning Chart (see the Appendix for a reproducible version of the B/D/A Questioning Chart). Ask them to take stock of what they are wondering and to contribute their questions to the chart before they began reading.

B/D/A Questioning Chart

What were you wondering?

Before Reading	During Reading	After Reading
Why would adolescents be more vulnerable to tobacco addiction?	Can teens really get hooked from the first cigarette?	Will we discover how to predict tobacco addiction?
How easy is it for adolescents to become addicted?	How many teens smoke?	How can we tell if one has an "addictive" personality?
How easy is it for adolescents to become addicted?	Is teen smoking on the rise?	Are cigarettes too available for purchase?
	What can schools do?	Will we ever eliminate dangerous habits like smoking?
	Why is there more smoking in movies?	

What do you understand now that you didn't understand before?

Teens can become addicted to tobacco almost immediately, even infrequent smokers, and as a result are highly likely to continue smoking into adulthood.

3 Next read aloud the first paragraph or so, and again, think-aloud about questions that have you wondering. These are entered in the "During Reading" center column of the chart. For example, you might wonder, Can teens really get hooked from the first cigarette? How many teens currently smoke? Is this number going up?"

Assign students to then work independently on reading the rest of the text, recording their questions about the material. Set a target number of questions (such as five for the passage) or recommend a question for every couple of paragraphs. Mandate a number of thick questions, to encourage students to go beyond merely clarification. When students have completed this phase, have them meet with partners to share their questions. Ask them to identify questions that were eventually answered by the author, and questions that still remain after reading.

4 The third phase involves those lingering questions after a text has been read. Emphasize that, as inquisitive people, we will likely finish a text and realize that some of our questions remain unresolved. Additional exploration and reading in the future will be necessary to flesh out satisfactory answers. These "hanging" questions are placed in the "After Reading" column. When the chart has been completed, solicit questions that students feel are particularly significant to guide class discussion of the passage. For instance, students might be wondering whether dangerous personal habits like smoking will ever really diminish in our culture.

5 Prompt students to inventory their learning by summarizing key ideas in the "What do you understand now that you didn't understand before?" box on the bottom of the chart. Again, ask students to share with a partner, and then generate a list of important understandings from the class on the board or overhead transparency.

6 Provide students with multiple opportunities to identify their own questions while learning. For example, ask students to list five things "they are wondering about" while reading a passage. Each "I wonder" could be written on a sticky note and affixed to the margin of the page. Or students could be given a "think-mark"—a bookmark for the chapter with slots for their five questions.

Advantages

- Students experience a significant and valuable role reversal where they become the questioners themselves.
- Students gain essential practice with and feedback on becoming question-posers rather than merely question-responders.
- Students are encouraged to be curious and critical readers who wonder about what a text is telling them.
- B/D/A Questioning Charts provide students with a visual reminder of the progress of their thinking as they explore a new text.

References

Bloom, B., Englehart, M., Furst, E., Hill, W., & Krathwohl, D.R. (1956). *Taxonomy of educational objectives: The classification of educational goals. Handbook I: Cognitive domain.* New York: Longman.

Brody, J. (2008, February 12). In adolescents, addiction to tobacco comes easy. *The New York Times*, D7.

Buehl, D. (2005, November). Thick and thin questions. *OnWEAC*. Retrieved from www.weac.org/News/2005-06/nov05/readingroomnov05.htm

Laverick, C. (2002). B-D-A strategy: Reinventing the wheel can be a good thing. *Journal of Adolescent & Adult Literacy, 46*(2), 144–147.

Brainstorming Prior Knowledge

What do you know about Antarctica? Earthworms? Ultraviolet light? Jane Austen? Chances are, if you were going to read a passage about any of these topics you would spend a few moments "reconnoitering" in your mind what you already know. You would take stock of your prior knowledge.

Suppose you are paging through a magazine and chance upon an article entitled "Lasers: The Promise of a 21st-Century Technology." What do you anticipate this author will talk about? Laser tools? Laser surgery? Laser scanners and printers? Laser treatments? Laser light displays? Laser weapons? The principles behind lasers as a beam of light?

Like any proficient reader, you predict the article's content by recalling pertinent prior knowledge that might relate to new material in the article. In the classroom, teachers need to assess what students already know about a topic and help them access this useful knowledge. Frontloading activities that help students connect to prior knowledge are necessary to jump-start learning about a topic (see the discussion on frontloading in Chapter 2).

Using the Strategies

Brainstorming strategies provide a useful framework for eliciting students' prior knowledge before learning. Several classroom variations may be used: List, Inquire, Note, and Know (LINK), List-Group-Label, or Alphabet Brainstorming.

LINK

LINK (Vaughan & Estes, 1986) is a brainstorming strategy that encourages student-directed discussion about their knowledge of a topic. Using this strategy involves the following steps:

1 Decide on a keyword or concept related to the material that will trigger responses from your students. Write this "cue" on the chalkboard or overhead transparency. Allow 3 minutes for the students to list on paper as many meaningful associations as come to mind. For example, the term *solar system* might trigger knowledge for a sixth-grade class preparing to read a science selection on this topic. Solicit an association from each student and write these around the cue term. Start with less confident students to increase their involvement and ensure that all students can contribute. When everyone has offered an association, allow students to respond with further associations. During this stage, student contributions are listed without any comments from either you or the students, including those offering the associations. Sixth graders, for example, will offer a rich assortment of associations for the cue term *solar system* (see the LINK for Solar System example).

2 Encourage students to inquire about the associations arrayed about the topic; ask them, "Which items are you wondering about?" Students may ask their peers for clarification or elaboration of some items or ask for examples or definitions. They may challenge some items. However, all inquiries are directed to one another, not to the teacher. Langer (1981) advocates that the teacher initiate the discussion by selecting a response and asking, "I'm wondering what made you think of...?" This prompts students to converse with one another as they explore their understandings.

3 During the inquiry process, students interact both to share and to extend their understandings of the topic. To help students assume this responsibility, establish some classroom ground rules. Remind students to be respectful of one another during their inquiries, taking care not to embarrass or belittle classmates as they examine or challenge items. Emphasize that we all "hear things that are not necessarily accurate." In the solar system example, students might question associations such as solar cells or solarium. The resulting discussion could establish a connection between the solar system (the sun and its orbiting bodies) and other important links with the sun (solar energy).

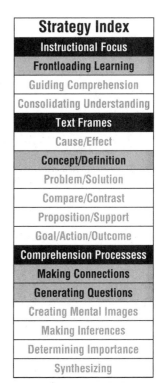

Strategy Index
Instructional Focus
Frontloading Learning
Guiding Comprehension
Consolidating Understanding
Text Frames
Cause/Effect
Concept/Definition
Problem/Solution
Compare/Contrast
Proposition/Support
Goal/Action/Outcome
Comprehension Processess
Making Connections
Generating Questions
Creating Mental Images
Making Inferences
Determining Importance
Synthesizing

LINK for Solar System

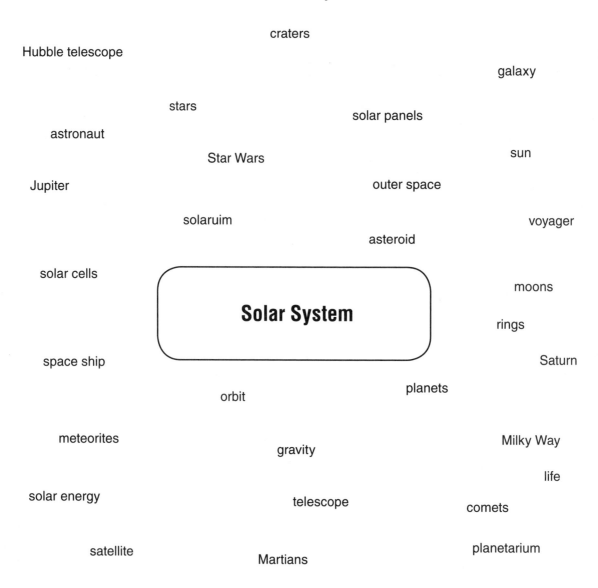

craters

Hubble telescope

galaxy

stars

solar panels

astronaut

Star Wars

sun

Jupiter

outer space

solaruim

voyager

asteroid

solar cells

Solar System

moons

rings

space ship

Saturn

orbit

planets

meteorites

Milky Way

gravity

life

solar energy

telescope

comets

satellite

planetarium

Martians

Source: Buehl, D. (1995). *Classroom strategies for interactive learning* (p. 65). Madison: Wisconsin State Reading Association.

4 When students have completed their inquiries and comments about the items, cover the items and ask students to turn over their papers and note what they have learned about the topic. One variation is to have them explain the concept. What they write is based on both their prior experience and the class discussion during the inquiry. Students are now ready to read the passage. After reading, ask them to note what they have learned from the new material.

List-Group-Label

List-Group-Label (Taba, 1967) is a more involved brainstorming strategy that is effective for students who have an adequate baseline of information about a topic. Using this strategy involves the following steps:

1 Decide on an appropriate cue word and give students 3 minutes to write as many words as they can associate with the term. For example, ask students to jot down associations for *amphibian* before studying this topic. List the associations on a chalkboard or overhead transparency. Ask for a quick justification for how each word or expression relates to the topic. For example, a list might include *frog, salamander, lives near water, toad, eats bugs, cold-blooded, ponds, aquarium,* and *slimy skin.*

2 When you have a sufficient list, have students work in cooperative teams to group items by common characteristics. Provide teams with small slips of paper so they can record items and physically shift them into groups. Students should aim for at least three items per group, although there may be misfit items that do not correspond with the others.

3 The final stage of this brainstorming activity involves categorization. Have students examine their groupings and decide on an appropriate label, which can be written on a slip of paper and used as a title for each sublist. Each team shares its categories and explains the rationale for organizing the lists. Labels for amphibian could include types, where they live, and characteristics.

Alphabet Brainstorming

Alphabet Brainstorming (Ricci & Wahlgren, 1998) is effective for students who have more extensive background knowledge. The resulting chart serves as a prompt for remembering terms, facts, or events (see the Alphabet Brainstorming chart used for a history class studying the 1960s).

1 Give each student or cooperative group a blank copy of the Alphabet Brainstorming chart (see Appendix for a reproducible version of the Alphabet Brainstorming chart). A history teacher embarking on a study of the 1960s used the general prompt: "The 1960s."

2 Students work with partners or in groups to generate a related term or meaningful association that begins with each letter of the alphabet. Ask students to fill in as many boxes as possible within a designated time period.

3 Ask students or groups to share their terms with the entire class and briefly justify how each term fits with the topic. In particular, students will want to hear if other groups came up with associations for difficult letters. In the 1960s example, some groups might have thought of "Malcolm X" for the usually problematic *X* slot on the chart.

Advantages

- Students prepare for the study of new material and anticipate the content based on what they already know. Students are more motivated to read material that is related to something they already know.

- Students share background knowledge with their peers so that all students can begin reading with some familiarity of the topic.

- Student misconceptions about the material that appear during brainstorming are in the open to be corrected during instruction.

- Students assume the responsibility for raising questions, seeking clarifications, and engaging in discussion about the topic.

Alphabet Brainstorming—The 1960s

A Apollo	B Beatles	C Civil Rights	D Drugs	E Easy Rider	F Flag Burning	G
H Hippies	I	J Jimi Hendrix	K Kennedy	L Long Hair	M Moon Walk	N Nixon
O	P Protests	Q	R Rock Music	S Sexual Revolution	T	U
V Vietnam	W Woodstock	X	Y	Z Mao Zedong		

Source: Buehl, D. (2001). *Classroom strategies for interactive learning* (2nd ed., p. 33). Newark, DE: International Reading Association.

- Students can revisit their lists after learning to add new information or to eliminate erroneous information.

References

Buehl, D. (1995). *Classroom strategies for interactive learning.* Madison: Wisconsin State Reading Association.

Buehl, D. (2001). *Classroom strategies for interactive learning* (2nd ed.). Newark, DE: International Reading Association.

Langer, J. (1981). From theory to practice: A prereading plan. *Journal of Reading, 25*(2), 152–156.

Ricci, G., & Wahlgren, C. (1998, May). *The key to know "PAINE" know gain.* Paper presented at the 43rd Annual Convention of the International Reading Association, Orlando, FL.

Taba, H. (1967). *Teacher's handbook for elementary social studies.* Reading, MA: Addison-Wesley.

Vaughan, J., & Estes, T. (1986). *Reading and reasoning beyond the primary grades.* Boston: Allyn & Bacon.

Chapter Tours

Notice how this next painting exhibits several characteristics of Monet's later masterpieces. The subject (water lilies), the brush technique, and the use of color—all are associated with canvases completed by Monet in the 1920s....

Think about your experiences being escorted on a guided tour of an art gallery, a museum, a national park, or a historical site. A guided tour provides a knowledgeable introduction to what is being viewed, helps you focus on what is interesting or important, offers insights or experiences that enhance appreciation, and provides a framework for understanding. In contrast, unless you are already quite knowledgeable, you will probably miss significant elements of the experience if you wander about by yourself. This is also true of students struggling to make sense of class textbooks. Chapter Tours can provide them with enough direction and background so that they can successfully learn what is important in their reading.

Using the Strategy

Chapter Tours, a frontloading technique, guides or talks readers through a chapter and points out features of the text that warrant special attention. An effective tour should set up readers for comprehension by stimulating connections to prior knowledge, self-questioning, imagining, inferring, determining importance, and ultimately, synthesizing understanding.

1 To underscore the importance of frontloading before reading, provide students with a short text that might appear obscure if they had not been alerted to the general topic. For example, display the following passage on an overhead transparency and provide students with enough time for a single reading.

Your first decision is to choose the size you desire. Once you have made your selection, examine the general shape to determine where to start. The initial incision is always at the top, and you should continue until you can lift it cleanly. The removal of the interior portion can be fun, although some people regard this as the least enjoyable aspect. Once the shell is empty, you can begin to craft a personality. Some prefer a forbidding likeness, while others follow a more humorous direction. Finally, arrange for a source of illumination.

Enjoy your results while you can, for your work will soon begin to sag.

Ask volunteers for hunches about the passage. As students offer their ideas, have them cite clues from the passage that triggered their theories. A variety of explanations about the selection may be offered and justified. Then allow students to reread the passage with the prompt *Halloween*. Students will quickly recognize that the passage describes carving a pumpkin into a jack-o-lantern.

Discuss with students frustrations they encountered when trying to read the passage without frontloading. Because students were not sure what part of their memory to access, they may not have been able to make sense of the text without the Halloween clue. Follow up with similar passages, each time encouraging students to search their memory banks for connections to apply to the material. Students will realize that reading is much more efficient and successful if they frontload before tackling a text.

2 Preview a typical textbook chapter to identify salient features that students might overlook during their reading. Many textbooks present information in a variety of visual formats other than print and offer numerous study aids that guide learning in a chapter. Yet, unless attention is specifically called to these text features, students often skip them while reading to complete an assignment. As part of the preview process, take special notice of ways the chapter forecasts text structure—cause/effect, for example—and how it signals key concepts and ideas.

3 Create a Chapter Tour that prompts students to think about these features

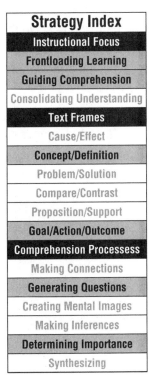

Strategy Index
Instructional Focus
Frontloading Learning
Guiding Comprehension
Consolidating Understanding
Text Frames
Cause/Effect
Concept/Definition
Problem/Solution
Compare/Contrast
Proposition/Support
Goal/Action/Outcome
Comprehension Processess
Making Connections
Generating Questions
Creating Mental Images
Making Inferences
Determining Importance
Synthesizing

as they use the book. For example, students reading a world history textbook can easily become immersed in the voluminous details and miss major themes or ideas. A Chapter Tour can help them focus on *changes* and *problems*, two concepts that predominate in history (see the Chapter Tour for History example).

4 Have students complete a Chapter Tour as an introduction to the textbook. An effective way of using a Chapter Tour is to allow the students to work with partners so they can verbalize what they are discovering about the way a specific textbook works. Develop variations of the Chapter Tour for subsequent chapters

---

Chapter Tour for History

Facts! Facts! Facts! History textbooks seem crammed with never-ending facts: names, dates, places, and events. This Chapter Tour will help readers see beyond the facts—to identify important changes that people have experienced and problems they have confronted. Learning about changes in the past can help us better understand who we are and the changes we have to deal with today. A Chapter Tour helps you discover major ideas and avoids close attention to details. Ask: "What's the point of all this?" "What are the important changes in the lives of these people?"

Surveying a Chapter Before Reading
To find out what a chapter is about, take a "tour" first.

1. What is the title of Chapter 24? (based on *World History: The Human Journey*, 2003).
   Chapter 24 is organized into four sections. List those sections below.

2. Go to the first two pages of Chapter 24. Notice each chapter begins with a time line. Select one item that happened during this time period that is familiar to you. Briefly share what you know about this item:

3. Find the red title at the bottom of the first page: "Build on What You Know." Each chapter begins with a main idea focus statement that introduces major changes emphasized in the chapter. What changes will be talked about in Chapter 24?

4. Now find the first page of Section 1. What country will you be reading about here?
   Notice on the left side the author provides some useful help in understanding this section. Examine the four "Read To Discover" statements first. Now list all the changes this country experienced.
   Also read the box: "Why It Matters Today." Why does the author say this section might connect to your life?

5. Find "The Main Idea" box at the beginning of this section. What problem is discussed in this section? Who will be trying to solve this problem?

6. Locate the introductory paragraph ("The Story Continues"), which will feature a quote from a primary source, material that was written during the time period covered by the chapter. There are many primary source quotes throughout the textbook. Quickly skim this paragraph, which will help to focus attention on what is included in the chapter.
   What person is quoted in this passage?
   What problems is she discussing?

7. Find a "Primary Source Eyewitness" box in this section, which also features a quote from the time period. Who is quoted here, and what change does this person want?

8. Quickly flip through the pages of the first section of Chapter 24. Notice that the material is divided into smaller topics, each identified by a heading. Write the four headings for this section. (Don't confuse headings [red] with subheadings [green].)

9. Look over the pictures in this chapter and think about problems and changes. Write down one thing you already know that is connected to one of the pictures.
   What is something about this chapter you are wondering as you think about the pictures?
   Find a picture of a person in a "History Maker" box. With what problems did this person deal?
   With what changes was this person involved?

10. This chapter features a number of graphic displays, like maps, charts, or tables. Find one chart in this chapter.
    What is the general topic of this chart? Examine it and decide: What change or changes is this chart detailing?

to remind students of critical elements in the text and to include additional aspects that you want brought to their attention.

5 Reinforce the necessity of getting a "first read" before undertaking any reading task. Use a sports analogy with students:

> Before a football quarterback runs a play, he takes time at the line of scrimmage to "read" the defense. He wants to know what to expect and he wants to make predictions of what might happen. He also wants to anticipate strategies he can use during the play to be successful.

A first read, or preview, is a self-guided Chapter Tour. This initial sweep through the material requires an active and aggressive mind-set that targets the following:

- **Topic**— What is the selection about? What do I already know about this topic? What do I predict I should know after reading this?

- **Main idea**—What is the point of this material? Why did the author write this? How might this material be useful to me? On what should I focus?

- **Major themes**—What are the key arguments or conclusions? If this material were summarized, what are the central thoughts that connect most of the details? What does this author apparently believe?

- **Structure**—How is this material put together? How is it sectioned or subdivided? Where do I need to allocate my most careful attention?

- **Salient details**—Are there any facts that call for special attention? What stands out in the material? Is there text in bold or italic type, quotations, or capital letters? Are there any key phrases that seem important? How familiar is this material? What details do I already know?

- **Style**—What do I notice about writing style? How complex are sentences? How dense is the vocabulary? How smoothly does the prose flow? How easy will this be to read?

- **Tone/attitude/mood**—Does the author have an attitude toward this material? Can I detect any emotion in the material? What tone can I sense—Anger? Humor? Enthusiasm? Criticism? Sarcasm? Irony? Reasoning? Persuasion? Inspiration? Explanation? If the author were doing a live presentation of this material, what would it be like?

Advantages

- Students learn to become frontloaders when they read.

- Students are conditioned to make predictions about a passage, and then read to confirm or reject them.

- Students are provided with an "expert guide" to alert them to what is most important in a chapter and to make more systematic use of reading aids provided within a textbook.

This strategy can be applied to text materials in all content areas and is appropriate for students from elementary through high school levels.

Reference

World history: The human journey. (2003). Austin, TX: Holt, Rinehart and Winston.

Suggested Readings

Cunningham, D., & Shablak, S.L. (1975). Selective reading guide-o-rama: The content teacher's best friend. *Journal of Reading, 18*(5), 380–382.

Wood, K.D., Lapp, D., & Flood, J., & Taylor, D.B. (2008). *Guiding readers through text: Strategy guides for new times* (2nd ed.). Newark, DE: International Reading Association.

Character Quotes

- Give me liberty or give me death!

- Ask not what your country can do for you; ask what you can do for your country.

- We have nothing to fear but fear itself.

- I have a dream that one day this nation will rise up and live out the true meaning of its creed.

  Or

- I'm the most terrific liar you ever saw in your life. It's awful. (Salinger, 1951, p. 16)

- One of my troubles is, I never care too much when I lose something—it used to drive my mother crazy when I was a kid. (p. 91)

- It was one of the worst schools I ever went to. It was full of phonies. And mean guys. You never saw so many mean guys in your life. (p. 170)

- Just because somebody's dead, you don't just stop liking them, for God's sake—especially if they were about a thousand times nicer than the people you know that're alive and all. (p. 174)

The power of expressive language! From the stirring rhetoric of Patrick Henry, John F. Kennedy, Franklin Roosevelt, and Martin Luther King to the introspective musings of Holden Caulfield in J.D. Salinger's *The Catcher in the Rye* (1951), our words are a significant way we reveal ourselves to others. Character Quotes (Buehl, 1994; adapted from Blachowicz, 1993) is a strategy that helps students develop insights about a character by examining what he or she says.

Using the Strategies

Character Quotes can be used to examine fictional characters in literature, real-life individuals in biographies, and authors—all who present themselves through their words. In addition, Reading With Attitude is an extension of Character Quotes that develops reader sensitivity to the author behind the words.

Using the Character Quotes strategy involves the following steps:

1 Preview the text to identify several quotes by a character, historical figure, or author that illustrate different facets of the individual's personality. Select quotes that encourage students to develop varying descriptions of the kind of person this individual might

be. Write each quote on a separate slip of paper or index card. For example, students preparing to read the classic *Anne Frank: The Diary of a Young Girl* (1995) will encounter an introspective adolescent who struggles with fears of being discovered while coping with the intense pressures of living in close proximity to her family and others (see the Character Quotes From *Anne Frank: The Diary of a Young Girl* example). Students in a history class studying the development of the American West can be introduced to an American Indian point of view through quotes taken from Nez Perce leader Chief Joseph's speech of surrender to United States government troops in 1877 (see the Character Quotes From Chief Joseph example).

2 Students work in cooperative groups, each group with a different quote to consider. Ask groups to generate as many words as possible that describe their impression of this person based on the quote. For example, groups working on quotes from *Anne Frank: The Diary of a Young Girl* might come up with *studious, sensitive, worried, resentful, witty, well educated, misunderstood, an outsider, gets picked on, dissatisfied, wants to be better, strong-willed, stressed out, depressed,* or *lonely.*

3 After each group has generated a list of descriptors, they read the group's quote to the entire class and share the list of character qualities and traits that the group associates with that character. They also talk about why they arrived at these traits. As they share, write the qualities and traits on an overhead transparency and inform the class that all quotes were uttered by the same individual.

4 Involve students in making generalizations about the character

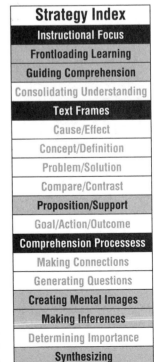

Strategy Index
Instructional Focus
Frontloading Learning
Guiding Comprehension
Consolidating Understanding
Text Frames
Cause/Effect
Concept/Definition
Problem/Solution
Compare/Contrast
Proposition/Support
Goal/Action/Outcome
Comprehension Processess
Making Connections
Generating Questions
Creating Mental Images
Making Inferences
Determining Importance
Synthesizing

Character Quotes From Anne Frank: The Diary of a Young Girl

- My report card wasn't too bad. I got one D, a C- in algebra and all the rest B's, except for two B+'s and two B-'s. My parents are pleased, but they're not like other parents when it comes to grades. They never worry about report cards, good or bad. I'm just the opposite. I don't want to be a poor student. (p. 17)

- Not being able to go outside upsets me more than I can say, and I'm terrified our hiding place will be discovered and that we'll be shot. That, of course, is a fairly dismal prospect. (p. 28)

- I don't fit in with them, and I've felt that clearly in the last few weeks. They're so sentimental together, but I'd rather be sentimental on my own. (p. 29)

- A few nights ago I was the topic of discussion, and we all decided I was an ignoramus. As a result, I threw myself into my schoolwork the next day, since I have little desire to still be a freshman when I'm fourteen or fifteen. The fact that I'm hardly allowed to read anything was also discussed. (p. 38)

- Mother and I had a so-called "discussion" today, but the annoying part is that I burst into tears. I can't help it... At moments like these I can't stand Mother. It's obvious that I'm a stranger to her; she doesn't even know what I think about the most ordinary things. (p. 41)

- They criticize everything, and I mean everything, about me: my behavior, my personality, my manners; every inch of me, from head to toe and back again, is the subject of gossip and debate. Harsh words and shouts are constantly being flung at my head, though I'm absolutely not used to it. (p. 44)

- Night after night, green and gray military vehicles cruise the streets. They knock on every door, asking whether any Jews live there. If so, the whole family is immediately taken away... It's impossible to escape their clutches unless you go into hiding. (p.72)

- In bed at night, as I ponder my many sins and exaggerated shortcomings, I get so confused by the sheer amount of things I have to consider that I either laugh or cry, depending on my mood. Then I fall asleep with strange feelings of wanting to be different than I am or being different than I want to be, or perhaps of behaving differently than I am or want to be. (p. 75)

Source: Frank, A. (1995). *The diary of a young girl: The definitive edition* (O. Frank & M. Pressler, Eds.; S. Massotty, Trans.). New York: Doubleday.

Character Quotes From Chief Joseph

- I want to have time to look for my children and see how many I can find. Maybe I shall find them among the dead. (p. 554)

- I am tired; my heart is sick and sad. From where the sun now stands, I will fight no more forever. (p. 554)

- You might as well expect the rivers to run backward as that any man who was born free should be contented penned up and denied liberty to go where he pleases.... (p. 555)

- Good words will not give my people good health and stop them from dying. Good words will not get my people a home where they can live in peace and take care of themselves. I am tired of talk that comes to nothing. (p. 554)

- We only ask an even chance to live as other men live. We ask to be recognized as men. We ask that the same law shall work alike on all men. (p.555)

- All men were made by the same Great Spirit Chief. They are all brothers. The earth is the mother of all people, and all people shall have equal rights upon it. (p.555)

- Let me be a free man—free to travel, free to stop, free to work, free to trade where I choose, free to choose my own teachers, free to follow the religion of my fathers, free to think and talk and act for myself—and I will obey every law, or submit to the penalty. (p. 555)

Source: Bailey, T. (Ed.). (1967). *The American spirit: United States history as seen by contemporaries* (2nd ed., pp. 554–555). Boston: D.C. Heath and Company.

or individual. Students work in their groups to write a preliminary personality profile of this character by drawing upon the qualities and traits listed by the entire class. The profile should contain four or five statements that integrate important qualities from the list.

Provide an opening stem as a template to assist students in organizing their personality profile (see the Template Frames strategy beginning on page 178). The following is the opening stem for a profile on Chief Joseph's quotes:

> Chief Joseph was the type of person who _____.
> He also seemed to be _____. Other traits of his personality included _____. His words show that he experienced _____.

5 Students read the story, biography, or other selection. After reading, students return to their personality profiles to discuss what new qualities or traits they might add and how they would change the profile to make it better match their understanding of the character or individual. Ask students to select further quotes from the text that provide new information about their character, or have them identify representative quotes that lead to understanding a second character or individual.

Reading With Attitude

Reading With Attitude (Buehl, 2004), an extension of Character Quotes, tunes readers in to the emotional content of a text and helps them detect author attitude and perspective. Using this strategy involves the following steps:

1 Introduce students to three ways of tracking emotions in a written text:

- **Character Emotions**—Readers notice emotions displayed by the people or characters featured in a text. (People/Characters feel...)
- **Reader Emotions**—Readers monitor their own personal emotional responses to what they are reading. (I feel...)
- **Author Emotions**—Readers recognize emotions expressed or implied by the author of a text. (The author feels...)

Inform students that some emotions in a text are readily apparent but frequently emotional content of a text is not directly stated and, as a result, must be inferred by a reader. In particular, readers of prose fiction need to be sensitive to an author's word choice as they search for "Character Emotions." The specific language chosen by an author can signal an implied emotional dynamic.

2 Provide practice in detecting all three kinds of emotion as they read. Ask students to mark or record on sticky notes any language and situations that indicate underlying feelings. For example, marking for "Character Emotions" reveals a number of significant hints about the relationship between the narrator in a short story—a young girl—and her father, which is never directly stated. Students then write down what they are wondering about the unstated emotions:

- "Would I like to see him?" (Why would there be a question whether the girl would want to see her father?)
- "Dad was fidgety." (Why? What was he feeling?)
- "I'd prepared for weeks." (Was she excited to be meeting her father? Anxious? Unsure?)
- "I realized his fingertips were squared off on top, like mine." (Was she wondering how much she was like her father?)
- "His eyes danced." (How did he feel about his many travels about the world?)
- "He sighed." (How was he feeling about not knowing his own daughter?)

(quotes from Wesselman, 1993, pp. 1–2)

3 "Character Emotions" and "Reader Emotions" are often the easiest for students to discern when reading a text. However, "Author Emotions" are in many cases less obvious and must be inferred. Authors may "lead" a reader toward certain ideas or conclusions that greatly influence how a text is understood and how a reader thinks about a topic. Some authors are upfront in communicating the perspective they bring to their writing so that readers know who is talking to them and can factor this insight into their understanding. But many authors leave their personal imprint on a text unstated so that readers must figure out on their own the extent an author's prejudices and experiences are reflected in their message. Therefore, have students identify "Author Emotions" by asking "Does the author have an attitude?" Students consider whether an author is displaying "attitude," such as a viewpoint, an opinion, a perspective, or a bias. Most students can understand or readily identify with "having an attitude" about something, and locating author attitude is an essential component to critical reading.

Prompt students to ask, when considering any written text, fiction or nonfiction, whether the author has an *attitude*. For example, while examining the following excerpt from a history textbook, they can ask themselves, Does the author have an attitude about César Chávez?

> One of the most notable campaigns for Latino rights in the 1960s was the farmworker struggle in California. César Chávez, a farmworker born in Arizona, was one of the principal leaders of this effort to improve the

lives of migrant workers.... Like Martin Luther King Jr., Chávez relied on nonviolence in the struggle for equal rights. Among other tactics, he used hunger strikes as a political tool. He fasted several times over the years to draw attention to the plight of farmworkers and to pressure employers to improve working conditions. (*History Alive! Pursuing American Ideals*, 2008, pp. 609–610)

Students may note favorable language, like "notable," "improve lives," and "nonviolence," as well as a respectful comparison to King, as indicators that the author has an approving attitude toward Chávez, and perhaps workers in general.

Advantages

- Students are introduced to several important facets of a character or individual's personality before they begin reading.
- Students are involved in actively predicting major themes and issues of a story or selection.
- Students become conditioned to search for implicit meanings of a text and strengthen their abilities to make inferences.
- Students tune in to the voice talking to them through print, so that they can become critical readers as well

as deepen their understanding. All students need extensive practice with a variety of texts to determine author perspective and bias, in order to determine the extent to which they can trust an author's judgment and version of "the truth."

References

Blachowicz, C. (1993, November). *Developing active comprehenders*. Paper presented at the Madison Area Reading Council. Madison, WI.

Buehl, D. (1994). You said it: Colorful quotes can be the voice of a character's soul. *WEAC News & Views, 29*(11), 21.

Buehl, D. (2004). Does the author have an attitude? *On WEAC In Print, 4*(5), 13.

Literature Cited

Bailey, T. (Ed.). (1967). *The American spirit: United States history as seen by contemporaries* (2nd ed., pp. 554–555). Boston: D.C. Heath and Company.

Frank, A. (1995). *Anne Frank: The diary of a young girl: The definitive edition.* (O. Frank & M. Pressler, Eds., S. Massotty, Trans.) New York: Doubleday.

History alive! Pursuing American ideals. (2008). Palo Alto, CA: Teachers' Curriculum Institute.

Salinger, J.D. (1951). *The catcher in the rye.* New York: Little, Brown.

Wesselman, K. (1993). House of snow. *Nimrod: International Journal of Prose & Poetry, 37*(1), 1–14.

Concept/Definition Mapping

Let's see...harbinger...um...presage...forerunner, herald...a person sent in advance to secure accommodations. I'm still not sure that I have a feel for this word harbinger.

"Look it up in the dictionary!" Students are conditioned throughout their schooling to follow this advice. But for many students, using the dictionary means fixating on very narrow and sometimes vague statements to define a word. These dictionary definitions contain little elaboration and may not connect at all to what students already know about a word. In contrast, Beck, McKeown, and Kucan (2002) recommend vocabulary instruction that is frequent, rich, and extended, and which engages students to reach beyond mere identification of a definition. Students need a classroom environment that prompts them to assume true ownership of words for more precise written and spoken expression.

Concept/Definition Mapping (Schwartz & Raphael, 1985) helps enrich understanding of a word or concept. Concept Definition Maps are graphic displays that focus attention on explaining the key components of a definition: the class or category, the properties or characteristics, and illustrations or examples. The strategy also encourages students to call on their personal knowledge when understanding new words.

Using the Strategy

Concept/Definition Mapping is an excellent strategy for teaching key vocabulary and concepts in all content areas. These graphic representations are especially useful for teaching academic vocabulary, sometimes referred to as *tier 3* words (see the discussion of tier 2 and tier 3 words in Student-Friendly Vocabulary Explanations, page 175). Using this strategy includes the following steps:

1 Display a blank Concept/Definition Map on an overhead projector (see the Appendix for a reproducible version of the Concept/Definition Map). Point out questions that a complete definition would answer: What is it? What is it like? What are some examples of it? Model how to use the Concept/Definition Map by selecting a familiar concept and soliciting the relevant information for the map from the class. For example, students responding to a map for *cheese*

might identify it as *food* or a *dairy product* (see the Concept/Definition Map example). Properties such as *is usually soft, is usually yellow or white, is made from milk*, and *is kept cold* could be entered into the boxes under "What is it like?" As examples of cheese, students might offer *cheddar, Swiss, mozzarella*, and *Gruyere*.

2 Present a new key term or concept from material students are learning. Have students work in pairs to create a Concept/Definition Map for the new concept. Instruct them to use information from the reading passage, a glossary or dictionary, or their own background knowledge to complete the map. For example, science students studying different climatic regions of the earth might be given the concept *tundra* to map (see the Concept/Definition Map for Science example). The textbook identifies *tundra* as one of several geographical regions. Have students note the properties of a tundra from the reading: has no trees; vegetation consists mostly of grasses, mosses, and lichens; has temperatures below freezing most of the year; and has permanently frozen ground called permafrost. Some students may draw from their background knowledge that reindeer and caribou are found in tundra regions. Have students locate examples of tundra on a world map in the textbook showing the different geographic regions: the tundra region is indicated in the arctic areas of the United States, Canada, Greenland, Norway, and Russia.

3 When students have finished constructing their Concept/Definition Maps, have them use the maps to write a complete definition for the concept in the "My Explanation" box. Emphasize that the definition should explain

Strategy Index
Instructional Focus
Frontloading Learning
Guiding Comprehension
Consolidating Understanding
Text Frames
Cause/Effect
Concept/Definition
Problem/Solution
Compare/Contrast
Proposition/Support
Goal/Action/Outcome
Comprehension Processess
Making Connections
Generating Questions
Creating Mental Images
Making Inferences
Determining Importance
Synthesizing

Concept/Definition Map for Cheese

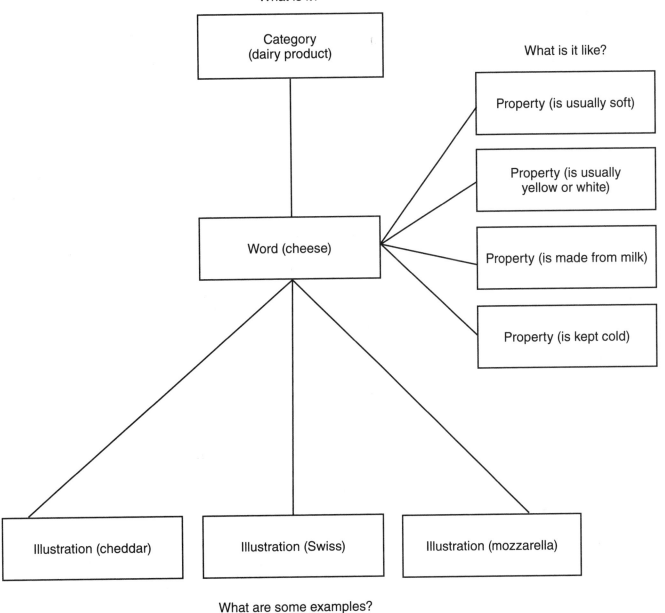

Topic (cheese)

What is it?

Category
(dairy product)

What is it like?

Word (cheese)

Property (is usually soft)

Property (is usually
yellow or white)

Property (is made from milk)

Property (is kept cold)

Illustration (cheddar)

Illustration (Swiss)

Illustration (mozzarella)

What are some examples?

My explanation of _____ (cheese) _____

Cheese is a dairy product that is made from milk. Some examples are cheddar, Swiss, and mozzarella. Cheese is usually soft, and most cheeses are yellow or white in color. You usually have to keep cheese cold so that it doesn't spoil.

Source: Buehl, D. (1995). *Classroom strategies for interactive learning* (p. 38). Madison: Wisconsin State Reading Association.

Concept/Definition Map for Science

Tundra

What is it?

geographical region

What is it like?

is treeless

temperature usually below freezing

tundra

has permafrost

lichens, grasses, mosses grow there

reindeer can be found there

northern Alaska	Arctic Region of Canada	northern Russia

What are some examples?

My Explanation of _____tundra_____

The tundra is a region of the earth that has temperatures below freezing most of the year. No trees grow there—only grasses, mosses, and lichens. The cold temperatures cause permafrost. The tundra is located above the Arctic Circle.

Source: Buehl, D. (1995). *Classroom strategies for interactive learning* (p. 38). Madison: Wisconsin State Reading Association.

the category of the word, its properties or characteristics, and specific examples, and will comprise several sentences instead of simple dictionary statements. For example,

> The tundra is a region of the earth that has temperatures below freezing most of the year. No trees grow there—only grasses, mosses, and lichens. The cold temperatures cause permafrost. The tundra is located above the Arctic Circle.

4 Assign students to create Concept/Definition Maps for other key terms and concepts from their reading that can be used as review and study for tests.

Advantages

- Students expand their understandings of key vocabulary and concepts beyond simple definitions.

- Students construct a visual representation of a concept's definition that helps them in remembering.

- Students are encouraged to integrate their background knowledge when forming a definition.

References

Beck, I.L., McKeown, M.G., & Kucan, L. (2002). *Bringing words to life: Robust vocabulary instruction.* New York: Guilford.

Buehl, D. (1995). *Classroom strategies for interactive learning.* Madison: Wisconsin State Reading Association.

Schwartz, R.M., & Raphael, T.E. (1985). Concept of definition: A key to improving students' vocabulary. *The Reading Teacher, 39*(2), 198–205.

Suggested Reading

Santa, C.M., Havens, L.T., & Valdes, B.J. (2004). *Project CRISS: Creating independence through student-owned strategies* (3rd ed.). Dubuque, IA: Kendall/Hunt.

Connect Two

The checkerspot butterfly—a colorful photograph splashed across the newsprint immediately snags your attention. A quick scan of the accompanying newspaper article reveals the following prominent vocabulary terms: *invasive, habitat, greenhouse gases, extinction, assisted migration, biodiversity, ecological, ice age, species, transported,* and *conservation biologist.* Consider for a moment how an author might put these terms into play in a news story about butterflies. Given what you know about each of these words, how might they contribute to the development of the author's message? Which terms might you expect to find linked in some way in this article? Perhaps *extinction* and *species,* or *biodiversity* and *habitat?* What other potential combinations occur to you?

As readers, we realize that a flow of significant vocabulary guides our thinking through written texts. Of course, our comprehension of these texts hinges on the knowledge of key vocabulary that we bring to our reading. But we are also called upon to tap into our partial knowledge of words, our hunches about words that are still unfamiliar to a degree, and our predictions about words based on our attempts to glean an overall sense of meaning from a passage. Finally, we realize that vocabulary words operate as semantic networks, not as isolated packets of definitional information. Words are better understood in conjunction with their companion words—"fellow-traveler" terms with which they share some relationship. In their natural environment, words do not exist alone; instead they are interwoven into extended language to craft meaningful communications.

Using the Strategies

Connect Two (Blachowicz, 1986) is a strategy that helps students explore the key vocabulary of a passage before they begin reading. It encourages students to make predictions about the probable meaning of a passage based on what they know or can anticipate about a number of keywords or terms. Then, when students begin reading, they have already previewed the major ideas of the text. A related strategy is Possible Sentences (Moore & Moore, 1986).

Using the Connect Two strategy involves the following steps:

1 Identify 10 to 15 key concepts or terms in material that students will be reading. Include terms that will be familiar, as well as those that may be obstacles in their reading. Focus on words that are related to important ideas in the story or selection. The words you choose to draw attention to should help guide readers through central ideas or events. Pay special attention to words that readers tend to encounter in written texts rather than through spoken language (tier 2 words; see page 175 in Student-Friendly Vocabulary Explanations for more discussion on these tiers). In addition, highlight words that represent academic concepts (tier 3 words). In our opening scenario, *invasive* and *migration* are examples of significant tier 2 words, and *biodiversity* and *habitat* are examples of important tier 3 words.

2 Present these words to students as a group, rather than as a series of stand-alone new vocabulary terms. Blachowicz (1986) suggests Exclusion Brainstorming as one method for initial exploration of a core group of words. For this activity, intersperse words that are *not* found in the text—and which do not necessarily seem consistent with topics in the reading—with the set of words you selected from the passage. In our butterflies example, we might provide the following array of words for students to examine: *invasive, habitat, cholesterol, greenhouse gases, extinction, assisted migration, teleprompter, biodiversity, ecological, asphalt, species,* and *conservation biologist.*

Introduce this set of words by noting that several were taken from a selection that the class will be reading (in this case, on the topic of the checkerspot butterfly). In groups, have them speculate which words are the odd ones that

Strategy Index
Instructional Focus
Frontloading Learning
Guiding Comprehension
Consolidating Understanding
Text Frames
Cause/Effect
Concept/Definition
Problem/Solution
Compare/Contrast
Proposition/Support
Goal/Action/Outcome
Comprehension Processess
Making Connections
Generating Questions
Creating Mental Images
Making Inferences
Determining Importance
Synthesizing

do not appear in the article and should be struck from the list. As students deliberate, they begin to anticipate possible themes of the butterfly article and to identify likely vocabulary that could communicate those themes. As students share knowledge about the words in this set, they are likely to decide that words like *cholesterol*, *teleprompter*, and *asphalt* do not seem as likely to be used as the others. The key dynamic here is the collaborative discussion about word knowledge, not that students discover all the superfluous terms. Some words that are actually in the article might be struck because these words might appear in unexpected ways in the text, or because students lack sufficient knowledge of them. Or students might suppose that *asphalt* belongs because a butterfly's habitat could be covered with asphalt).

3 Present the key vocabulary arranged into two columns on the chalkboard or overhead transparency. Place words that might be more challenging or unfamiliar in Column A (see the Connect Two for Science example). Related but more common words are listed in Column B. Students work with partners to create five sets of pairs, each pair consisting of a link between a word from each column. For each pair, they must explain how the two words might be meaningfully connected. Then students create a sentence that uses the two words. These sentences should represent ideas that students predict might occur in an article on butterflies that contains such a core group of words.

For example, *extinction* from Column A might be paired with *global warming* from Column B. The explanation of this pair's connection might be: "global warming is making it harder for some plants and animals to survive, which could cause their extinction." A predictive sentence illustrating this pair could be: *Global* warming is threatening to cause the extinction of the checkerspot butterfly. Of course, other partners could pair these terms differently. *Greenhouse gases* might be paired with *global warming* or *polar bears* with *extinction*. The intent behind Connect Two is to engage students in conversations about their vocabulary knowledge that focus on relationships between words as they might occur within a topic of study.

4 Students read the text. Ask them to notice how the author employed the words in Columns A and B.

5 When they have completed their reading, students continue their vocabulary exploration. Select six to eight of the terms to receive more in-depth emphasis. For example, you might select: *invasive, habitat, assisted migration, range, extinction, biodiversity,* and *conservation biologist*. Partners then write statements using each word to summarize one important understanding about the topic. Each statement is built around a different key term, and each statement must say something different about the topic. When these statements are completed, students will have practiced their new vocabulary by embedding these terms into a summary of the article about the checkerspot butterfly. A sample summary might begin as follows:

> Invasive plants have taken over places in the San Francisco Bay area, replacing the plants that the checkerspot butterfly depends on to live. The habitat for the checkerspot butterfly has changed, and fewer of them can be seen in the San Francisco Bay area. One proposal to help the butterfly is assisted migration, which involves moving the butterflies to a new area which has the habitat they need.

This phase of vocabulary development asks students to experiment with integrating these words with their own language, in a highly contextualized manner, by talking about their understanding of a now-familiar passage. Because they have the author's use of the word as a model, they are more apt to be comfortable using the words themselves.

Possible Sentences

Possible Sentences (Moore & Moore, 1986) is a variation that involves students in discovering the accuracy of their predictions about key vocabulary. Using this strategy involves the following steps.

1 List target vocabulary on the board or on an overhead transparency. With partners, have students write a series of sentences that could possibly appear in the reading (see the Possible Sentences for Social Studies example). For terms that are unfamiliar, encourage students to predict a probable meaning and to construct possible sentences. For example, students preparing to read a passage on the ancient Greeks might know that the Parthenon was a temple with many statues, and that the Greeks did a lot with architecture, philosophy, and the arts. They may not know

---

Connect Two in Science

Checkerspot Butterfly

Column A	Column B
invasive	ice age
habitat	transported
greenhouse gases	range
extinction	climate
assisted migration	preserves
biodiversity	global warming
ecological	grassland
species	carbon dioxide
conservation biologist	polar bears

Possible Sentences for Social Studies

Chapter 4: Greek Culture

Key Terms

Hellenic Age	Plato
architecture	philosophy
Parthenon	The Republic
democracy	theater
tragedies	Aristotle
the arts	statues
temple	Father of Biology

Possible Sentences

DK   1. The Hellenic Age was a time of many tragedies.

T   2. The ancient Greeks did a lot with architecture, philosophy, and the arts.

T   3. The Parthenon was a temple with many statues.

F   4. The Greeks had a democracy and their government was called The Republic.

F   5. Plato was called the Father of Biology.

DK   6. Greek theater performed plays by Aristotle.

Key:

T = True based on the reading.

F = False based on the reading; needs to be rewritten.

DK = Don't Know; not mentioned in the reading

---

about Plato and Aristotle, so they would offer guesses based on the key terms.

2 Have students read the passage and check the accuracy of the possible sentences. They should evaluate each possible sentence in terms of whether it is true (the text backs up their prediction), false (the text presents a different use of the terms), or don't know (the statement can be neither proved nor disproved based on the text). For example, some possible sentences in the ancient Greece example are directly contradicted by the text: the reading reveals that Aristotle was not the Father of Biology, and *The Republic* is a work by Plato and not the name of the Greek government. Other possible sentences were not clearly dealt with in the text. For example, many of Aristotle's activities were detailed, but any connection with Greek theater was not mentioned.

3 After students have read the passage and evaluated their possible sentences, they again work with partners to rewrite their sentences to be consistent with the reading. Have students locate relevant portions of text in order to defend their corrections. For example, sentence 4 might be "repaired" by students to read, "Plato created a perfect model for a government that he called The Republic." Students may find that some statements need to be expanded to two or three sentences in order to accurately reflect the text. Students may also generate new sentences to add to the original group. Emphasize that exact statements copied from the text are unacceptable; students need to paraphrase their understandings of these terms in their own words.

Advantages

- Students become acquainted with key terms and vocabulary from a passage before they begin to read.

- Students are encouraged to draw on their partial knowledge of words to speculate about possible meanings in the context of a core group of words about a theme or topic.

- Students encounter new vocabulary as "extended families" of words that are related to each other, rather than as definitions that need to be memorized.

- Students are involved in a process that helps them to establish their purposes for reading.

- Students activate what they know about information before they read and are able to share background knowledge with their classmates.

References

Blachowicz, C.L.Z. (1986). Making connections: Alternatives to the vocabulary notebook. *The Journal of Reading, 29*(7), 643–649.

Moore, D.W., & Moore, S.A. (1986). Possible sentences. In E.K. Dishner, T.W. Bean, J.E. Readence, & D.W. Moore (Eds.), *Reading in the content areas: Improving classroom instruction* (2nd ed., pp. 174–179). Dubuque, IA: Kendall/Hunt.

Suggested Reading

Readence, J.E., Moore, D.W., & Rickelman, R.J. (2000). *Prereading activities for content area reading and learning* (3rd ed.). Newark, DE: International Reading Association.

Different Perspectives for Reading

"That's not what I got out of that article!" Two individuals sparring over a piece of text that both have read is a frequent occurrence. Look at the potential for spirited discussion that arrives each day in the morning newspaper—an editorial about the glass ceiling for women executives, an exposé on the flaws of capital punishment, a movie review of the most recent action blockbuster, an article about substituting holistic health practices for drug treatments, a discussion of the mayor's comments about raising bus fares, a travel column recommending must-see spots in Europe, a feature article on the need for higher standards in schools, a report about a group of teenagers who are lobbying the city for a skateboard park, an analysis of the role of "soft" money in politics—the list goes on.

What might be your impressions in each of these reading situations? Chances are, you would read using a variety of personal "lenses," which would create a perspective derived from your experiences, values, and attitudes to guide your comprehension of the text. Socioeconomic status, gender, political persuasion, age, ethnic identity, marital status, career history, educational background, specific life experiences—all factor into your perspective as you read. Thus, two people can read the same article and come away with different but equally valid interpretations of what the text means.

Because students, too, are individuals with different background experiences, beliefs, and understandings about the world, no two students will read and comprehend a passage in the same way. A student whose grandparents are dairy farmers will understand a passage about organic milk in a decidedly different way than a student whose only connection to cows may be a cartoon. Likewise, a student who has visited Arizona will comprehend a story about the desert with a different appreciation than a student who has never left New York City. Strategies that broaden perspective about a topic will help students read with a greater depth of comprehension and appreciation.

Using the Strategy

Different Perspectives for Reading (McNeil, 1984) uses a graphic organizer to guide students through multiple readings of a text so that they factor in different thinking perspectives in addition to their own. Using this strategy involves the following steps:

1 After appropriate frontloading instruction, students read a story, article, or selection for the first time.

2 Identify different perspectives for a second reading of the text that are connected to the important ideas or concepts of the passage. For example, different perspectives in a world history textbook passage about the French Revolution might include those of a merchant, a peasant woman, a revolutionary, a parish priest, and a nobleman. For fictional material, assign students the perspective of characters other than the narrator in a story. For example, in the novel *To Kill a Mockingbird* by Harper Lee, the perspective is that of the young girl, Scout; however, other perspectives to consider are those of her brother, Jem; the family cook, Calpurnia; the elderly neighbor, Mrs. Dubose; the lawyer, Atticus Finch; the wronged man, Tom Robinson; or the phantom neighbor, Boo Radley.

3 Introduce the Different Perspectives Graphic Outline on the overhead projector and provide students with individual copies (see Appendix for a reproducible version of the Different Perspectives Graphic Outline). Divide the class into cooperative groups of three or four and assign each group a different perspective. Ask students to identify the issues, feelings, effects, or concerns surrounding a particular perspective. For students studying the French Revolution, ask them to wonder, Why would the revolution be a concern for a priest? A merchant? How would the revolution affect the needs of a peasant woman? A

Strategy Index
Instructional Focus
Frontloading Learning
Guiding Comprehension
Consolidating Understanding
Text Frames
Cause/Effect
Concept/Definition
Problem/Solution
Compare/Contrast
Proposition/Support
Goal/Action/Outcome
Comprehension Processess
Making Connections
Generating Questions
Creating Mental Images
Making Inferences
Determining Importance
Synthesizing

Different Perspectives Graphic Outline

Your Perspective on ___the French Revolution___

Role ___Peasant woman___

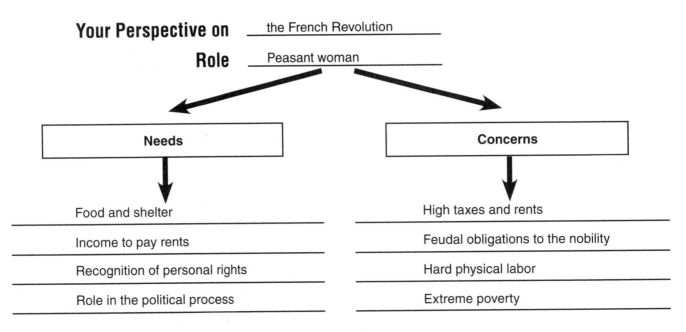

Needs

Food and shelter

Income to pay rents

Recognition of personal rights

Role in the political process

Concerns

High taxes and rents

Feudal obligations to the nobility

Hard physical labor

Extreme poverty

Read and React

Text Statements → **Your Reactions**

—Peasants were forced to pay one tenth of their income—a tithe—to Catholic church

—Nobility paid low or no taxes, collected dues from peasants, had highest positions in government & army

—Peasants worked long and hard but had no voice in making or changing laws

"We are starving and can't afford this 'tax' to the church; also what if we don't believe in this religion?"

"I resent how we do all the work and the nobles get all the rewards. We must change to a fairer system!"

"The Third Estate is 97% of the population, and mostly us peasants. We deserve a voice. Liberty, Equality, Fraternity!"

Summary Position Statement

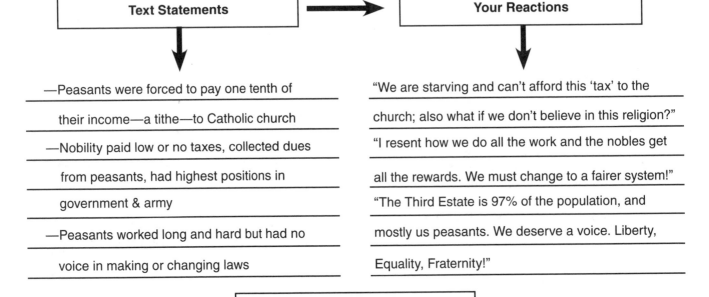

"We peasants represent most of the people of France, but we have no power and no rights. As a result, we live in extreme poverty with little food. The nobility has all the rights and advantages, and we are forced to support them with our hard work and rent payments, and they make us give one-tenth of our tiny income to the church. Things need to change in France!"

nobleman? Students might decide that a priest would need respect for the religion, income for the church, and parishioners. Nobility would be concerned about loss of estates, decreased political power, and possible execution. Merchants would need economic and political stability, markets for their products, and lower taxation. They would be concerned with constant change in the government and periods of lawlessness.

4 Have students re-read the material to look for specific statements or information that would be of special interest to their perspective. Have them write this information on the graphic outline, along with comments about their assigned perspective. For example, students re-reading the history passage from a peasant woman's perspective might react as follows: How can we peasants be expected to provide the church with one-tenth of our income when we are already in poverty and starving? (see the Different Perspectives Graphic Outline for the French Revolution example).

5 Discuss with students new insights gained through looking at material from a variety of viewpoints. To bring their thoughts together, ask students to write a position statement summarizing the feelings of an individual with a particular perspective. Include this statement on the bottom portion of the graphic outline.

Advantages

- The strategy reinforces that a number of legitimate conclusions and generalizations may be drawn from a specific text.

- Students read with more emotional attachment while using this strategy and develop empathy for points of view other than their own.

- Students are given a structure to re-read materials and to pick out ideas and information that they may have overlooked in the first reading.

- Students are given practice in selecting specific information that relates to alternative ways of looking at a text.

Reference

McNeil, J.D. (1984). *Reading comprehension: New directions for classroom practice*. Glenview, IL: Scott Foresman.

Suggested Reading

Cook, D.M. (Ed.). (1989). *Strategic learning in the content areas*. Madison: Wisconsin Department of Public Instruction.

Discussion Web

Consider the array of political discussions in which you have participated. At times you undoubtedly have been involved in passionate and highly emotional exchanges; at other times, quietly reasoned, earnestly argued conversations have taken place. All such discussions reflect a basic underlying principle, that oft-repeated truism: There are two sides to every question. Through exchanges with others we have the opportunity to refine our thinking, respond to challenges to our viewpoints, and acknowledge alternative ideas.

Teachers know that classroom discussions are an important way to encourage students to think. But involving the entire class in discussion is difficult. Too often, only a few students are willing to contribute, and as a result they monopolize the conversation. What starts as a discussion ends as a dialogue between the teacher and a handful of students. Meanwhile, the rest of the class sits passively—perhaps not listening to or not paying attention to what is being said. However, the Discussion Web (Alvermann, 1991) is a strategy designed to include all students in active participation in class discussion.

Using the Strategy

The Discussion Web incorporates all four facets of communication (reading, writing, speaking, and listening) and takes advantage of cooperative learning to give students multiple opportunities to interact. Using this strategy involves the following steps:

1 Choose a selection for student reading that develops opposing viewpoints, such as a story that elicits conflicting interpretations of a character's actions or an article that deals with controversial issues. Frontload instruction by activating relevant background knowledge for the selection and setting their purposes for reading (see Brainstorming Prior Knowledge beginning on page 55).

2 After students read the selection, introduce the Discussion Web and a focusing question for discussion (see the Appendix for a reproducible version of the Discussion Web). For example, students reading a history textbook passage on the Industrial Revolution might be asked, "Did the Industrial Revolution help working people?" (See the Discussion Web for the Industrial Revolution example.) Students in a literature class reading *The Red Badge of Courage* by Stephen Crane might be asked, "Was Henry Fleming a coward for running?" Middle school students reading the novel *Hatchet* by Gary Paulsen might be asked, "Could Brian have survived in the wilderness without the hatchet?"

3 Assign students to work in pairs to develop the opposing sides of the question. As they work, they flesh out the arguments for both sides on a blank Discussion Web, going back to the text as needed. During this phase, the emphasis is on "fact-finding"—detailing the strongest possible arguments on both sides of the Web. These "yes" and "no" statements provide the reasons for supporting or rejecting the central question. Remind students to set aside their personal beliefs to ensure that both positions are represented fairly.

After analyzing the actions of the main character in *The Red Badge of Courage*, for example, students may outline the following arguments about his cowardice:

Henry ran at the beginning of the battle, he misled others about his running, and he felt shame for running. However, Henry was experiencing his first battle, he had never before been under fire, many others ran as well, and there was much confusion during the battle.

4 After partners complete the preliminary work on their Discussion Webs, assign each set of partners to collaborate with another pair, forming a new group of four. Ask them to deliberate toward a consensus on the question. Additional arguments on both sides of the question are added to the Discussion Web at this time, and when the group

Strategy Index
Instructional Focus
Frontloading Learning
Guiding Comprehension
Consolidating Understanding
Text Frames
Cause/Effect
Concept/Definition
Problem/Solution
Compare/Contrast
Proposition/Support
Goal/Action/Outcome
Comprehension Processess
Making Connections
Generating Questions
Creating Mental Images
Making Inferences
Determining Importance
Synthesizing

reaches a conclusion, it is written at the bottom of the Web. For example, one group might conclude that in *Hatchet*, although Brian could have gotten fire from other means and may have adapted to his plight by using different strategies, he probably would not have survived without the hatchet. A second group might argue that Brian's ingenuity and common sense involving the hatchet could have been applied in other ways, which would have helped him survive without it.

5 Each group of four students is now ready to present its conclusions to the entire class. Allow three minutes for a spokesperson from each group to discuss one reason for their conclusion, which reduces the likelihood that the last groups to report will have no new ideas to offer. Encourage spokespersons to mention any dissenting viewpoints from their group discussions. In a discussion about the Industrial Revolution, some groups will decide that industrialization was progress and that working people ultimately benefited from innovations in industry. Other groups will likely deplore the unsafe and unhealthy conditions in which people worked and their exploitation by factory owners.

6 Students are now prepared to write their own personal responses to the focusing question. The Discussion Web provides an organized guide to

Discussion Web for the Industrial Revolution

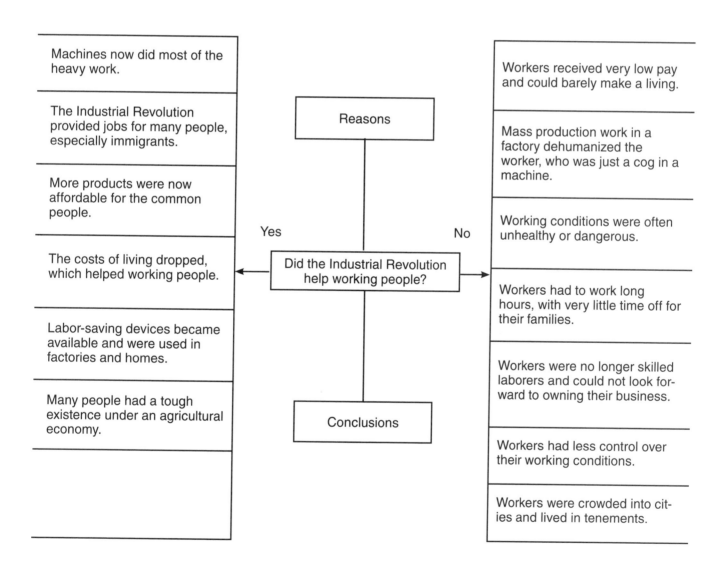

Machines now did most of the heavy work.

The Industrial Revolution provided jobs for many people, especially immigrants.

More products were now affordable for the common people.

The costs of living dropped, which helped working people.

Labor-saving devices became available and were used in factories and homes.

Many people had a tough existence under an agricultural economy.

Reasons

Yes   No

Did the Industrial Revolution help working people?

Conclusions

Workers received very low pay and could barely make a living.

Mass production work in a factory dehumanized the worker, who was just a cog in a machine.

Working conditions were often unhealthy or dangerous.

Workers had to work long hours, with very little time off for their families.

Workers were no longer skilled laborers and could not look forward to owning their business.

Workers had less control over their working conditions.

Workers were crowded into cities and lived in tenements.

Source: Buehl, D. (1995). *Classroom strategies for interactive learning* (p. 44). Madison: Wisconsin State Reading Association.

information and arguments that may be included in the writing. Students are thus able to develop their own ideas as well as reflect on the contributions of their classmates as they write about the question.

Advantages

- Students are active participants in discussion and develop collaboration skills.
- Students have a framework for evaluating both sides of an issue or question, and they are encouraged to process opposing evidence and information before asserting their viewpoints.
- Students write using well-organized support for their positions.

References

Alvermann, D.E. (1991). The discussion web: A graphic aid for learning across the curriculum. *The Reading Teacher, 45*(2), 92–99.

Buehl, D. (1995). *Classroom strategies for interactive learning.* Madison: Wisconsin State Reading Association.

Double-Entry Diaries

Consider a typical personal reading experience—for example, a magazine cover story on women and heart disease. As you read, you encounter a wealth of important information—startling statistics, extensive scientific studies, suggested precautions, and recommended actions. Although the article mentions details already known to you, much is new knowledge, some of which may even surprise you or change what you had believed about this topic.

As a proficient reader, you engage in reading experiences like this many times a day. Somehow, often without thinking about it, you glide through a particular text, picking out salient elements and sorting them into a meaningful condensation of the message. As you read, you make sure it makes sense, you double-check your understanding, and you pull your thoughts together—summarizing the gist of the passage, drawing some conclusions, and generalizing about themes, ideas, and implications.

This process of synthesizing meaning really involves your mind operating on parallel tracks while reading. You are most aware of the *what* of reading—what this article is about, what is most important, what you should remember, what you should do with the information. Yet your mind is also involved in the *how* of reading—the ongoing thinking you must do to get at the *what*. You think of how this text connects to and extends your previous knowledge on a topic. You think of questions not yet answered as you wonder about what you read. You think about things that are not expressly stated as you make inferences and predictions. Reading comprehension is, ultimately, the result of the thinking you do when you are engaged with a text.

Students are often unaware of their thinking as they read, especially the thinking that can guide and enhance their comprehension. Strategies which prompt this thinking, and which encourage students to notice *how* they are reading, can strengthen their comprehension abilities as they tackle the various texts for classroom learning.

Using the Strategy

Double-Entry Diaries (Tovani, 2000) use reader responses to prompt students to employ essential comprehension behaviors such as making connections to background knowledge, creating mental images, posing questions, making inferences, and clarifying confusions when thinking about classroom texts.

Using this strategy involves the following steps:

1 Double-Entry Diaries are a version of two-column (or Cornell) note-taking and are tailored for students to monitor their comprehension. Double-Entry Diaries are an excellent option for students when reading materials that cannot be marked, such as textbooks or class sets of novels.

Introduce Double-Entry Diaries by asking students to divide a sheet of paper into two vertical columns by folding it lengthwise in half. The left column is reserved for specific information from a text, such as a short passage, factual information, or a summary. The right column accords students space to provide written responses that correspond to the text material they selected for the left side. The result is a series of important textual references and the students' personal reactions and connections to them.

For example, a history teacher might lift some segments from the textbook to model this process with students. Using the overhead projector, the teacher might record the passage: "Immigrant workers trapped on the upper floors during the Triangle Shirtwaist fire jumped to certain deaths rather than remaining in the flaming factory." On the right side, the teacher records her thinking: "I am reminded of the 9-11 tragedy at the World Trade Center in New York City, when people also leaped to their deaths to escape the fire." The teacher is modeling how her background knowledge has connected to a textbook account of a historical event and how

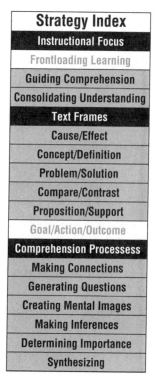

Strategy Index

Instructional Focus
Frontloading Learning
Guiding Comprehension
Consolidating Understanding
Text Frames
Cause/Effect
Concept/Definition
Problem/Solution
Compare/Contrast
Proposition/Support
Goal/Action/Outcome
Comprehension Processess
Making Connections
Generating Questions
Creating Mental Images
Making Inferences
Determining Importance
Synthesizing

her knowledge helps her understand this historical occurrence and makes it more meaningful. Emphasize during this interaction with students that proficient readers constantly seek to use their personal knowledge to help them make sense of new information.

2 Tovani (2000) recommends a focus on one specific comprehension behavior in the right column during the initial stages of using Double-Entry Diaries. The example in Step 1 models asking students to make connections to what they are reading by considering how what they know might relate to new information. In addition, students should verbalize how their personal connections contributed to a greater understanding of a passage. For this activity, the teacher could instruct students to label the right column, "This reminds me of...."

Other comprehension behaviors that could form the focus for the right column of a Double-Entry Diary include the following:

- Questioning: "I wonder...."
- Making inferences: "I figured out that...."
- Clarifying: "I am confused because...."
- Determining importance: "This is important because...."
- Visualizing: "I would describe the picture I see in my mind as...."

For example, a biology teacher might use a Double-Entry Diary to guide students to determine importance by asking them to fill in the right side of the column using the prompt "This is important because...." (see the Double-Entry Diary on Bacteria example).

3 After sufficient practice, students can track multiple comprehension processes using Content/Process Double-Entry Diaries (Harvey & Goudvis, 2007). Content/Process notes are a natural extension of Text Coding (see page 180), which involves students in marking texts to track their comprehension by noticing their thinking processes as they were reading. The "R" code signifies that the reader was reminded of background knowledge that connects to the text;

"Q" represents a question the reader was wondering about at a given point in the text; "V" notes a spot where the reader could especially visualize what was being described; "I" is an inference as the reader adds to meaning based on hints provided by the author; and "?" denotes a point of confusion.

Notes follow the split-page format: the left side for important "Content" from a selection and the right side for "Process"—the thinking noticed during reading. For students, these two columns can be labeled "What I Learned" (Content) and "What I Was Thinking" (Process). Walk students through this note-taking process by modeling entries in both columns as you extract key information for the left side, and recognize what you were thinking in the right side. As you think aloud about the passage, it is likely that you will alternate from one column to the other, at times emphasizing the content of the text and then registering your thoughts about the material.

The "What I Learned" (Content) column focuses on the author—what did I learn from the author that I felt was important? In contrast, the "What I Was Thinking" (Process) column focuses on the reader—what thoughts occurred to me as I read that helped my understanding of this text? Although the Content column will likely feature similar information recorded by students, entries in the Process column will be highly varied and will illustrate the vast breadth of possible thinking that occurs to individual readers.

4 Content/Process notes are especially advantageous for reading assignments that will challenge students. Using the Content/Process note-taking system, students can keep track of what they judge to be key ideas and facts while logging some of their thinking. For example, students in a science course might read a section from their textbooks on hurricanes and tropical storms and use Content/Process Notes to examine their thinking on the text (see the Content/Process Notes for Hurricanes example.) Pair students and ask them to share what they thought was most important and what they were thinking as they read. Ask partners to see if they can clarify any of the confusions that might have emerged during the reading. Elicit from students any

---

Double-Entry Diary on Bacteria

Text passage and page number	This is important because....
p. 325—"Heterotrophic bacteria are unable to make their own food, so they feed on plant and animal matter."	These bacteria get rid of waste, like dead plants and animals. Bacteria recycle unneeded stuff that would otherwise pile up on earth.

Source: Buehl, D. (2001). Double, double your learning. *OnWEAC In Print, 2*(2), 13.

Content/Process Notes on Hurricanes

What I Learned	What I Was Thinking
• Is a low pressure area with strong winds and heavy rain	R—I remember a movie that featured a fishing boat in a hurricane, "The Perfect Storm"
• Winds can blow 120 kilometers per hour or more	Q—I wonder what that speed would be in miles?
• Greatest damage is from currents called storm surges which push walls of water inland	V—I can really see this happening, the waves smashing on the shore, knocking over trees and buildings
• Hurricanes are similar to cyclones, with the wind spiraling toward the center.	I—It seems the author is saying that hurricanes are like ocean tornadoes
• Center is called the "eye" of the storm, where there is no rain and almost no wind	Q—I wonder why it's called the "eye"? I—The "eye" seems a safe area

Source: Buehl, D. (2003, May). What were you thinking? *OnWEAC In Print, 3*(9), 13.

"?" spots that still remain after their discussions with their peers.

With practice, students can begin to use Double-Entry Diaries as an ongoing method of tracking their thinking. They can be adapted for use with partners or small groups as students work to construct meaning from difficult material. Encourage students to use this strategy when they struggle with especially challenging texts, and as a study technique to review for exams.

Advantages

• Students are conditioned to be active thinkers as they read, and they are reminded of comprehension strategies such as accessing prior knowledge, raising interesting and clarifying questions, and considering what information is most significant.

• Students begin to assume personal responsibility for their comprehension, and they develop facility with a variety of essential strategies for making sense from classroom materials.

• Students have written records of their thinking, which they can rely upon during class discussions, when reviewing for exams, and when seeking clarification from the teacher and other classmates.

• This strategy reinforces that comprehension is a dynamic process that combines what an author offers with what a reader brings to a text.

References

Buehl, D. (2001). Double, double your learning. *OnWEAC In Print, 2*(2), 13.

Buehl, D. (2003). What were you thinking? *OnWEAC In Print, 3*(9), 13.

Harvey, S., & Goudvis, A. (2007). *Strategies that work: Teaching comprehension for understanding and engagement* (2nd ed.). Portland, ME: Stenhouse.

Tovani, C. (2000). *I read it, but I don't get it: Comprehension strategies for adolescent readers*. Portland, ME: Stenhouse.

First-Person Reading

How many times has this happened to you? You are in the company of another person—a spouse, perhaps, or a friend. This individual is seated near you, increasingly preoccupied by the act of reading. A couple of attempts to initiate conversation go nowhere. You busy yourself with a solitary activity of your own. And when you look up again, your reading companion has vanished!

Well, not exactly physically departed, but "gone" nevertheless. Certainly, he or she is no longer sharing this space and time with you. Your companion has become completely lost in a good book, and has disappeared into the lines on the pages, at this moment living vicariously the events and experiences being spun by the words of an author.

We have all experienced times when our imaginations were so stimulated by what we were reading that we were transported in our minds into the literary terrain we held in our hands. It almost felt like we were there, in person, ourselves. Our imaginations are essential to our comprehension of written texts. Cued by the author's language, we create our personalized versions of the people, the locations, and the events we encounter as readers. And because we are different people, tapping into different life experiences, our imaginations do not lead to identical interpretations of how things look, sound, taste, smell, or feel.

Using the Strategies

Three classroom strategies—Eyewitness Testimony Charts, First Impressions, and You Ought to Be in Pictures—encourage students "to read themselves" into a text.

Eyewitness Testimony Charts

Eyewitness Testimony Charts are a 3-column graphic organizer that prompts students to imagine events in their reading as if they were present themselves. Using this strategy involves the following steps:

1 Begin with a pre-planned live interaction with another person, which your students witness. For example, you might ask a colleague to walk into your classroom and initiate a short but spirited argument with you. After your collaborator leaves, turn to your students and ask them to quickly write down their "eyewitness" accounts of what they just observed. Caution them not to share their recollections, but to draw exclusively on their personal memories.

2 Ask students to exchange their accounts with a partner, again without conversation. As they read their partner's statement, ask students to be alert for specifics their partners included that they omitted and for any discrepancies between these individual versions of the event. Finally, allow them an opportunity to clarify with each other what they agree they observed.

3 With the entire class, solicit the elements of a reliable eyewitness account. As they talk about their experiences with this activity, students will likely relate that some witnesses were more discerning and noticed more details. Acknowledge that eyewitnesses might disagree in their interpretations but should agree on "the facts" of the event. Inform students that accounts that are inconsistent with the facts are deemed unreliable.

4 Have students read a selection and distribute three-column Eyewitness Testimony Charts (Buehl, 2008; see the Appendix for reproducible versions of the Eyewitness Testimony Chart). The first column ("I was there") identifies the aspects of the selection that form the focus of the eyewitness testimony. The middle column ("The Author's Words") represents "the facts" that each testimony should be based on. The third column ("My Version") is reserved for how each individual student imagined this part of the author's message.

For example, students reading the classic Edgar Allen Poe short story, "The Cask of Amontillado," might be asked to write

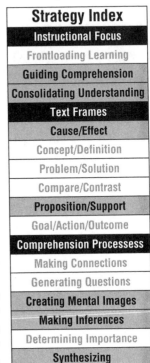

Strategy Index

Instructional Focus
Frontloading Learning
Guiding Comprehension
Consolidating Understanding
Text Frames
Cause/Effect
Concept/Definition
Problem/Solution
Compare/Contrast
Proposition/Support
Goal/Action/Outcome
Comprehension Processes
Making Connections
Generating Questions
Creating Mental Images
Making Inferences
Determining Importance
Synthesizing

their eyewitness accounts of the scene of the crime, drawing upon the author's language to create in their imaginations the vaults of the Montresor palazzo (see Eyewitness Testimony Chart on Poe Story example). Imagined personal details, like "it was so cold I was shivering" or "it was totally creepy with all those shadows of old skeletons flickering on the stone walls," add uniqueness to these personal eyewitness accounts. Students should write their versions as they imagine it would have been had they been there in person. The "The Author's Words" column prompts students to attend closely to descriptive language and important details, so that their versions show fidelity to the written text. Ask students to share their versions with partners, and also notice points of agreement on the "facts" of the text (the author's words).

First Impressions

First Impressions (Buehl, 2008) provides a variation of this activity, which again asks students to assume a first-person perspective as they read. Using this strategy involves the following steps:

1 Distribute a blank First Impressions Chart to students (see the Appendix for a reproducible version of the First Impressions Chart). As they begin to read a selection, ask students to pause to notice their first impressions of a person, place, or event. Students record the author's description under "The Author's Words" and their impressions to the right. These are entered in the "First" segment at the top of the chart (see the First Impressions on Poe Story example). Like the Eyewitness strategy, students are accountable for grounding their impressions in the facts of the selection.

2 Students continue reading the selection. As they read further and discover more, their impressions are likely to deepen or perhaps take a different turn. At an appropriate spot, ask students to pause again to inventory the author's words and to talk once more about their impressions. These are recorded in the middle "Next" segments of the chart.

3 At the end of the selection, students revisit their impressions and add their final comments based on additional information from the author. The First Impressions strategy engages students in recording how their impressions of a person, setting, or event evolved. The first reactions represent their initial impressions, and subsequent entries show how their impressions progressed or changed. For the Poe example, students could be asked to track their impressions of the victim, Fortunato, as if they were directly acquainted with the details of the story.

You Ought to Be in Pictures

Remember paging through an old family photo album? As you gazed at pictures of your kinfolk, taken

---

Eyewitness Testimony Chart on Poe Story

I Was There (and can describe...)	The Author's Words ("The author wrote...")	My Version ("I saw, heard, felt, experienced...")
The setting of this crime—the ancient vaults of the Montresor family	Down long and winding staircase Damp ground of catacombs Cavern walls Extensive vaults Long walls of piled skeletons Niter hangs like moss Drops of moisture trickle Casks & puncheons in recesses Range of low arches Kept descending & descending Deep crypt with foul air Flames from flambeaux Bones thrown down on earth Walls of solid granite	The Montresor vaults were dug deep into the ground under their mansion. To get there you had to carefully walk down a very long and winding staircase. Soon you were in total darkness except for the torches you carried. Down in the catacombs it was like a cemetery cave, with a dirt floor and stone walls, and skeletons and bones everywhere, some stacked up and some just thrown about. It was cold and very wet, and water dripped down from the ceiling, and the air was horrible to breathe. You kept going down and down, and had to bend down under these arches, and your torch kept shining on all those skulls and bones....

First Impressions of *Fortunato*

	The Author's Words	My Impressions
First	Pride in wine knowledge Carnival season, wore tight-fitting striped dress & conical cap & bells Accosted with excessive warmth, drinking Insisted check out the amontillado instead of Luchesi, who he said can't tell sherry from amontillado.	My first impression was that Fortunato seemed like a sort of silly person, and that was how he was dressed, like a jester or clown. He seemed to drink a lot and want others to believe he was a wine expert. He has a very high opinion of himself and talked this Luchesi down so that he gets the honor of checking the amontillado. Maybe he just wanted more drink. He was pretty drunk, loud, pushy, and braggy.
Then	Gait unsteady; intoxication Coughed; unable to talk for several minutes Refused to go back from catacombs Continued to drink Called Luchesi an ignoramus	He was very drunk and kept drinking while in the crypt and made rude comments about Luchesi. He seemed he have health problems, because he had these coughing fits, and I don't think the damp catacombs were good for him, but he wouldn't leave. I think he still wanted to show off his wine knowledge (big ego!) but he was also getting more to drink.
Finally	Stood stupidly bewildered Too astounded to resist Low moaning cry after fettered to wall Loud, shrill screams and then silence Sad voice, said "very good joke" Said, "for the love of God."	He didn't catch on what was happening until he was chained and being plastered in. He seemed stunned that someone was so angry with him. Then he lost it and starting moaning and screaming. He seemed to panic and then become depressed, and finally, he tried to pretend it was a joke. He didn't beg until the end, though, and he never asked why this was being done. Maybe he had finally figured it out.

perhaps a century or more ago, you probably found yourself pausing periodically and imagining what life was like for those people. What were the daily conditions like for growing up on a cattle ranch in New Mexico in 1896? How has the landscape changed since then? What was the country like for your great-grandparents who emigrated to North America in the 1880s? Who in a particular photo is most like you?

Photographs can evoke a sense of mood and convey meaningful information that communicates far beyond written description. The old adage "a picture is worth a thousand words" explains why textbook editors undertake the expense of including many photographs and other visuals in the layout of a chapter. Unfortunately, students taking the "quick trip" through a textbook section—endeavoring to finish the reading and complete the assignment—may overlook these rich sources of insight on the content. In addition, students may regard the textbook as personally uninviting and distant, merely as paragraphs of dense information. Taking time to guide students through a thoughtful examination of photographs can help them connect to concepts and successfully tackle learning new material. You Ought to Be in Pictures (Buehl, 2000) is

a strategy that encourages students to imagine themselves within the context of a photograph. Using this strategy involves the following steps:

1 Look for vivid photographs that connect with your curriculum. Some outstanding photographs already may be provided in the textbook students are reading. Check other textbooks, reference sources, and newspapers and magazines. Search for photographs to which your students can make a personal connection. To display photographs, use an overhead transparency, PowerPoint, or images projected from a website.

2 Select a photograph that will introduce or extend important ideas or concepts for a unit of study. Guide students in their viewing of the photograph by stimulating their mental imagery and suggesting a personal connection to events portrayed in the picture. For example, to prepare students in a history course for studying the Great Depression of the 1930s in the United States, identify a photograph that illustrates some key themes of the time period, such as a Dorothea Lange photograph from the U.S. Great Depression Era (which can be found online at memory.loc.gov). Using the photograph, take students through the following

Photograph From the Depression Era

Source: Lange, D. (1938). *Family walking on highway* (Library of Congress American Memory Collection). Retrieved August 5, 2008, from memory.loc.gov

guided imagery exercise (see Guided Imagery, beginning on page 90).

> During the period of the Great Depression, many people, especially farmers, lost their land and were forced out on the road. You are looking at a Library of Congress photograph of a homeless family in Oklahoma in 1938.
>
> First, examine the location of the photograph and note as many details as possible. What do you observe about the countryside? About the land? The plants and vegetation? The road? What time of year might it be? What does the climate appear to be like? What type of day does it seem to be?
>
> Now focus closely on each person in the photograph. Pay particular attention to what each person is wearing. Look at the way family members carry themselves, their posture, or their facial expressions.
>
> Next, choose one individual in the photograph and imagine you are this person. What might you be thinking while this was happening? Describe what you might be feeling, what emotions you might be experiencing. What has the day been like for you? Imagine what might have happened before the scene presented in the photo. What do you see happening later during this day and following days?

3 Guided imagery using photographs provides an excellent opportunity for students to record observations and thoughts in writing. Using the Depression example, give students the following writing prompt:

> It is now many years later. You are showing this photograph of your family to a grandchild. What would you tell this child about your memories of that day? Write what you would share as an entry in your notebook.

After students respond in writing, have them first share their observations with a partner. Then ask for volunteers to read their entries to the class. Students who have chosen the same individual with whom to identify will hear and compare classmates' musings about that individual during that difficult time. Students will delve into the Great Depression unit with much more empathy for the great personal dramas of the time and more personal involvement in the material. For example,

> I remember I was so small that Papa plunked me in the wagon. At first I thought it was a great long wagon ride and I would giggle and shriek every time we went over a bump. It was really hot, but I only had one set of clothes to wear. If we happened past a farm with vegetables, we would try to snatch something to eat, but Papa wouldn't eat with us. He used to say, "The bank didn't take my dignity."

This strategy can be adapted for use with photographs that do not feature people. For example, with science pictures, suggest that students are personally witnessing what is portrayed in the photo and guide them through noticing details as if they were actually viewing the scene.

Advantages

- "First-Person" comprehension strategies stimulate students to fire up their imaginations as if they were actually participating in the events described in a written text.

- Students become accustomed to paying closer attention to author details that can trigger sensory responses.

- Students develop personal interpretations of people, locations, and events that they encounter in their reading; they add their personality to the author's words.

- Students encounter key ideas through pictures before reading, increasing their motivation to learn more about the topic and priming them to learn from text materials that may otherwise be regarded as cold and impersonal.

References

Buehl, D. (2000). You ought to be in pictures: Using photos to help students understand past. *WEAC News and Views, 35*(8), 14.

Buehl, D. (2008). First person reading. *On WEAC.* Available online: www.weac.org/news/2007-08/feb08/readingroom.htm

Lange, D. (1938). *Family walking on highway* (Library of Congress American Memory Collection). Retrieved August 5, 2008, from memory.loc.gov

Follow the Characters

The face of a massive stone statue suddenly shifts, producing a gloomy opening. Through this fissure, a hideous slithering form emerges. The basilisk, a serpent with fangs dripping with venom, begins to uncoil its lethal, tree-trunk sized body. Inexorably, with piercing evil eyes, the snake advances for the kill.

What would you be feeling if this were happening to you? What was Harry Potter feeling? Exciting fiction can put us on the edge of our chairs, it can rile up our emotions and place us vicariously in the midst of the action. In the climatic scene described above, based on J.K. Rowling's (1999) *Harry Potter and the Chamber of Secrets*, Harry confronts his nemesis, Lord Voldemort, and the murderous basilisk. And what was Harry feeling as this scene unfolds? Certainly, our imaginations as readers are a great help. When we consider how we would feel if we were facing such a predicament, we can empathize with a character in a story. In addition, authors help us gauge the emotions of a passage through their use of well-chosen language. Thus Rowling guides us through this scene by referring to Harry with phrases such as "horror-struck," "fear spreading up his numb legs," "trembled," "running blindly sideways," and so forth. An author's choice of words provides readers with cues that help us access the emotions of a text.

Change and conflict are two constants of life that underlie fictional literature. Tracking the emotional content of a text is a particularly effective strategy for examining how characters handle change and conflict. Developing sensitivity to emotional subcurrents—what a character is feeling and thinking and how this affects actions and responses from others—can spark inferential thinking and help students develop insight into an author's point of view.

Using the Strategy

Follow the Characters (Buehl, 1994) is a strategy that cues students to understand stories through character analysis. Students organize key information about a character into a visual outline that can help them develop an interpretation of an author's theme or message (see the Follow the Characters graphic). The strategy is appropriate for both short stories and longer works of fictional literature, as well as biographies, autobiographies, and other nonfiction works that feature descriptions of individuals. Using this strategy involves the following steps:

1 Review the basic components of story structure (see Story Mapping beginning on page 166). Establish that stories have a setting, characters, plot events, a conflict, and a resolution. As students understand a story, they develop an interpretation of what the story might mean to the author (possible theme) and what the story means to them as readers.

2 Use the role of detective as a metaphor to help students conceptualize the process of character analysis. Ask students how a detective goes about solving a mystery, and they will likely answer that a detective looks for clues and investigates people. Emphasize the detective frame of mind as a way to discover the theme of the story. For clues about an author's viewpoint in a story, students should "follow the characters" by tuning in to what a character does or says and what others do or say about the character. Students should pay special attention to the role of the character in the story's conflict and whether this role changes the character in any way.

3 Place a blank Character Analysis Grid on the overhead projector and model with students using a familiar story, such as a fairy tale or a selection students have read previously (see the Appendix for a reproducible version of the Character Analysis Grid). For example, most students can relate to the story of Cinderella, which has appeared in various guises in a number of recent movies. They may know that the major conflict in this fairy tale is between Cinderella and her stepmother and stepsisters. Elicit information about Cinderella from

Strategy Index
Instructional Focus
Frontloading Learning
Guiding Comprehension
Consolidating Understanding
Text Frames
Cause/Effect
Concept/Definition
Problem/Solution
Compare/Contrast
Proposition/Support
Goal/Action/Outcome
Comprehension Processess
Making Connections
Generating Questions
Creating Mental Images
Making Inferences
Determining Importance
Synthesizing

the students to fill in the grid. Record her actions (works hard, scrubs floor, doesn't complain); record her thoughts and words (asks to go to the prince's ball, wishes she could attend, does not tell prince who she is); record others' views of her (is treated like servant, is told she is less worthy than her stepsisters, is denied chance to go to ball, is treated like a princess by fairy godmother and prince); and record the changes she undergoes during the story (she begins to believe in herself, she starts to stand up for herself). Help students to articulate a theme for the story, such as "Hard work and honesty will be ultimately rewarded."

4 Students are now ready to apply the Character Analysis Grid to a work of literature. For example, students in an English language arts class who read the dramatization of the classic novella *A Christmas Carol* by Charles Dickens (Horovitz, 1979) would analyze the major character, Ebenezer Scrooge, who is visited by a series of spirits who convince him to see the mistakes of his life (see the Character Analysis Grid example). After students read the play, have them work with partners to complete the conflict ring and first three quadrants: What does the character do? What does the character say or think? How do others feel about the character? Note that "others" might also include the author, story narrator, and characters in the story.

5 Team each pair of students with a second set of partners, forming cooperative groups of four to work on the fourth quadrant: How does the character change? Students should use the information recorded in the first three quadrants to formulate the changes experienced by the character and list them as before-and-after comparisons. Emphasize that authors communicate important insights to readers through the ways in which characters change. As students examine Scrooge's actions and thoughts, they will find that his internal conflict about how he has lived his life changes him—he is gradually transformed from a nasty, ill-tempered, greedy miser into a charitable and outgoing benefactor of others. Have each student group write their version of the theme of the story based on their analysis of the character's changes. Students might express the theme of *A Christmas Carol* as, "One's wealth is measured in friendships and good deeds, instead of merely money."

6 Ask students to complete multiple Character Analysis Grids for fictional works such as novels, which feature more than one major character. These can be compared to analyze the way an author treats different characters and what this might signal about an author's ideas and themes.

Follow the Characters

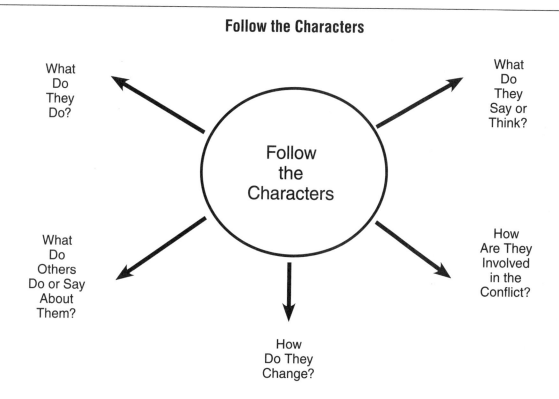

What Do They Do?

What Do They Say or Think?

Follow the Characters

What Do Others Do or Say About Them?

How Are They Involved in the Conflict?

How Do They Change?

Source: Buehl, D. (1995). *Classroom strategies for interactive learning* (p. 47). Madison: Wisconsin State Reading Association.

Character Analysis Grid

Story: *A Christmas Carol*

1. What does the character do?

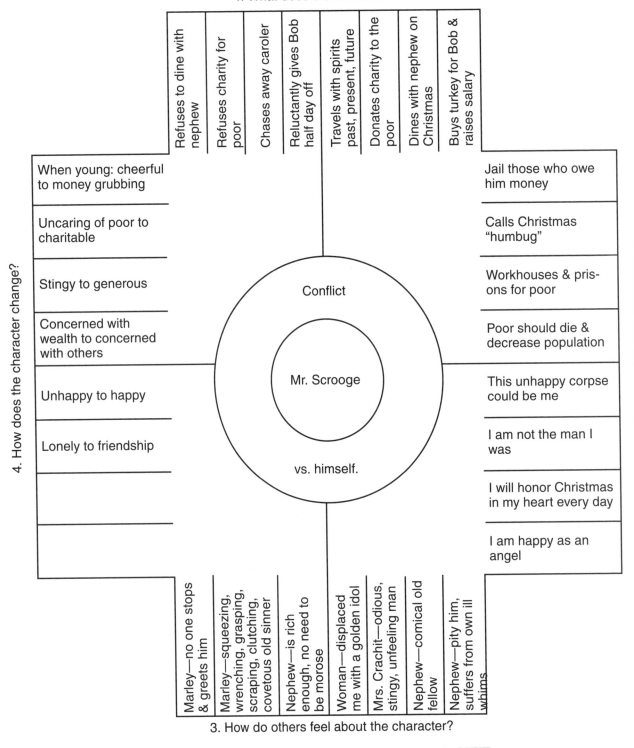

1. What does the character do? (top row):
- Refuses to dine with nephew
- Refuses charity for poor
- Chases away caroler
- Reluctantly gives Bob half day off
- Travels with spirits past, present, future
- Donates charity to the poor
- Dines with nephew on Christmas
- Buys turkey for Bob & raises salary

4. How does the character change? (left column):
- When young: cheerful to money grubbing
- Uncaring of poor to charitable
- Stingy to generous
- Concerned with wealth to concerned with others
- Unhappy to happy
- Lonely to friendship

Conflict: Mr. Scrooge vs. himself.

2. What does the character say or think? (right column):
- Jail those who owe him money
- Calls Christmas "humbug"
- Workhouses & prisons for poor
- Poor should die & decrease population
- This unhappy corpse could be me
- I am not the man I was
- I will honor Christmas in my heart every day
- I am happy as an angel

3. How do others feel about the character? (bottom row):
- Marley—no one stops & greets him
- Marley—squeezing, wrenching, grasping, scraping, clutching, covetous old sinner
- Nephew—is rich enough, no need to be morose
- Woman—displaced me with a golden idol
- Mrs. Crachit—odious, stingy, unfeeling man
- Nephew—comical old fellow
- Nephew—pity him, suffers from own ill whims

5. Author's theme or point of view:
One's wealth is measured in friendships and good deeds, instead of merely money.

Advantages

- Students are provided with a systematic way to analyze a story to help them articulate possible meaning and the author's themes.
- Students learn to recognize the central roles that conflict and change play in character development.
- Students develop a visual outline of major elements in a story that can help them articulate the author's theme or point of view.

References

Buehl, D. (1994). Persona: Character analysis sheds light on story's meaning. *WEAC News & Views, 29*(10), 21.

Buehl, D. (1995). *Classroom strategies for interactive learning.* Madison: Wisconsin State Reading Association.

Literature Cited

Horovitz, I. (1979). A Christmas carol: Scrooge and Marley. In *Prentice Hall literature, grade 7* (pp. 740–806). Boston: Pearson Prentice Hall.

Rowling, J.K. (1999). *Harry Potter and the chamber of secrets.* New York: Scholastic.

Suggested Reading

Beck, I.L., & McKeown, M.G. (1981). Developing questions that promote comprehension: The story map. *Language Arts, 58*(8), 913–918.

Guided Imagery

You weren't there, in the logging camps of the Northwest in the 1870s, to hear the crack of axes against towering pines, to witness the trudging draft horses as they snaked 16-foot logs along forest trails, to inhale the steamy rich aromas of a camp dining hall preparing platters of roast beef and baked chicken, baskets of biscuits, and line-ups of fruit pies. You weren't there, embedded as a miniature visitor in the stalks of slender sprouts of corn as they continued their growth from a seed into a mature plant, to observe firsthand the life cycle of a plant as it eventually produced its own seeds to perpetuate the species for another season. You weren't there, in the fervently inventive mind of author J.K. Rowling, as she conjured up an entire world and culture, populated with a host of compelling characters and sinister villains, and spun an unfolding storyline of intrigue and adventure.

You weren't there. But sometimes it seemed like you were. As readers, we do far more than decipher words on a page. Ultimately, reading triggers a vicarious reality, as we recreate for ourselves how things are, or were, or could be, even though we are not actually experiencing them "in the moment." And sometimes we even transcend the physical act we call reading—that conscious awareness that our eyes are processing lines of print—and we are transported in our minds to somewhere else, as if we are immersed in a live event. That bionic DVD player in our heads kicks in, and we feel as if "we were there."

It is our imaginations that take us beyond those abstract symbols arrayed as visual information by someone who is employing language to help us "get it"—a story, an idea, an explanation, a depiction. It's as if authors are saying, "You weren't there, but if you follow what I am telling you, you can almost see it, hear it, smell it, taste it, feel it." Yet if you ask many of our students "what do you see when you read," they will respond as if this was a trick question. "Words, of course," they will answer. Many students regard reading as mostly a word identification exercise, and as a result, their comprehension suffers. They struggle with picturing in their imaginations what an author is using language to convey. Comprehension involves animating the abstract language of written texts with life experiences.

Using the Strategy

Guided Imagery (Gambrell, Kapinus, & Wilson, 1987) is a strategy that triggers visualization for students as they read and learn. Guided Imagery can be used either to prepare students for a reading or to deepen their understanding after they have read. For example, Guided Imagery could introduce a history passage by helping students visualize hardships experienced by settlers traveling west across the Great Plains in North America. Or students in a science class may first need to examine a passage on photosynthesis to acquire some basic knowledge before they could successfully visualize the process inside a plant. Using this strategy involves the following steps:

1 Start with a variety of "imagination tune-ups." Wilhelm (2004) recommends a progression of visualization activities. First, encourage students to become precise observers. Bring an interesting object to class and ask students to examine it carefully, to handle it, to notice everything they can about it. A unique item might be especially effective. Cue students to inspect the item from the perspective of a reporter, a person who perceives something with enough detail so that he or she can reliably describe it to others even though the item is no longer present. After sufficient viewing time, have students close their eyes and imagine the item, with as much specificity as they can. Students can then be asked to describe the item to a partner, or to quickly sketch the item from memory. A variation of this activity involves pairing students and providing a different item for each partner to examine. Partners would not see each other's items. Each student then attempts to assist their partner in

Strategy Index
Instructional Focus
Frontloading Learning
Guiding Comprehension
Consolidating Understanding
Text Frames
Cause/Effect
Concept/Definition
Problem/Solution
Compare/Contrast
Proposition/Support
Goal/Action/Outcome
Comprehension Processess
Making Connections
Generating Questions
Creating Mental Images
Making Inferences
Determining Importance
Synthesizing

imagining the unseen item by capitalizing on their powers of observation.

Next, have students transition to imagining objects that are not physically present but are commonplace elements of their lives. For example, you might ask students to imagine they are each standing in a room in their homes. What one object captures their attention? Instruct them to zero in on that object and try to perceive it in great detail. Again, have students practice with a partner translating their images into descriptive language.

Extend practice from an emphasis on imagining particular objects to the unfolding of scenes in our "mind's eye." Ask students to run action sequences in their imaginations, with all their senses alert. For example, ask students to imagine a basketball, then the basketball being dribbled, and hearing the sounds it makes while noticing how the basketball feels on their hands each time it bounces up to them. Then ask them to replay in their imaginations a short series of events on a basketball court, involving people in movement.

2 Have students preview a reading selection. Classroom texts often strike students as an endless parade of terms and facts. Emphasize that they should give special attention to pictures, drawings, or graphics that are included with the text. This is especially important for science or social studies texts, which typically feature a number of visual elements that enhance information. As students notice these visual elements, they begin to see what the material is about. You also may wish to use other sources for pictures that will stimulate the students' imaginations (see You Ought to Be in Pictures, page 83). For example, before biology students tackle the dense prose of their textbook, the teacher can take them through a short Guided Imagery exercise on fungi (see the Guided Imagery for Science example). After students imagine the fungi, they are directed to a photograph in their textbook to see how close their imaginations approximated the actual item.

3 Tell the students to close their eyes and turn on their imaginations. Introduce a Guided Imagery exercise by giving them some background on the situation they will be visualizing. Encourage them to make use of all their senses as they imagine—sight, sound, smell, physical sensation, taste, and emotion. Suggest an image to students one sentence at a time, and pause for several seconds after each sentence to allow them time to process what you are saying and to visualize the picture. To prepare students for a reading about the rigors of farming in the Great Plains in North America during the 1880s (see Guided Imagery for Social Studies example), begin with the following:

Guided Imagery for Science

Fungi

Imagine the air moving through the room. As the air slowly circulates, imagine that you can see that on these air currents are carried thousands of microscopic, round, bead-like spores.

These spores are looking for an opportunity to grow. They are like tiny little seeds, searching for a food source that will enable them to grow and live. If they locate a food source with enough moisture, they can grow.

As you imagine them drifting by, notice that loaf of bread on the counter. The plastic bread bag has been left open.

The drifting spores get closer and closer. Some of them begin to land on a slice of bread.

Watch carefully as tiny little strings of cells began to grow from a spore. More and more cells grow out, farther and farther from the spore.

Soon there are so many of them that they appear as a tangled mass of little strings; these are growing denser and denser as they feed off the bread. Imagine you see some of them with little hooks that attach to the bread fibers. They continue to wind outward and outward.

You can now start to see with the unaided eye a velvety fuzz appearing on the surface of the bread. What colors are you seeing now?

Source: Buehl, D. (2001). *Classroom strategies for interactive learning* (2nd ed., p. 60). Newark, DE: International Reading Association.

"Imagine being a homesteader on the Great Plains in the late 19th century. You are alone, and you see the prairie much the way it was before the settlers came."

Ask students to share their reflections about what they were imagining during the exercise. What did they notice with their imaginations? Do they have any questions about what they were attempting to visualize? This would be an excellent opportunity to have students write about what they visualized as a way of summarizing their insights.

4 Provide frequent opportunities for students to experiment with responding to author language to trigger mental images. Wilhelm (2004) suggests using imagery-rich texts as short read-alouds to develop sensitivity to author language. Read a vividly written selection to your students and pause periodically to comment on how you are imagining what the author is relaying in words. These think-alouds underscore that an author relies on readers to fire up their imaginations

Guided Imagery for Social Studies

The Great Plains

Imagine that you are in Nebraska. It is summer, 1867, and you are standing in the midst of rolling prairie for as far as you can see in all directions.

Look around and see that no trees, buildings, or other human beings are in sight.

Notice the wind gently swaying the 2-foot tall prairie grasses back and forth.

Feel the 90-degree heat from the hot noon sun as it beats down upon you.

Breathe in the dust and pollen from the grasses around you and imagine wiping the grimy sweat from your forehead.

Notice the tired ox standing next to your single-bladed steel plow.

See yourself trudging over to the plow and placing your hands on its rough wooden handles.

Watch the hard-packed deep black prairie soil turn over from your plow blade as you struggle along behind the ox.

Feel the blisters on your hands as they grip the plow handles.

Imagine the strain in your back muscles and in your arms and legs as the plow jerks you along.

Labor your way over a small hill, and in the distance notice the small hut made with thick squares of prairie sod.

Leave the plow and slowly make your way closer to the hut, noticing it in greater and greater detail.

Bend your head as you enter the dark, dank sod hut, and slowly pace around on the hard dirt floor.

Source: Buehl, D. (2001). *Classroom strategies for interactive learning* (2nd ed., p. 60). Newark, DE: International Reading Association.

find it advantageous to portray their thinking nonverbally in addition to talking about what they imagine using language.

5 As students gain practice in visualizing, have them create their own Guided Imagery exercises in cooperative groups or with partners, taking turns describing what they visualized. Or ask students to use a Movie Clip strategy, to make decisions from the perspective of a movie director and select a segment of a text that is rich in mental imagery. The student "directors" then pitch to their studio how this material would appear if it were filmed.

In addition, lead students in discussions of text visuals provided by an author to supplement comprehension. Authors recognize that, at times, telling may not be sufficient, and readers would be better able to use their imaginations if pictures, drawings, charts, or other visual displays are included. With texts lacking visuals, ask students to suggest the visuals they feel would aid readers in accessing their imaginations. Students can be asked to draw these visual extensions on sticky notes to be affixed to the page next to the appropriate text.

Advantages

- Imagination activities nurture readers who use visual, auditory, and other sensory connections to fashion personal mental images of an author's message.
- Students who place inordinate attention on "reading the words" are prompted to enliven their reading by unleashing their imaginations.
- Students develop an eye for evocative language, which stimulates the development of increasingly more sophisticated mental images.
- Students read with a deeper engagement with a text, and they personalize their reading through individual interpretations of how things might appear if they experienced them.
- Students create vivid mental images of ideas and concepts that help them remember information longer.

References

Gambrell, L.B., Kapinus, B.A., & Wilson, R.M. (1987). Using mental imagery and summarization to achieve independence in comprehension. *Journal of Reading, 30*(7), 638–642.

Wilhelm, J.D. (2004). *Reading IS seeing: Learning to visualize scenes, characters, ideas, and text worlds to improve comprehension and reflective reading.* New York: Scholastic.

Suggested Reading

Lazear, D. (2003). *Eight ways of teaching: The artistry of teaching with multiple intelligences* (4th ed.). Thousand Oaks, CA: Sage.

to breathe life into the words on the page. After modeling, continue to pause, but now prompt the students to generate their own mental images. Occasionally, encourage students to quick-sketch images that come to mind or to elaborate what they are imagining to a partner. Quick-sketches are just that—quick—and are not carefully drawn artistic renditions. Some students

Hands-On Reading

And now, the moment of truth. You've lugged the box in from the car, unpacked the contents, and arrayed the obligatory hodge-podge of tools around you. A do-it-yourself project, long overdue, is finally scheduled to be tackled. Another installment in home improvement is imminent. So where do we start. Ah yes, the directions. From amidst the clutter of bubble wrap and obscure-looking unassembled parts, you snatch the product booklet. And inevitably, your blood pressure starts to head northward.

Hmm...assembly and instructions, Turn-of-the-Century ceiling fan...canopy and down rod...slot of hanger ball snapped into chip of bracket... the motor blue wire and tangerine wire attached to... Wait! Tangerine wire? Goes where? Who ever heard of tangerine wires!

The do-it-yourself nightmare—you are poised to undertake a project, and the enthusiasm you have kindled begins to fizzle as you are confronted with the inevitable set of incomprehensible directions and obscure illustrations. You wonder, Who writes this stuff anyway?

Imagine for a moment the author who wrote these guidelines for installing a ceiling fan. Who does this writer think will be reading these instructions? What does the writer think readers will already know? What expectations does the writer apparently have about readers' abilities to make sense of this document? What could the writer have done to make the writing more accessible? Is it any wonder that after reading directions such as these, many readers would toss the directions aside and try to "wing it" through their project?

Eventually, the task described above is satisfactorily accomplished, but most of us likely encountered frustrations along the way. We realize that for our efforts to be successful, we have to engage in a special kind of reading—technical reading—that contrasts with the reading routines we follow when we bury ourselves in a pleasurable novel, study a textbook, or peruse magazine articles. Technical reading is undertaken for a very pragmatic purpose: step-by-step guidance for how-to-do-it tasks. Hands-on projects require hands-on reading.

As adults, we recognize the need for technical reading strategies in a variety of daily contexts. Directions for filling out tax forms, care and maintenance instructions in product manuals, help sites for computer software, and the like all mandate reading for pragmatic purposes. Students encounter technical reading demands frequently in school, and like adults, they often find them challenging. Steps to follow in a classroom procedure, such as a science lab, involve technical reading. So does much of the reading in applied technology, computers, business education, family and consumer education, and health and fitness courses.

Using the Strategy

Hands-On Reading (Buehl, 2002) focuses students on coping with the particular demands of technical nonfiction. Because readers frequently find themselves overwhelmed by dense, functional writing, this strategy anticipates the need for problem-solving while reading. Using this strategy involves the following steps:

1 Introduce technical nonfiction as a special text genre. Technical nonfiction tends to exhibit the following characteristics:

- Technical texts are usually very terse. Because it is assumed that an individual is reading only to act on the information, little background is provided. Technical texts generally follow a "just the facts" approach.

- Technical texts usually follow a goal/action/outcome text organization. That is, the reader is usually provided with a clear goal for reading (for example, to bake a lemon meringue pie, to integrate visuals into a word-processing document, or to build a cedar chest). The reader is then presented a sequence of steps to follow. Typically, some description or illustration of the expected outcome is also included.

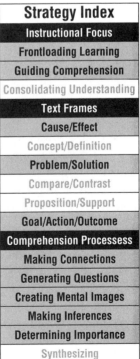

Strategy Index

Instructional Focus
Frontloading Learning
Guiding Comprehension
Consolidating Understanding
Text Frames
Cause/Effect
Concept/Definition
Problem/Solution
Compare/Contrast
Proposition/Support
Goal/Action/Outcome
Comprehension Processess
Making Connections
Generating Questions
Creating Mental Images
Making Inferences
Determining Importance
Synthesizing

- Technical texts are usually laden with content-specific vocabulary. Because these texts are very direct and concise, terminology may be used without definition or explanation. Technical texts expect that the reader will already be familiar with much of the vocabulary and perhaps experienced with the procedures being outlined.

- Technical texts tend to be highly visual. Diagrams and illustrations frequently accompany the written information. Readers may have to infer meanings and functions of some of the technical vocabulary by examining labeled pictorials. Information presented visually may be not adequately repeated in written form.

- Technical texts rarely give any consideration to motivating or entertaining the reader. Technical texts are viewed only as a means toward an end. Readers consult them only to the extent necessary to satisfactorily accomplish a task. Language is chosen to be as precise and straightforward as possible. As a result, technical texts strike readers as dry, impersonal, and blunt.

2 Given the nature of technical nonfiction, readers need to adopt reading strategies especially tailored for comprehension of technical material. Begin by brainstorming with students problems that readers typically experience with technical nonfiction. Students will likely comment that the texts are difficult to understand, they make extensive use of terms that are not well known, they are not clearly written, the visuals are hard to decipher, and they don't provide enough useful information. Like adults, students will probably lament that such texts don't use "friendlier" English. Finally, students may comment that they despair of making sense from some of these documents, so they may be tempted to toss the text aside and attempt to complete the project by relying on their personal background knowledge and common sense.

Unfortunately, proceeding without reading can be a hit-or-miss proposition. The task may be done improperly, it may take longer than necessary, or the student may become discouraged and give up on the project.

3 Outline Hands-On Reading as a strategy for reading technical nonfiction. Hands-On Reading assumes that readers will be "doing" while they are reading, manipulating or examining objects when these items are featured in the text. Hands-on reading follows a start-again, stop-again approach to a written text, as readers set documents aside to attempt to translate instructions into action, returning to the text to confirm their understandings or to transition into the next stage. Emphasize the following steps for Hands-On Reading of technical texts:

- **Size up the task**—Start by surveying the text to obtain a general sense of what needs to be done and what the final outcome should look like. What exactly does it appear the reader needs to do with this information?

- **Clarify vocabulary**—What key terms are used in the text? Which of these terms are already known, and which are unfamiliar? What aids does the text provide to assist a reader with key terms? What can a reader do if the text does not adequately elaborate critical vocabulary?

- **Scan the visuals**—Examine any visual information provided in the text. The diagrams and drawings should help the reader visualize the process to be followed in completing the task. Compare the visual information to the actual objects with which you will be working.

- **Look out for cautions**—Some projects will be ruined if the steps are not followed exactly as prescribed. In other cases, readers may make a serious error, or even expose themselves to danger, if steps are ignored or done in improper sequence.

- **Read and apply**—Begin reading and undertaking the task in phases. Read the first segment, clarify the message, and apply the information. Hands-On Reading assumes a recursive spiraling through a technical text: read a segment, apply the information "hands on," re-read to confirm the actions taken or to clarify misunderstandings, continue to read the next segment, and so forth.

- **Collaborate**—Hands-On Reading usually requires a degree of problem solving. Therefore, a major component of this reading strategy is interaction with fellow learners. Re-reading segments and verbalizing understandings with a partner is a natural problem solving routine for adults grappling with technical nonfiction.

4 Students work with partners to read and apply information from classroom technical material.

Advantages

- Students learn independent routines for learning from technical texts rather than over-reliance on teachers to provide all the information.

- Students become more flexible in their approach to various text genres, realizing that some texts need to be read, and re-read, in parts rather than straight through.

- This strategy is appropriate for most technical non-fiction texts in all content disciplines, but especially for courses that feature "applied" reading as central to the curriculum.

Reference

Buehl, D. (2002). Putting it all together. *OnWEAC In Print*, *3*(4), 13.

History Change Frame

The Vikings emanated from the Scandinavian peninsula at the end of 800 A.D. and regularly plundered the inhabitants of northern Europe over the course of the next century. With their high-prowed, shallow-draft vessels, the Vikings created the perfect attack ship, which allowed them to sail long distances under a variety of oceanic conditions. Not only did they pillage monasteries and communities in the British Isles and France, but also they became permanent settlers. The Vikings created the duchy of Normandy, for example, which eventually evolved into the country of France.

For many students, history lessons like this one seem to be a never-ending series of facts: names, dates, places, or events. What is the point? Students begin to make more sense of history when they use facts to help them understand important changes people have experienced and how changes contribute to problems people confront. Learning about these changes helps students better understand human society and what we have to deal with today.

The Thinking Like a Historian project (Mandell & Malone, 2007) focuses history instruction on essential questions related to this change dynamic: What changed and what remained the same? Who or what made change happen? What were the effects of change? Who supported and who did not support these changes? Who benefited from the change and who did not?

Teaching students to read history materials with a problem/solution frame of mind enables them to cue into the major changes discussed in a chapter or text. The History Change Frame (Buehl, 1992; see the History Change Frame example) is a frontloading strategy that helps students get a chapter overview without becoming bogged down in the details of what they are reading. The History Change Frame guides comprehension by focusing attention on groups of people who confront problems and cope with change.

Using the Strategy

The History Change Frame is an excellent strategy to use with students in history class when introducing a reading. Using this strategy involves the following steps:

1 Select several time periods to be covered in class. In a brainstorming exercise, ask students who they expect will be featured in a reading for each time period. Emphasize that they should think of groups of people, not individuals: What groups of people would you expect to read about in a chapter on the American Revolution? The growth of industrialization? The Vietnam War? As students consider what they know about each of these time periods, their responses might include angry colonists and the British; factory owners, workers, and labor unions; and protesters, the U.S. Army, the French colonial government, and communist guerrillas.

2 Hand out student copies of the History Change Frame Graphic Organizer (see the Appendix for a reproducible version) and introduce the graphic on an overhead transparency. In your discussion, note that the study of history involves stories of people who deal with change and address problems. Factual details in a textbook chapter are presented to help readers understand the problems and the actions taken to solve these problems. Highlight the categories of change that are commonly featured in history texts. Cue students to be especially sensitive to anything involving change within a section or chapter, such as the following:

- **Population**—Increases or decreases in a geographical area or changes in composition with regard to factors like age distribution or ethnic identity.

- **Technology**—New inventions or other innovations that affect the way things are done in a society.

- **Environmental**—Changes in the physical geography of an area or in weather patterns.

- **Economic**—Changes in how people make a daily living and in their standard of living.

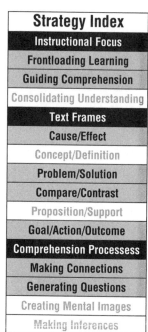

Strategy Index
Instructional Focus
Frontloading Learning
Guiding Comprehension
Consolidating Understanding
Text Frames
Cause/Effect
Concept/Definition
Problem/Solution
Compare/Contrast
Proposition/Support
Goal/Action/Outcome
Comprehension Processess
Making Connections
Generating Questions
Creating Mental Images
Making Inferences
Determining Importance
Synthesizing

- **Political**—Changes in the type of government, the nature of the leaders, elections, laws, court decisions, treaties, and wars.

- **Beliefs**—Changes in or opposition to what people believe, including religious beliefs, ideas and views, and values.

3 Assign students a chapter to preview. Have them survey the chapter to determine the groups that are the focus of the material. Model this process by thinking aloud as you examine the title, headings and subheadings, chapter objectives, advance organizers, primary source excerpts, pictures, and graphics. Determine with students who "the players" are in the chapter. Who is featured? Do not accept individual names during this phase but rather ask students to generalize groups of people who will be involved in the action.

4 Ask students to continue surveying the chapter, looking for clues about problems the groups of people might be encountering: What problems did the peasants face in feudal Europe? Nobles? Monarchs? What problems concerned women in the Progressive Age in the United States? African Americans? Muckrakers? Interestingly, students will discover that some groups featured in the chapter may be causing problems that other groups must deal with: Who experienced problems because of the crusaders? Who experienced problems because of the kings who believed in divine rights? Who experienced problems because of the dissidents arguing for reformation of the church?

5 As students read, have them work with a partner to complete a blank History Change Frame Graphic Organizer. Have them analyze information from the text that describes the changes and problems for each group of people. Ask students to identify actions taken by groups to solve their problems. For example, changes that affected American Indians in the latter half of the 19th century included population (the demographic shift resulting from a huge influx of settlers of European ancestry), geographical (ranching and farming altered the prairie and the buffalo were depleted), technological (the railroad and more advanced weapons), economic (mining of gold and other minerals), and political (the passage of the Homestead Act, which promised affordable land to settlers). Conflict also resulted from the drastically divergent worldviews and beliefs of American Indian nations and settlers.

6 Discuss with students how changes affect people in different ways. For example, both the building of the Transcontinental Railroad and the passing of the Homestead Act affected three groups of people in the American West: How did the railroad cause different

History Change Frame

Source: Buehl, D. (1995). *Classroom strategies for interactive learning* (p. 57). Schofield: Wisconsin State Reading Association.

problems for Plains Indians, cattle ranchers, and prairie farmers? How about the Homestead Act? Students come to realize that the effects of changes vary depending on which group of people is considered. Sometimes a change benefits one group and causes problems for another (see the History Change Frame for the American West example). For example, the railroad clearly benefited ranchers but was detrimental to the lifestyles of Plains Indians. The Homestead Act opened the floodgates to farmers heading west but was resisted by both cattle ranchers and Indian nations.

Advantages

- Students are provided with a visual overview that helps them sort through a wealth of information and recognize important points of a reading selection.

- Students come to see that the information included in a history chapter is not a series of randomly selected facts.

- Students see how the information fits together and have a construct for making sense of what they read.

History Change Frame for the American West

Group	What Problems Did They Face	What Changes Affected These People	What Did They Do to Solve Their Problems?
Plains Indians	• Less land to live on • Disappearance of buffalo • Conflicts with settlers • Many were killed	• Population—Increased numbers of settlers coming West • Economic—Discovery of gold and other metals • Political—Homestead Act • Technological—The railroads	• Fought the settlers and soldiers • Agreed to treaties • Left reservations • Changed their way of life
Cattle ranchers	• End of the open range • Conflicts with Plains Indians • Conflicts with farmers and sheep ranchers	• Population—More settlers who wanted to farm and fence off the prairie • Political—Homestead Act • Technological—The railroads	• Got help from army against Plains Indians • Range wars • Accepted fenced prairie
Prairie farmers	• Conflicts with Plains Indians • Conflicts with cattle ranchers • Hardships of the prairie	• Political—Homestead Act • Environment—Harsh weather • Technological—The railroads • Economic—Recessions	• Got help from army against Plains Indians • Fenced in the prairie • Adapted to conditions—Harsh weather, new machines

Source: Buehl, D. (1995). *Classroom strategies for interactive learning* (p. 58). Schofield: Wisconsin State Reading Association.

The problem/solution text frame enables students to see patterns in history and to develop a coherent understanding of what history is and why it is studied.

The History Change Frame provides an excellent blueprint for writing assignments and other follow-up activities. Relevant information is clearly organized to allow relationships to be established and comparisons to be made.

References

Buehl, D. (1992). A frame of mind for reading history. *The Exchange. Newsletter of the International Reading Association Secondary Reading Special Interest Group, 5*(1), 4–5.

Buehl, D. (1995). *Classroom strategies for interactive learning.* Schofield: Wisconsin Reading Association.

Mandell, N., & Malone, B. (2007). *Thinking like a historian: Rethinking history instruction.* Madison: Wisconsin Historical Society.

History Memory Bubbles

Napoleon invaded Russia. The Marshall Plan helped Europe. The Sumerians wrote in cuneiform. George Washington stopped the Whiskey Rebellion. W.E.B. Du Bois was a founder of the National Association for the Advancement of Colored People. Charles I was executed during the English Civil War. The Mormons settled in Utah.

Facts—students reading history textbooks encounter a dizzying and seemingly endless array of factual information. For many, learning about history soon defaults to short-term memorization of isolated facts. The larger context of historical themes and ideas remains murky at best, and after a test is over, information is promptly jettisoned from their memories as the students begin anew with the next chapter.

In contrast, proficient readers search for connections and relationships among information as they study. Instead of becoming engulfed by a torrent of disjointed facts, they seek the flow of the information. In history textbooks, that flow often follows a problem/solution text frame.

Using the Strategy

History Memory Bubbles (Buehl, 1998) are a variation of concept mapping that emphasizes problem/solution relationships in history (see also the History Change Frame strategy). Using this strategy involves the following steps:

1 Emphasize to students that history does not consist of isolated facts, but instead tells stories of various groups of people who cope with problems and changes. Have students analyze key vocabulary or facts in terms of their connection to a problem/solution text frame: What is this fact? What does it have to do with problems discussed in the chapter? What does it have to do with solving these problems? What does it have to do with changes highlighted in this chapter? For example, the term *graft* is a key concept in studying politics during the later half of the 19th century in the United States. Whose story is graft a part of? What does graft have to do with problems during this time? How did people try to solve graft? What changes occurred because of graft?

2 Have students identify key terms or facts from a history selection that they have read. For example, students might earmark the following terms as central to corrupt politics in the post–Civil War era in the United States: *Gilded Age, robber barons, city bosses, political patronage, graft,* and *Civil Service Act.* Ask students to concentrate solely on information that focuses attention on key themes and ideas, not on background detail (see Chapter 4 discussion of Fact Pyramids). Students typically would learn such terms as isolated historical facts by scanning the chapter to locate and memorize minimal details associated with each term. Their assignments may resemble disconnected "blurbs" of information, such as: "*The Gilded Age* is a book by Mark Twain." "The Tweed Ring was a group of dishonest elected officials in New York City." "Political patronage was the practice of exchanging political jobs for political support." In contrast, this strategy engages students in developing meaningful associations around changes and problems.

3 Place a transparency of a blank History Memory Bubble on the overhead projector (see the Appendix for a reproducible version of the History Memory Bubble) and model using a key term such as *city bosses.* In addition to identifying the term, ask students to consider the problems connected to this term and list them on the History Memory Bubble under "Problems": bribes, election fraud, robbing the city treasury, and exchanging jobs and contracts for votes (see the History Memory Bubble on the Topic of City Bosses example). As shown, city bosses like the Tweed Ring caused reformers to emerge who prosecuted these crimes, which connects this concept to solutions for the

Strategy Index
Instructional Focus
Frontloading Learning
Guiding Comprehension
Consolidating Understanding
Text Frames
Cause/Effect
Concept/Definition
Problem/Solution
Compare/Contrast
Proposition/Support
Goal/Action/Outcome
Comprehension Processes
Making Connections
Generating Questions
Creating Mental Images
Making Inferences
Determining Importance
Synthesizing

History Memory Bubbles
on the Topic of City Bosses

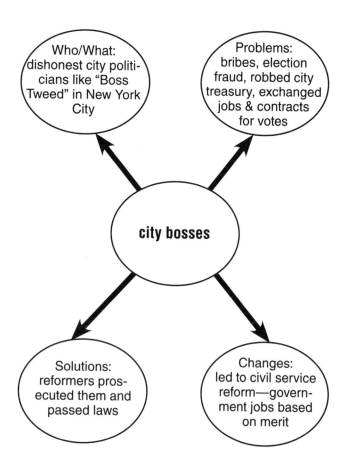

Source: Buehl, D. (1998). Memory bubbles: They help put information into context. *WEAC News and Views*, *33*(7), 13.

problems. As a result, a major change was instituted: Civil Service reform mandated awarding of jobs based on merit.

4 Have students work with a partner to create History Memory Bubbles for the remainder of the targeted terms. When they finish, invite volunteers to share their Memory Bubbles with the entire class. As part of this process, students will discover that corresponding information may not be available to fill all four bubbles for every term or fact. After practicing this strategy, students can be asked to create Memory Bubbles independently as they learn new material. They will begin to perceive interlinking relationships among key terms as they flesh out several Memory Bubbles for a unit of study.

Advantages

- Students see connections that guide them toward remembering information in the context of larger issues and ideas.

- Students are engaged in establishing the significance of key factual material encountered in history textbooks.

- Students examine history terms as concepts that involve a number of connecting variables rather than memorize a single isolated fact about an important term.

- History Memory Bubbles may be assigned as a homework activity and for study preparation for chapter exams.

Reference

Buehl, D. (1998). Memory bubbles: They help put information into context. *WEAC News and Views*, *33*(7), 13.

Inquiry Charts

The Etruscans: The Etruscans invaded Italy about 600 BC. They settled in an area by the Tiber River they called Rome. The Etruscans were farmers and they also traded with cities like Carthage. They built roads and cultivated the land. The Gauls defeated the Etruscans and sacked Rome in 390 BC.

Teachers will have no trouble spotting the generic, rote, encyclopedically derived report unfolding in this example. Unfortunately, much student research results in uninspired, litany-of-facts writing. But what about the interesting stuff? What might you really be wondering? What questions might arise about the ancient Etruscans that more research might answer? What was life like in an Etruscan community? What did they believe? And what impact did these people have on the succeeding Roman civilization? Inquiry Charts, also known as I-Charts (Hoffman, 1992), emphasize research as a process of inquiry based on a reader's curiosity, rather than a mere collection of isolated bits of information.

Using the Strategy

The I-Chart prompts the generation of meaningful questions that focus research and organize writing and other projects. I-Charts are suitable for a whole-class, small-group, or individual inquiry. Using this strategy involves the following steps:

1 Select a topic studied in the curriculum and brainstorm with students things about this topic they might be wondering. As you solicit possible questions to explore, look for a mix of "thin" and "thick" questions (see the discussion in the B/D/A Questioning Charts strategy beginning on page 52). Note that thick questions tend to be most promising for further investigation. Ask the class to choose three or four of the most interesting questions, which will provide direction for student inquiry.

2 Introduce the I-Chart by modeling how to use this tool to organize information on chart paper or the chalkboard. Also provide students with individual, blank I-Charts (see the Appendix for a reproducible version of the I-Chart). Record the chosen questions in the boxes along the top. For example, a music teacher wants her musicians to become more knowledgeable

about jazz before students begin rehearsing a jazz piece for performance. After an array of questions has been generated, the class chooses four on which to center their inquiry: How did jazz music get started? What kinds of music is jazz related to? What are the basic elements of jazz music? How has jazz influenced other music? (see the I-Chart for Jazz example).

3 Brainstorm any preexisting knowledge about the topic. Ask students to offer what they know or have heard about jazz and have them indicate which question on the chart this information might answer. Knowledge not germane to the questions can be placed in the column labeled "Other Important Information." This process uncovers any misconceptions about a topic that will be confronted as students learn more.

Most music students know that jazz is associated with African American culture and that New Orleans, Louisiana, USA, is regarded as a founding city. They may offer that rock music is related to jazz and comment that instruments such as the saxophone, used with performers such as Bruce Springsteen, are often regarded as jazz-type instruments. Louis Armstrong and Duke Ellington might be musicians who are known to some students, although others might put forth contemporary artists like Kenny G. or Diana Krall as an example of a jazz musician. Their awareness of jazz clubs, which does not fit under the target questions, is recorded in the "Other Important Information" column.

4 Provide access to a variety of materials, including websites and newspaper and magazine articles, for students to consult to answer their target questions. Have students work in cooperative groups, with each group consulting a different source. The

Strategy Index
Instructional Focus
Frontloading Learning
Guiding Comprehension
Consolidating Understanding
Text Frames
Cause/Effect
Concept/Definition
Problem/Solution
Compare/Contrast
Proposition/Support
Goal/Action/Outcome
Comprehension Processess
Making Connections
Generating Questions
Creating Mental Images
Making Inferences
Determining Importance
Synthesizing

I-Chart for Jazz

Topic: Jazz	Q1: How did jazz music get started?	Q2: What kinds of music is jazz related to?	Q3: What are the basic elements of jazz?	Q4: How has jazz influenced other music?	Other important information	New questions
What we know:	African Americans New Orleans	Rock music	Improvisation	Rock—Bruce Springsteen has instruments like saxophone	There are jazz clubs in New Orleans, Duke Ellington, Kenny G.	
Source: Book—*A New History of Jazz* (Shipton, 2008)						
Source: *American Heritage* Magazine						
Source: Website— www. allaboutjazz. com						
Summaries						

Source: Buehl, D. (2001). *Classroom strategies for interactive learning* (2nd ed., p. 68). Newark, DE: International Reading Association.

target questions will guide students as they decide which material in a source is useful and which is extraneous. Have each group record their information on sticky notes, one fact per note, which are affixed to the chart paper or chalkboard under the appropriate question. Color-coded sticky notes make it easier to identify the source from which the information was taken. As notes are added to the I-Chart, it becomes clear whether enough information has been discovered and whether each question has been answered adequately.

As students consult sources on jazz, they discover a variety of facts and information to address their questions: Blues, a music with which they may be less familiar, is a precursor of jazz, as are work songs and gospel songs. Ragtime is an early form of jazz. These facts are entered in the Question 2 column on the I-Chart. Students place information according to the specific source in which they found it, although some information is contained in all sources, which is also indicated on the I-Chart. Students are surprised to learn that classical music has been influenced by jazz, and they record information about George Gershwin and Leonard Bernstein in the Question 4 column. As they read about jazz compact disc clubs and jazz radio stations, a new question emerges from their research: How popular is jazz today?

5 Ask students to synthesize information from each question into a summary. Sometimes contradictory material is uncovered, which also needs to be acknowledged. Summarization provides a transition from inquiry to writing, as students decide on main idea statements for each question and organize pertinent details.

6 Students are now ready to write about their topic, and they proceed to discuss each question and the information that relates to it. Each vertical column may comprise a paragraph or, with more sophisticated inquiry, a section of a written discussion of the topic. Students also may wish to respond to one or two additional questions that occurred to them as they delved into their sources, which can be added to either the "Other Important Information" or "New Questions" columns.

Advantages

- As students become more independent, they can develop individual I-Charts that focus their inquiry and organize their notes.

- Student writing is less likely to be a rambling compendium of facts and is more likely to be centered on the significant questions that they had a role in developing.

- Students receive guided practice in synthesizing and summarizing information.

- Students use multiple sources that provide a variety of information as a basis for an inquiry project rather than answering identical questions based on a single source.

- This strategy is especially well suited for web-based inquiry projects.

References

Buehl, D. (2001). *Classroom strategies for interactive learning* (2nd ed.). Newark, DE: International Reading Association.

Hoffman, J.V. (1992). Critical reading/thinking across the curriculum: Using I-charts to support learning. *Language Arts, 69*(2), 121–127.

Shipton, A. (2008). *A new history of jazz: Revised and updated edition.* London: Continuum International Publishing.

Interactive Reading Guides

Go to the big oak tree in the center of the park. Walk 20 paces in the direction the lowest limb is pointing. Go to the large speckled rock. Under the rock...

Most of us have participated in a treasure hunt. We were given a series of instructions or clues that led to several locations. At times we had to pause and think about a clue, and it helped to collaborate with others. If we followed all the instructions carefully, we would discover the spot that contained the "treasure"—the whole point of the hunt.

Getting the point of a reading assignment, however, is a difficult task for many students. They are confounded by the large amount of information they encounter in textbooks and find it difficult to differentiate key ideas from background detail. Students could benefit from a few clues to direct them through the text.

The Interactive Reading Guide (Wood, 1988) is an excellent strategy to guide comprehension of text materials. Unlike typical study guides, which sometimes can be completed by skimming for facts and details, Interactive Reading Guides are carefully constructed to prompt all essential comprehension thinking—making connections, generating questions, creating mental images, inferring, determining importance, and synthesizing. In addition, Interactive Reading Guides assume collaborative problem-solving—students work with partners or small groups as they read rather than after they read.

Using the Strategy

Interactive Reading Guides make it possible for students to learn from text materials that may be too difficult for independent reading. Using this strategy involves the following steps:

1 Preview the reading assignment to determine priorities for learning and locate possible pitfalls for understanding. Be especially concerned with difficulties struggling readers might have with the material. Notice salient features of the text that students might overlook such as pictures, charts, and graphs. Determine any mismatch between students and text. Does the author assume knowledge that some students might lack? Does the author introduce ideas and vocabulary without sufficient explanation or examples? Does the author use language or sentence style that may be difficult for some students?

2 Construct an Interactive Reading Guide for students to complete with partners or in cooperative groups. Design the guide to cue students to thoughtfully engage in understanding and to support the learning of challenging material. At times, you will want to ask students to inventory their prior knowledge as they consider what an author expects them to already know. In addition, prompt them to raise questions, rather than merely answer them. Some tasks should trigger students' imaginations as a tool for understanding what an author is saying. Students should be asked to grapple with implicit as well as explicit elements of comprehension, and the guide should avoid requiring students to respond to "bottom of the fact pyramid" items (see Chapter 4). Finally, students should be asked to sum up their understandings and consider conclusions or generalizations that can be drawn from their reading.

3 Divide the passage into segments—those to be read orally by individuals to their group, those to be read silently by each student, and those less important that can be skimmed. Use the guide to frontload additional background information or encourage students to brainstorm what they already know about the topic.

For example, in a biology class, a government natural resources publication on water conditions in streams may be too difficult for students to read independently. Instead, the teacher "jigsaws" (Aronson et al., 1978) the text among the cooperative groups; each group reads a different segment of the material.

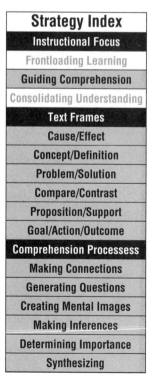

Strategy Index

Instructional Focus
Frontloading Learning
Guiding Comprehension
Consolidating Understanding

Text Frames
Cause/Effect
Concept/Definition
Problem/Solution
Compare/Contrast
Proposition/Support
Goal/Action/Outcome

Comprehension Processess
Making Connections
Generating Questions
Creating Mental Images
Making Inferences
Determining Importance
Synthesizing

Interactive Reading Guide for Biology

Water Clarity and Sediments (pages 11–12)

1. This article will talk about factors that influence the health of streams and rivers. <u>Entire group:</u> Make a list of things you already know that can affect how healthy a stream might be for fish and other animals.

2. Look at the drawing of the fish at the top of the page. *Stream troublemakers* are mentioned. <u>Entire group:</u> Predict what two examples of "stream troublemakers" might be.

3. A keyword in this article is *clarity*. <u>Student A:</u> Read paragraph 1 out loud to your group. <u>Rest of group:</u> Decide what *water clarity* means and write your group's definition. Imagine you were a fish: Decide what would be the best type of water for you, according to paragraph 1.

4. Paragraph 2 talks about the *color* of a stream. <u>Entire group:</u> Skim this paragraph silently. Locate two things that can change the color of water in a stream.

5. Paragraph 3 is the main point of your article. <u>Student B:</u> Read paragraph 3 out loud to your group. <u>Rest of group:</u> Summarize what effect algae and sediments have on water.

6. The next section describes *algae*. <u>Entire group:</u> Read Paragraph 4 silently. Look for the following key ideas on algae:

    • What kinds of streams are most likely to have algae?
    • What exactly is algae?
    • What color is water that has a lot of algae?
    • Where in your community might you find algae?

7. <u>Student C:</u> Read paragraph 5 out loud to your group. <u>Rest of group:</u> Decide what kinds of things could become *sediment* in a stream. Which of these kinds of sediment might be a problem in your community?

8. <u>Entire group:</u> Read paragraph 6 silently. Look for ways sediment gets into streams. Summarize what these ways are and write them here.

9. <u>Entire group:</u> Skim paragraphs 7, 8, & 9 silently. Imagine you were a fish: Decide which source of sediment sounds the worst to you. Explain why.

10. Sediment and algae make water cloudy. Cloudy water causes trouble for fish. The next paragraphs tell five reasons why. <u>Student A:</u> Read paragraphs 10 & 11 silently. <u>Student B:</u> Read paragraphs 12 & 13 silently. <u>Student C:</u> read paragraph 14 silently. Then share the five reasons why cloudy water is bad for fish and write them in your own words below.

Note: From Irvin, Judith L., Douglas R. Buehl, & Ronald M. Klemp. *Reading and the high school student: Strategies to enhance literacy* (2nd ed., p. 73). Published by Allyn and Bacon, Boston, MA. Copyright © 2007 by Pearson Education. Reprinted by permission of the publisher.

Interactive Reading Guide for History

Section A: Section 1: Coming to America (pages 122–126)

1. <u>Both Partners:</u> Skim paragraph 1 silently. <u>Individually:</u> Locate one name of a famous immigrant you have heard of and briefly write something you know about this person. <u>Both Partners:</u> Share what you know about the person you selected.

2. <u>Both Partners:</u> Read paragraphs 2 & 3 silently. Decide together: Why were so many "common people" motivated to come to the United States?

3. <u>Partner A:</u> Read paragraph 4 out loud. <u>Partner B:</u> As you listen, decide: How did ship companies try to attract people to sail to America? <u>Both Partners:</u> Think of at least two reasons why poor people might be attracted by these offers.

4. <u>Partner B:</u> Read paragraph 5 out loud. <u>Partner A:</u> As you listen, decide: What are two ways poor people found the money for sailing to America?

5. <u>Both Partners:</u> Read paragraphs 6 & 7 silently. Decide together: Look for evidence that these immigrants were very poor.

6. <u>Both Partners:</u> Read paragraphs 8 & 9 silently. Decide together: Describe three bad conditions for immigrants on the ships.

7. <u>Partner A:</u> Paragraph 10 is a direct quote by an immigrant. Read it out loud. <u>Partner B:</u> Summarize why this person would leave Italy and risk coming to America.

8. <u>Both Partners:</u> Skim paragraphs 11 & 12 silently. Decide together: Write one sentence which summarizes the tough times immigrants had on the ships.

9. <u>Both Partners:</u> Examine the photograph on page 126. <u>Individually:</u> Imagine you are one of the immigrants leaving this ship. Which person would you select? Based on what you have learned in this section, write a diary entry about what traveling on this ship was like for you.

10. <u>Both Partners:</u> Share your diary entries when you have finished writing.

Source: Buehl, D. (2003). Reading and writing enhances learning in all classes. In Southern Regional Education Board (Ed.), *Literacy across the curriculum: Setting and implementing goals for grades six through 12* (p. 109). Atlanta, GA: Southern Regional Education Board.

Each group is provided a separate Interactive Reading Guide so that each group becomes expert on a particular segment about water: clarity, acidity, temperature, and amount of dissolved oxygen available in the water (see the Interactive Reading Guide for Biology example). The Interactive Reading Guide helps students manage an otherwise formidable task. Later, students can analyze a local stream for four crucial water variables that affect fish, using the guides to remind them of the key information needed for their analysis.

In another example, for a history class, an Interactive Reading Guide helps students navigate a challenging article on immigration to supplement a history textbook (see the Interactive Reading Guide for History example).

4 Have each group use the completed guides as an outline to create written summaries of their understandings or to report their findings to the whole class.

Advantages

- Students are conditioned to read materials at different rates for varying purposes, reading some sections carefully and skimming others.
- Students use partners as resources for tackling challenging reading assignments and discussing the material while they read.

- Struggling readers are especially supported by the use of Interactive Reading Guides.
- Completed Interactive Reading Guides serve as organized notes for classroom discussions and follow-up activities and also make excellent study guides for examinations.

References

Aronson, E., Blaney, N., Stephin, C., Sikes, J., & Snapp, M. (1978). *The jigsaw classroom*. Beverly Hills, CA: Sage.

Buehl, D. (2003). Reading and writing enhances learning in all classes. In Southern Regional Education Board (Ed.), *Literacy across the curriculum: Setting and implementing goals for grades six through 12* (pp. 101–125). Atlanta, GA: Southern Regional Education Board.

Irvin, J.L., Buehl, D.R., & Klemp, R.M. (2007). *Reading and the high school student: Strategies to enhance literacy* (2nd ed.). Boston: Allyn & Bacon.

Wood, K.D. (1988). Guiding students through informational text. *The Reading Teacher, 41*(9), 912–920.

K-W-L Plus
(Know/Want to Know/Learned)

Say you are planning a trip to another country. As you prepare an itinerary, you consider what you already know about the country. As you sort through various travel guides, articles, maps, and brochures, you plot activities and designate places to visit. At this point you probably think to yourself, What don't I know that I would like to learn more about? After you have immersed yourself in resources, you take stock of what you have learned about the destination and act on this knowledge by constructing an itinerary that matches your desires and priorities.

This scenario represents a very purposeful and pragmatic reading event. A persistent challenge for teachers is to encourage students to adopt a similar attitude—to be active thinkers who "use" the texts that they read. Chapter 1 detailed essential characteristics of comprehension, which are exemplified in this travel-planning scenario. Before you started reading, you considered what you already knew about a topic, you generated questions that got you wondering about this topic, and you anticipated what else you might need to know. Then you used your reading to satisfy your curiosity, answer your questions, and deepen your knowledge. You had a personal agenda for reading, a clear idea of what you were looking for, and when you finished you could evaluate whether you learned what you were seeking.

The K-W-L Plus strategy (Carr & Ogle, 1987) is a classic instructional practice that prompts all the thinking embedded in comprehension. Using this strategy helps students activate what they already know before they begin a reading assignment. A natural offshoot of this student activity is the generation of questions they would like to have answered. Students use the text to confirm and enhance their knowledge and to satisfy their questions. The strategy also helps students to organize what they have learned when they are finished reading.

Using the Strategy

K-W-L (Ogle, 1986) is an acronym for What I *Know*, What I *Want* to Know, and What I *Learned*. The strategy involves the use of a three-column graphic organizer that becomes the students' study guide as they read. The graphic organizer is effective as a worksheet and can be displayed on a chalkboard or an overhead transparency. The "Plus" stage (K-W-L Plus) engages students in categorizing and summarizing the work they have collected in the graphic organizer.

1 Write the main topic of a story or selection at the top of the K-W-L grid (see the K-W-L for Rattlesnakes example). Ask students to contribute what they know or have heard about the topic. Acknowledge that some of the things we "have heard" may not be accurate, but we use texts to confirm or revise our understandings. Students could do this prior knowledge brainstorming individually, with partners, or in cooperative groups. Record student contributions in the first column "K—Know." Students preparing to read a science selection about rattlesnakes might contribute the following: *poisonous, fangs, diamondbacks, live in deserts,* and *shake rattles as warning.* A story about sled dogs might elicit *huskies, live in the far north, harnessed as teams, transportation on snow and ice,* and *Iditarod.*

2 Next, ask students what they are wondering about this topic. Again, students can engage in this phase individually, with partners, or in cooperative groups. In addition to wondering if specific items recorded in the "W" column might be true, students will likely be curious about a variety of other questions. Solicit these questions and record them in the middle column "W—Want to Know." For instance, the students studying rattlesnakes wanted to know, Are all rattlesnakes poisonous? What happens to you if you are bitten? Do people often die? Do rattlesnakes always rattle before they strike? Do they live in our area? What do they look like?

3 Students read the story or selection. As they read, ask them to put a

Strategy Index
Instructional Focus
Frontloading Learning
Guiding Comprehension
Consolidating Understanding
Text Frames
Cause/Effect
Concept/Definition
Problem/Solution
Compare/Contrast
Proposition/Support
Goal/Action/Outcome
Comprehension Processess
Making Connections
Generating Questions
Creating Mental Images
Making Inferences
Determining Importance
Synthesizing

K-W-L for Rattlesnakes

K (Know)	W (Want to Know)	L (Learned)
• They have sharp fangs.	• What medicine stops the poison?	
• They are poisonous.	• What do they look like?	D—Rattle is set of horny pieces joined together
• They shake their rattles before striking.	• Are all rattlesnakes poisonous?	A—All are poisonous
• Diamondbacks are a type.	• Will you die if you get bitten by a rattlesnake?	P—Bite can be fatal to small children
		P—Some bites can kill adults
• They live in holes.	• Do all rattlesnakes rattle before biting?	A—Often warn before biting
• They eat mice.	• Do any live in our area?	L—28 varieties found from Canada to South America
		L—Most found in deserts
		L—Some found in Midwest
		D—Member of the pit viper family
		A—Young snakes are born live rather than from eggs

Categories of Information:

1. Where they live (L—Location)
2. What they do (A—Abilities)
3. How they look (D—Description)
4. How they affect people (P—People)

Source: Buehl, D. (1995). *Classroom strategies for interactive learning* (p. 61). Madison: Wisconsin State Reading Association.

check mark next to any item in the "K" column confirmed by the author and to put a line through any item contradicted by the author. In addition, students jot down answers to questions in the "W" column that they discovered in the text. These can be recorded on their personal worksheets in the "L—Learned" column.

4 When the students have completed their reading, focus their attention on the third, or "L" column. Some of the items written in this column will represent information that answers questions in the "W" column. In addition, ask students to offer new information they discovered in the reading and record this on the grid.

One variation is to create a graphic organizer that features an added fourth column. For this version of the strategy, reserve the "L" column for answers that were learned to the questions in the "W" column. The new fourth column is labeled "N—New Learning." Information that students deem important, but which

did not surface in the "K" or "L" column, is added here as new learning.

5 Guide students in categorizing their knowledge (this is the "Plus" stage of the strategy). With partners or in groups, ask students to sort all information in the "K" and "L" columns (and "N" column if this variation is used) by deciding what items might meaningfully be placed with others. They then decide upon a label for each grouping. Categories for rattlesnakes might include where they live (location), what they do (abilities), how they look (description), and their effects on people (people). Experienced students may complete this step independently, but many students will need guidance and direction in organizing the new information.

6 When the K-W-L grid is complete, create a concept map that brings together all the information under each category, designed by either the whole class or by

Concept Map for Rattlesnakes

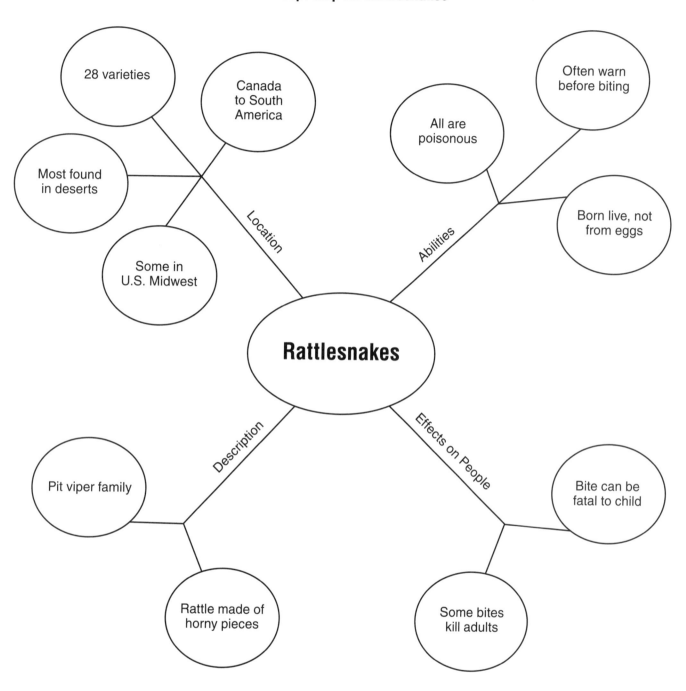

Source: Buehl, D. (1995). *Classroom strategies for interactive learning* (p. 62). Madison: Wisconsin State Reading Association.

students working in pairs or groups (see the Concept Map for Rattlesnakes example; see the Appendix for a reproducible version of the Concept Map). This synthesizing step organizes the information, so that students can express their understandings in writing assignments or other projects. Questions from the "W" column that are not answered by the reading are regarded as "hanging questions"—questions we inevitably have

after a learning episode that may provide the basis for future investigation and reading.

Advantages

- K-W-L Plus provides teachers with an inventory of students' background knowledge about a topic and reminds students what they already know.

- Class prior knowledge is "pooled," as students who know less about a topic are included in interactive conversations with students who bring more knowledge to the reading.
- Students are prompted to take an inquiring mindset toward reading, to "use" a text to address their questions as well as confirm and refine their previous understandings.
- Students are guided into meaningful organization of new information in order to synthesize their understandings.
- Student misconceptions about the topic are revealed and addressed during instruction.

- K-W-L Plus can be used as a strategy for lessons in social studies, science, math, and other subject areas.

References

Buehl, D. (1995). *Classroom strategies for interactive learning*. Madison: Wisconsin State Reading Association.

Carr, E.M., & Ogle, D. (1987). K-W-L Plus: A strategy for comprehension and summarization. *Journal of Reading, 30*(7), 626–631.

Ogle, D.M. (1986). K-W-L: A teaching model that develops active reading of expository text. *The Reading Teacher, 39*(6), 564–570.

Magnet Summaries

Consider for a moment a team of scientists sifting through mounds of data from a host of experiments. What sense could be made out of such a formidable body of information? Amidst this wealth of material, the group of researchers must decide, What does all this mean? Eventually, after carefully examining and analyzing their data, they will be able to develop an interpretation, a theory, a definition of "the big picture" that emerges from all the disparate slivers of detail. These scientists, like proficient readers, are able to synthesize.

As adults, on the job as well as in other aspects of daily life, we are bombarded by information that needs to be condensed in order to be understood. As readers, we constantly rely on synthesizing—the distillations by various experts, analysts, writers, and of course, ourselves—to render a bulk of information manageable for understanding.

Synthesizing takes place when a reader steps back from a text, sums up what is important, and goes on to make a generalization, create an interpretation, draw a conclusion, posit an explanation. When proficient readers talk about a piece of meaningful text—a discussion about a newspaper article, for example, or a book club chat about a novel—they don't just repeat what the text said. In addition they offer their personal "take" on a selection: "That's not the way I read it." "This is what I think the author was getting at." "I think the character acted this way because...." In essence, proficient readers pause periodically, reflect, ponder the meaning of a text, and then eventually exclaim, "Aha! I get it!"

One key component of synthesizing is summarizing. Students often have a difficult time summarizing what they read. Typically students may produce a string of disconnected pieces of information or segments of a story but overlook major themes or main ideas. Synthesizing combines summarizing—the ability to focus on the most important ideas and information—with a reader's perspective.

Using the Strategy

The Magnet Summary (Buehl, 1993) is a strategy that helps students rise above the details and construct meaningful summaries in their own words. Magnet Summaries involve the identification of key terms or concepts—magnet words—from a reading, which students use to organize important information into a summary. Using this strategy involves the following steps:

1 To summarize, a reader must identify the most important ideas and omit details of lesser significance. An effective summary also includes paraphrasing—reinterpreting what was read in the reader's own words. As a prelude to summarizing, ask students to retell what they have read. Initial retellings, especially with younger students or struggling readers, can take on a rambling quality, a clear indicator that the teller has not yet developed the facility to "cut to the chase." Likewise, some retellings may be unduly terse; too much is left out.

To help students focus during retellings, emphasize that all important elements or ideas need to be included, and that "smaller" details can be left out. When they are done, their retelling should make sense to the listener. Students may also splice in personal commentary and reflections, so that their summaries begin to incorporate other aspects of synthesis. Paired reviews can be an excellent classroom vehicle for retellings (see Paired Reviews beginning on page 121). Have partners take turns retelling what they have been reading (or watching in a video or listening to during a classroom presentation).

Oral paraphrasing practice can help students become comfortable with composing written summaries. Asking students to express their thinking in writing is a critical step in teaching them to summarize. Writing helps students realize what they have learned and provides them with a visual record of their thinking. Writing also allows students to continue

Strategy Index
Instructional Focus
Frontloading Learning
Guiding Comprehension
Consolidating Understanding
Text Frames
Cause/Effect
Concept/Definition
Problem/Solution
Compare/Contrast
Proposition/Support
Goal/Action/Outcome
Comprehension Processess
Making Connections
Generating Questions
Creating Mental Images
Making Inferences
Determining Importance
Synthesizing

to refine their thinking as they revisit their thoughts to clarify and expand their understandings. Learning log journal entries provide an excellent transition into written summaries (see the section Learning Logs in the Quick Writes strategy on page 142). Classroom journaling encourages students to be more preoccupied with the dynamics of summarizing rather than with the mechanics of writing.

2 Introduce the idea of magnet words to students by inquiring what effect a magnet has on certain metals. Just as magnets attract those metals, magnet words attract information. To illustrate, ask students to read a short portion of their text assignment, looking for a key term or concept to which the details in the passage seem to connect. After students finish reading, solicit from them possible magnet words, commenting that these "attract" information in the passage. Note that magnet words frequently appear in titles, headings, or may be highlighted in bold or italic print, but caution students that not all words in bold or italic are necessarily magnet words.

Write the magnet word on the chalkboard or overhead transparency sheet. Ask students to recall important details from the passage that are connected to the magnet word. As you write these details around the magnet word, have students follow the same procedure on an index card. Allow them a second look at the passage so they can include any important details they may have missed.

Ninth-grade students studying a U.S. history section on the westward movement of settlers may decide on the magnet word *Homestead Act*. Key details surrounding this concept might include *160 acres*, and *farm for 5 years* (see the Magnet Summaries for History example).

3 Ask students to complete the reading of the entire passage. Distribute three or four additional index cards to each student for recording magnet words from the remaining material. For younger students, indicate that they should identify a magnet word for each paragraph or section following a heading. In cooperative groups, have students decide on the best magnet words for the remaining cards. Have them generate the important details for each magnet word. When the groups are finished, each student will have four or five cards, each with a magnet word and key related information.

4 Model for students how the information on one card can be organized and combined into a

sentence that sums up the passage of text. The magnet word should occupy a central place in the sentence. Omit any unimportant details from the sentence.

Have students return to their cooperative groups to construct sentences that summarize each of their remaining cards. Urge students to combine information into one sentence, although it may be necessary to construct two sentences for a particular card. They may decide to omit some details if they judge them to be of secondary importance. Have students write their sentences on scratch paper first. Then instruct them to put the final version of each sentence on the back of the appropriate card and underline the magnet words. For example, the card for the Homestead Act might be summarized as follows:

> Many people went west because of the <u>Homestead Act</u>, which gave 160 acres to people if they farmed them for 5 years.

5 Direct students to arrange the sentences in the order they wish their summary to read. At this point, the sentences will need to be altered so they flow smoothly from one to the other. Model inserting connectives and other language that integrates the sentences into a summary. At this point students should also judge whether all the important ideas have been included, and whether anything further can be deleted. Students can then test their summaries by listening to how they sound when they are read aloud. The following example is a Magnet Summary for a history passage on life in the Great Plains in the 1880s:

> Many people moved west because of the Homestead Act, which gave them 160 acres if they farmed this land for 5 years. But in the Great Plains, people had hardships from the very hot and very cold weather, and their crops failed due to drought and insects. Therefore farmers needed to do dry farming, so they dug wells, made windmills, and changed the way they plowed to grow wheat. The farmers' homes on the prairie were sod houses, called soddies, because there were no trees. The people were lonely because the houses were far from one another.

Advantages

- Students learn to prioritize what they need to remember, and develop facility in separating main ideas from supporting details.

- Students flesh out their understandings of key vocabulary and ideas.

Magnet Summaries for History

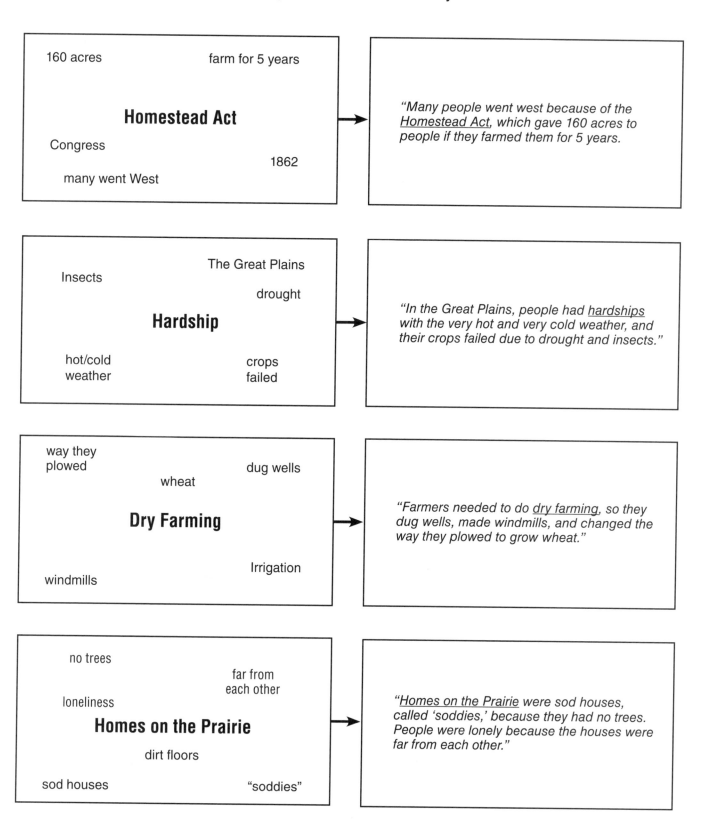

160 acres   farm for 5 years

Homestead Act

Congress

                                    1862

many went West

"Many people went west because of the <u>Homestead Act</u>, which gave 160 acres to people if they farmed them for 5 years."

                    The Great Plains
Insects
                        drought

Hardship

hot/cold   crops
weather   failed

"In the Great Plains, people had <u>hardships</u> with the very hot and very cold weather, and their crops failed due to drought and insects."

---

way they
plowed   dug wells
        wheat

Dry Farming

                                Irrigation
windmills

"Farmers needed to do <u>dry farming</u>, so they dug wells, made windmills, and changed the way they plowed to grow wheat."

---

no trees
                    far from
                    each other
loneliness

Homes on the Prairie

            dirt floors

sod houses   "soddies"

"<u>Homes on the Prairie</u> were sod houses, called 'soddies,' because they had no trees. People were lonely because the houses were far from each other."

Source: Buehl, D. (1995). *Classroom strategies for interactive learning* (p. 68). Madison: Wisconsin State Reading Association.

- Students gain practice in reducing texts to their most essential elements, allowing them to reflect on their personal understandings of what a text means.

References

Buehl, D. (1993). Magnetized: Students are drawn to technique that identifies key words. *WEAC News & Views, 29*(4), 13.

Buehl, D. (1995). *Classroom strategies for interactive learning.* Madison: Wisconsin State Reading Association.

Suggested Readings

Hayes, D.A. (1989). Helping students GRASP the knack of writing summaries. *Journal of Reading, 33*(2), 96–101.

Vacca, R.T., & Vacca, J.L. (2007). *Content area reading: Literacy and learning across the curriculum* (8th ed.). Boston: Pearson Allyn & Bacon.

Math Reading Keys

An angle ∠ is formed by two rays with the same endpoint. The rays are the sides of the angle. The endpoint is the vertex of the angle. One way to measure an angle is in degrees. To indicate the size or degree measure of an angle, write a lowercase m in front of the angle symbol, as in $m\angle A=80$. (Adapted from Bass, Charles, Hall, Johnson, & Kennedy, 2007, p. 36)

Um...let's see here. An angle is formed when two rays, which are straight lines, come together and touch. The parts of the angle are the rays, which are the sides, and the vertex, which is the point where they touch. The size, or how big the angle is, is indicated by degrees. I wonder how degrees in angles compare with degrees in temperature?

Increasingly, mathematics texts and assessments require students to use reading as a means to learn and demonstrate knowledge. But as the geometry example illustrates, math texts present special challenges for students. Math language is very precise and compact—each sentence conveys a heavy load of conceptual information. Textbook authors emphasize previous learning; readers are expected to bring a great deal of prior knowledge to their reading in math. In particular, readers are assumed to be fluent in using the discourse of math vocabulary. In addition, many students bring a mind-set that math is only the manipulation of numbers. They glide over math text in an attempt to jump right into solving problems and rely on the teacher to clear up misunderstandings. Therefore, students must take a different approach to reading math texts compared with social studies, science, or literature.

Using the Strategy

The Math Reading Keys strategy (Buehl, 1998) provides a protocol for helping students understand the unique features of math text as readers and learners. Using this strategy involves the following steps:

1 Use Questioning the Author (QtA) to introduce math reading strategies (see the Questioning the Author strategy beginning on page 137). Especially significant questions for math are, What does the author assume that I already know? What previous math concepts does this author expect me to remember? Students need to approach math text with careful

deliberation and constantly confirm their understandings, especially of math terminology.

2 Model how to read a challenging section of text. Reproduce a few pages from a textbook on an overhead transparency sheet and have students follow in their textbooks as you think aloud. Highlight *hidden knowledge*—spots where the author thinks that readers have sufficient knowledge and therefore need no further explanation. For example, a passage on absolute value in a pre-algebra text states,

> Integers are the set of whole numbers, including 0, and their opposites. The sum of two opposite integers is zero. One way to add integers is to use absolute value. The absolute value of a number is its distance from 0. The absolute value of −4, written as |−4| is 4; and the absolute value of 5 is 5. If the signs are the same: find the sum of the absolute values. Use the same sign as the integers. If the signs are different: find the difference of the absolute values. Use the sign of the integer with the larger absolute value. (Adapted from Bennett et al., 2008, p. 60)

Your think-aloud on this passage might unfold as follows:

Integers—the authors tell me what these are, whole numbers and their opposites. The authors must think I know what whole numbers are, because they don't define them. They give examples (0, 4, −4, 5) and I remember that whole number means it is not a fraction or decimal. Absolute value seems a key idea here, and this seems a little confusing, so I better reread this part carefully: "distance from 0." I know a number can go either way from 0, positive or negative, so absolute value seems to be the number of places from 0. Absolute value looks like it will always be expressed as a positive number, because it reflects how many places from 0.

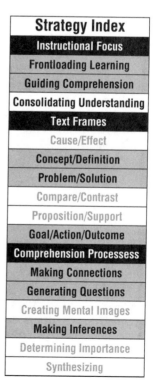

Strategy Index

| Instructional Focus |
| Frontloading Learning |
| Guiding Comprehension |
| Consolidating Understanding |
| **Text Frames** |
| Cause/Effect |
| Concept/Definition |
| Problem/Solution |
| Compare/Contrast |
| Proposition/Support |
| Goal/Action/Outcome |
| **Comprehension Processess** |
| Making Connections |
| Generating Questions |
| Creating Mental Images |
| Making Inferences |
| Determining Importance |
| Synthesizing |

Math Reading Keys Bookmark

1. Read carefully to make sure each sentence makes sense.

2. Summarize what you read in your own words. Reread parts that you are not able to summarize.

3. When you encounter tough words, think of easier words that mean that same thing and substitute them.

4. Discuss with a partner what you read

   a. to make sure you understand

   b. to clear up things you don't understand

5. Look for

   a. things the author assumes you already know

   b. things you have learned in math before

6. Read with a pencil

   a. to work any examples provided

   b. reread after working the examples

7. Write and store your own definitions for key terms in a notebook.

Source: Buehl, D. (1998). Making math make sense: Tactics help kids understand math language. *WEAC News and Views, 34*(3), 17.

3 Hand out copies of the Math Reading Keys Bookmark (see the Math Reading Keys Bookmark), and point out how your think-aloud followed the steps in the Bookmark. Use an analogy such as reading the operating manual for a piece of equipment or reading instructions for assembling an item. Often these documents are frustrating to read, so it is tempting to discard them and figure out what to do on your own, running the risk of making an important or costly error. Instead, it may be necessary to read the material several times, consult with another person, or eventually translate the confusing instructions into something you can understand.

4 Pair students with partners to read together portions of math text during class time. Typically, such reading is assigned as independent work, and many students skip it and attempt to solve problems by following examples in the text. As students follow the math keys and reach points of confusion, they check with their peers and practice verbalizing their understandings.

5 Encourage students to compile their own explanations of key terms in a notebook or on index cards. Students often discover that terms not sufficiently explained in a chapter are equally unclear in the book's glossary. For example, the precise glossary definition of *scientific notation*—a streamlined way of representing extremely large or small numbers—can be explained in a more student-friendly way (see the Translating Math Terms Into Student-friendly Explanations example; see also the Student-Friendly Vocabulary Explanations strategy beginning on page 175). Urge students to treat difficult math language the same way as they would a foreign language. For example, once they translate a sentence from Spanish into English, it makes more sense. They must also get into the habit of translating "math into English" so that it, too, is personally meaningful. This step combines the precision of math vocabulary, which is essential, with synthesizing personal understanding, which is necessary for comprehension.

6 Have students create a classroom dictionary of key math terms. Have students work with partners to write student-friendly explanations that can be voted on by the entire class. The explanations for each term voted as the easiest to understand are placed on a word wall as the official classroom dictionary. One option is to fold sheets of letter-size card-stock paper in half to form individual "flip-charts," which are tacked to the word wall. The math term with its precise definition is placed on the front. When the card is flipped up, students will find their student-friendly explanation.

Advantages

- Students learn strategies that can aid them in understanding conceptually dense text.

- Students are encouraged to consider how effectively an author has communicated information and to solve problems when things are not clear.

Translating Math Terms Into Student-Friendly Explanations

Front
of
card

> ### Scientific Notation
> A number is written in scientific notation when it is of the form $c \times 10^n$ where $1<c<10$ and n is an integer

Back
of
Card

> ### Explanation of Scientific Notation
> A way of writing very large or very small numbers, so you don't have to put down all the zeros.
> Very large number (has positive exponent):
> 4,500,000,000 (we say it as four and a half billion)
> In scientific notation: 4.5×10^9
> Very small number (has negative exponent):
> 0.000000003 (we say it as 3 billionths)
> In scientific notation 3×10^{-9}

Note: Scientific notation definition from Larson, R., Boswell, L., Kanold, T.D., & Stiff, L. (2007). *Algebra* 1, p. 512. Evanston, IL: McDougall Littell.

- Students learn to translate text into more personal and understandable language and to make connections to prior knowledge.
- Students learn to collaborate as problem solvers of challenging texts rather than merely relying on the teacher to tell them the information.

References

Bass, L.E., Charles, R.I., Hall, B., Johnson, A., & Kennedy, D. (2007). *Geometry*. Boston: Pearson/Prentice Hall.

Bennett, J.M., Chard, D.J., Jackson, A., Milgram, J., Scheer, J.K., & Waits, B.K. (2008). *Pre-algebra*. Austin, TX: Holt, Rinehart and Winston.

Buehl, D. (1998). Making math make sense: Tactics help kids understand math language. *WEAC News and Views, 34*(3), 17.

Buehl, D. (2001). *Classroom strategies for interactive learning* (2nd ed.). Newark, DE: International Reading Association.

Larson, R., Boswell, L., Kanold, T.D., & Stiff, L. (2007). *Algebra 1*. Evanston, IL: McDougal Litell.

Suggested Reading

Beck, I.L., McKeown, M.G., Hamilton, R.L., & Kucan, L. (1997). *Questioning the author: An approach for enhancing student engagement with text*. Newark, DE: International Reading Association.

Mind Mapping

Drive down Leonardo Street for about 10 blocks until you come to the second set of lights. Turn left onto Raphael and go about 3 blocks until you see a Supermart. Continue another 1/2 block and take the first right. You are now on Botticelli Boulevard, which winds through a subdivision and then along a heavily wooded park. When you come to the railroad intersection, go about 1/4 mile until you see the Lutheran Church. Take a sharp left on Van Gogh and....

What we really need here is a map! Maps are visual representations designed to guide us to our destinations. They allow us to perceive how the necessary information is connected within the context of the larger picture. They let us see where we are going and alert us to important signposts along the way. Likewise, students find that visual representations—maps—displaying major concepts and their relationships can make journeys through textbook chapters more navigable. Buzan (1991) describes visual representations or graphic organizers that demonstrate connections among key concepts and ideas as Mind Maps.

Using the Strategy

Mind Maps are structured outlines that can effectively introduce new material to students (Barron, 1969; Tierney & Readence, 2004). Using this strategy involves the following steps:

1 Analyze a passage that students will read in terms of the important ideas and concepts. Next, identify key facts and vocabulary from the reading students will use for developing an understanding of these concepts. Ignore any difficult terms in the text not essential to learning the central ideas, so that students don't get sidetracked by terms that are only of secondary importance when they read. For example, as a science teacher peruses a chapter on glaciers in an earth science textbook, she decides upon the following central concepts:

- Glaciers are moving masses of ice.
- Glaciers have had great impact on the features of the Earth.
- Glaciers have periodically covered much of the land surface of the Earth.

Key vocabulary for this chapter might be *ice front, erosion, lateral, ground, terminal moraines, till, drumlin, esker, kame, kettle,* and *ice age.*

2 Organize key concepts and vocabulary into a Mind Map that shows relationships and connections among the terms (see the Mind Map for Glaciers example). Include visual elements such as arrows, boxes, circles, pictorial representations, or other creative touches to make the Mind Map more vivid and memorable. In addition to specific vocabulary featured in the reading, include relevant terms that the students already know. These familiar "verbal landmarks" will help students recognize how the material fits into their current background knowledge of the subject. In the glacier example, add glacial features that may be known to many students, and include references to global warming that students could relate to this concept.

3 Present the map to the class to frontload learning the new material. Show an overhead transparency of the Mind Map to the entire class or provide students with individual copies to discuss as a small-group activity. Encourage students to speculate on the meanings of new vocabulary words and the nature of the relationships among concepts. Stimulate discussions with open-ended questions such as, What can you tell me by looking at this overview?

One effective method to encourage investigation of the Mind Map is the Expert/Novice variation of the Think/Pair/Share strategy (see the Paired Reviews strategy beginning on page 121). Have students work as partners, with one student designated as the Expert, the other as the Novice. When both have had ample opportunity to examine the map, the

Strategy Index
Instructional Focus
Frontloading Learning
Guiding Comprehension
Consolidating Understanding
Text Frames
Cause/Effect
Concept/Definition
Problem/Solution
Compare/Contrast
Proposition/Support
Goal/Action/Outcome
Comprehension Processess
Making Connections
Generating Questions
Creating Mental Images
Making Inferences
Determining Importance
Synthesizing

Mind Map for Glaciers

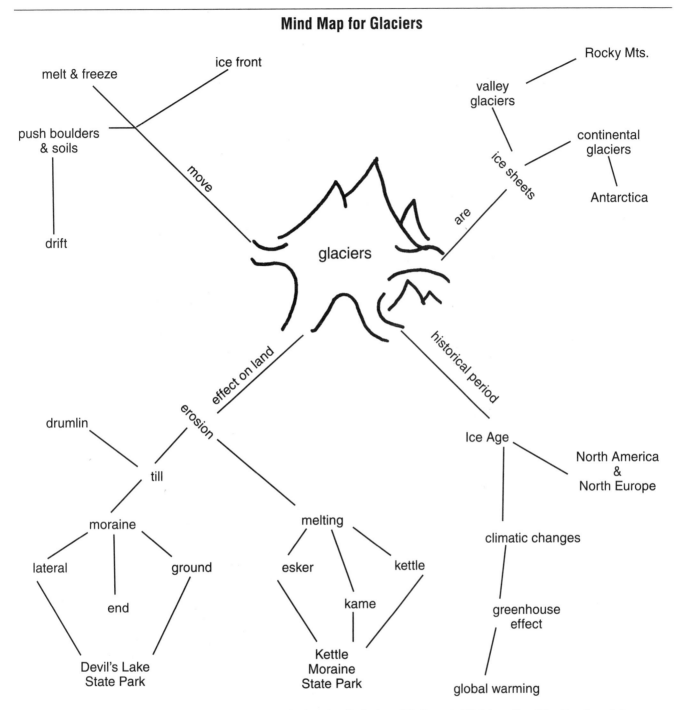

Source: Buehl, D. (2001). *Classroom strategies for interactive learning* (2nd ed., p. 86). Newark, DE: International Reading Association.

Expert describes what the topic is about by systematically going through the Mind Map, and the Novice talks about elements that remain confusing.

4 Recommend to students that they consult their Mind Maps while reading the new selection. To prompt the use of these Mind Maps as guides, ask them to add new terminology, both from the text and from their experiences as they make connections while reading. After reading, have students return to their small groups to incorporate into the maps any additional important ideas and terms.

5 After students have practice with Mind Maps, they can use the strategy in a variety of ways:

• Students can add illustrations to represent key terms, and color code each offshoot of information from the central concept with highlighter pens.

- Students can create their own Mind Maps using a list of important concepts and terms. This is especially effective in helping students to see relationships within material they have just read and can be done both individually and in small groups.
- Students can select their own list of important concepts and terms from a passage and create a Mind Map that represents their understanding of the relationships. In addition, they can add to the map information from their background knowledge.
- Students can be assigned to map a chapter and present the overview to fellow students as a way to introduce a new reading.
- Students can use the Mind Map to write a summary of the material, in order to synthesize understanding.

Mind Maps visually display key ideas and help students see the whole picture of an informational text.

Advantages

- Students encounter and discuss new vocabulary before reading a challenging passage.
- Students have a visual outline of major ideas and relationships among important pieces of information to guide them as they read.
- Students are encouraged to consider how their prior knowledge fits into the new material they will study.

References

Barron, R. (1969). The use of vocabulary as an advance organizer. In H.L. Herber & P.L. Sanders (Eds.), *Research in reading in the content areas: First year report* (pp. 29–39). Syracuse, NY: Syracuse University Reading and Language Arts Center.

Buzan, T. (1991). *Use both sides of your brain: New mind-mapping techniques* (3rd ed.). New York: Plume.

Tierney, R.J., & Readence, J.E. (2004). *Reading strategies and practices: A compendium* (6th ed.). Boston: Allyn & Bacon.

Paired Reviews

"Time Out!" In the midst of a frantically paced basketball game, a player's hands signal a *T*. At a crucial juncture during a football game, a coach wants the clock stopped. Often during athletic competitions, coaches and players need to pause the proceedings to take stock of events and plot adjustments necessary for a successful outcome.

Students, too, can benefit from a pause in the action. At times during the flow of new learning, students need to signal time out so they can collect their thoughts and reflect on their understandings. Like athletes, students may need to catch up, raise questions, clear up confusions, and set their minds for what will happen next.

Proficient readers know that understanding is not a one-step process. Often, we need to revisit what is being learned to make sure we understand. Therefore, a momentary pause clears up uncertainties and helps to mentally reconstruct material so that it makes sense. Reflecting, clarifying, and paraphrasing are automatic responses during learning.

However, many students cling to the habit of reading new material only once, whether they truly understand it or not. They may become preoccupied with completing an assignment rather than pondering the meaning of a passage. As a result, students' reading becomes a race to get done and close the book, and they retain only a vague notion of what was read. Classroom strategies that encourage review and reflection are a necessary step for synthesizing understanding.

Paired Review strategies enhance clarifying and paraphrasing skills and establish regular patterns of brief interruptions, which allow students to process what they are learning.

Using the Strategies

Steps for using five Paired Review strategies—the 3-Minute Pause (McTighe, in Marzano et al., 1992), Paired Verbal Fluency (Costa, 1997), Think/Pair/Share (McTighe & Lyman, 1988), Reflect/Reflect/Reflect (Costa, 1997), and Line-Up Reviews (Buehl, 2003)—are outlined in the sections that follow.

3-Minute Pause

During the 3-Minute Pause, students engage in the following three modes of thinking:

1. Summarizing what they have learned
2. Identifying interesting aspects or what they already know
3. Raising questions about what they find confusing or do not understand

Using this strategy involves the following steps:

1 Introduce the 3-Minute Pause by asking students to imagine themselves working at a computer, perhaps writing a story or essay. Then, after an hour, students quickly stand and turn off their computers. Many students will gasp and ask incredulously, "Without saving?" Some will blurt out that an hour's worth of work is gone forever. Some may offer instances when they neglected to save and irretrievably lost work they had labored over and subsequently had to redo. Recount personal instances when you were lax in saving and lost your work. Computer manuals recommend that you save frequently so that unexpected problems do not wipe out your work.

Extend the analogy to classroom learning. If you do not pause every few minutes to think about what you are hearing, viewing, or reading, then you are not saving or retaining the information. New information may be stored in memory banks for a limited period, but much of it will be heard, seen, or experienced and then forgotten soon after. By pausing every 10 or 15 minutes to think through new material, emphasize that you are in effect beginning to save it in your memory.

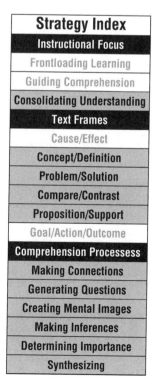

Strategy Index

Instructional Focus
Frontloading Learning
Guiding Comprehension
Consolidating Understanding
Text Frames
Cause/Effect
Concept/Definition
Problem/Solution
Compare/Contrast
Proposition/Support
Goal/Action/Outcome
Comprehension Processess
Making Connections
Generating Questions
Creating Mental Images
Making Inferences
Determining Importance
Synthesizing

2 Have students choose partners for a lesson or unit. Each pair decides who is Partner A and Partner B. When a 3-Minute Pause is called, either A or B is selected to summarize, question, and identify interesting information for his or her partner. Use a stopwatch to time the 3 minutes, which will accentuate the urgency of moving directly to task in order to complete the duties within a specific time period. For example, in a history class viewing a film on Gandhi's nonviolent protests, pause the film after 7 to 10 minutes for reflection.

3 During the pause, Partner A summarizes key points and Partner B comments on both familiar and confusing material. At the next pause, reverse these roles.

Paired Verbal Fluency

Paired Verbal Fluency is a similar strategy that provides practice in "summing up" what has been read or learned. Students take turns reviewing with a partner what they learned from a reading, a video, a class presentation, or a discussion. Using this strategy involves the following steps:

1 Pair students as Partner A and B. Partner A begins by recounting something memorable or interesting in the material and talks steadily for 60 seconds, while Partner B listens. After 60 seconds, tell the partners to switch and change roles. Partner B cannot repeat anything recalled by A.

2 When Partner B has talked for 60 seconds, tell the partners to switch again. Now, Partner A has 40 seconds to continue the review. Again, stipulate that nothing stated by either partner can be repeated. Announce another switch in which Partner B gets a 40-second turn.

3 Follow the same pattern, allowing each partner 20 seconds to recap. This strategy is a fast-paced way for students to summarize their learning. The no-repeat rule forces partners to dig deeper into the information and to listen carefully during the review rather than mentally rehearsing what to say during a summary. Time periods can be adjusted to fit the needs of the students, and when the activity is completed, confusions or questions that surfaced during the review can be addressed. Allowing students access to their notes or textbook during the review is optional.

Think/Pair/Share

This strategy is an extended version of the 3-Minute Pause strategy. Using this strategy involves the following steps:

1 Provide students with a specific question or issue to consider, allowing them a short wait time to ponder their thinking individually.

2 Have students discuss the topic in pairs. In addition to discussion, ask students to engage in other types of thinking during this phase such as reaching a consensus on an issue, solving a problem, or arguing an opposing position.

3 As a variation of Think/Pair/Share, have one partner assume the role of Expert, as though he or she were explaining new content to a Novice. The Expert must talk about material so that a person unfamiliar with the information can understand it. Concepts and vocabulary unknown to a Novice must be translated so that they make sense. The Novice asks clarifying questions and repeats what is understood about the content to the Expert, who verifies whether the Novice has understood correctly and clears up any misunderstandings.

As students become more independent, have them practice the Expert role with people outside of class. For example, a student studying chemistry might explain the day's concepts to a parent. The challenge is to translate the technical language of chemistry into layman's terms. If a parent understands, the student knows that the content has been successfully paraphrased.

Reflect/Reflect/Reflect

As students become more comfortable retelling what they learned, engage them in Reflect/Reflect/Reflect, a more sophisticated strategy for paraphrasing and clarifying. The strategy involves dividing students into groups of three. Each member of the triad, Partners A, B, and C, takes a turn assuming the roles of Authority, Reporter, and Observer (see the Reflect/Reflect/Reflect Outline). To help students understand the roles, ask them to imagine a news program in which a Reporter interacts with an Authority about a topic (or show a short film clip of such an interaction). Ask students to notice how the Authority presents information and personal thoughts about the topic; the Reporter at times summarizes the Authority's words and asks clarifying questions, or delves into the Authority's attitudes and emotions; and the Observer (the TV watcher) takes stock of what the Authority is saying and what the Reporter is summarizing and clarifying. At times the Observer may want to declaim at the screen, "But what about...?" or "That's not exactly right!" Using this strategy involves the following steps.

1 Allow the Authority 2 minutes to talk about a part of the reading material that was interesting, familiar, confusing, or perhaps difficult to learn. Assign the

Reporter the task of paraphrasing what the Authority says. Ask the Observer to comment on the accuracy of the paraphrasing and about whether any important information was omitted.

2 Students read the next passage. Partners switch to different roles and proceed as they did in Step 1. But this time, the Reporter must not only paraphrase the Authority's remarks, but must clarify them by asking questions. The Observer evaluates the paraphrasing and comments on whether questions were clarified.

3 Again, students read the next portion of text. Partners now assume the third role, with the Authority continuing as before. This time the Reporter does three things: paraphrases, asks questions to clarify, and identifies emotions exhibited by the Authority, such as excitement, frustration, confusion, or disagreement. This step brings empathy with a fellow learner into the interaction. The Observer completes the activity as before, commenting on the paraphrasing, clarifying, and empathizing.

Line-Up Reviews

The Line-Up Review (Buehl, 2003) is an especially effective strategy for exam review. Students can be asked to predict one specific piece of information they think might appear on an exam, describe it, and note on an index card why it is important to know. To avoid the same material appearing on the cards, you can assign different sections of a unit or chapter to groups of students. The Line-Up (students line up facing a progression of different review partners) allows them a chance to revisit a number of important concepts and engages students in summing up their understandings. Using this strategy involves the following steps:

1 Students respond to a particular prompt on an index card, which will then be shared with their peers. As a result, students should be cautioned to write clearly and legibly, because others will also be reading their cards. For example, students may be asked to describe something important they have learned or read that many people may not know. On the back of the card, they write why they believe this item is of particular significance.

2 When they have completed their cards, students form two lines of equal numbers so that each person is facing a partner. The students in Line A proceed first, sharing their cards with their partners in Line B. After Line A students have discussed the item on their card for one minute, the roles are reversed and the Line B students share their cards for one minute.

Reflect/Reflect/Reflect Outline

Step 1. Partner A—Authority—presents information and personal thoughts about information.

Partner B—Reporter—summarizes information presented by Authority ("I heard you say...").

Partner C—Observer—comments on presentation and summary (Was anything missed or incorrectly stated?).

Step 2. Switch Roles
Partner B—Authority—presents information and personal thoughts about information.

Partner C—Reporter—summarizes information presented by Authority ("I heard you say...") and asks questions to clarify or get more information ("I was wondering...").

Partner A—Observer—comments on presentation and summary (Was anything missed or incorrectly stated? Is anything still unclear?).

Step 3. Switch Roles
Partner C—Authority—presents information and personal thoughts about information.

Partner A—Reporter—summarizes information presented by Authority ("I heard you say...") and asks questions to clarify or get more information ("I was wondering...") and notes emotions ("You seem to feel...").

Partner B—Observer—comments on presentation and summary (Was anything missed or incorrectly stated? Is anything still unclear?).

Source: Buehl, D. (2001). *Classroom strategies for interactive learning* (2nd ed., p. 90). Newark, DE: International Reading Association.

3 After both students have talked, the partners swap their cards and everyone in Line B moves down to the next student to their left (of course, the person on the far end of Line B must circle back to the head of the line to link up with a new Line A partner). Each student now has a new card to share and a new partner. After this second round of sharing, partners swap cards again, and Line B shifts to the left one more time. In this way, students have an opportunity to verbalize a number of concepts and ideas with several of their peers. Line B can keep shifting to the left until students have had perhaps 8 to 10 different partners and cards to review.

Line-Up Reviews promote careful listening because students realize that they will soon be repeating what their partners tell them to another student. Therefore, they are also encouraged to clarify what their partners tell them, to ask questions if they are confused about any details, or to assist a partner who is struggling with understanding a card. The strategy has the additional advantage of coordinated movement, as students get to talk on their feet, which can provide a welcome active transition between class activities.

Advantages

- Students come to realize that learning does not happen all in one step, but that they need to visit new material several times as they continue to explore it.

- Students are reminded that merely hearing, viewing, or reading is not enough; they also must pause periodically to think about what they are experiencing.

- Students must verbalize their understandings to others and to themselves.

- Students are encouraged to use classmates to help construct personal meaning from important content, as well as to clarify and remember new information.

- Students receive continued practice in reducing what they are learning to meaningful summaries, which emphasize key ideas rather than an accumulation of information.

- These strategies also can be used for eliciting student knowledge about a topic before introducing a new lesson.

References

Buehl, D. (2003). Wait. Let me think about that. *OnWEAC In Print, 3*(10), 13.

Costa, A.L. (1997). *Teaching for intelligent behavior.* Davis, CA: Search Models Unlimited.

Marzano, R.J., Pickering, D.J., Arredondo, D.E., Blackburn, G.J., Brandt, R.S., & Moffett, C.A. (1992). *Dimensions of learning teacher's manual.* Alexandria, VA: Association of Supervision and Curriculum Development.

McTighe, J., & Lyman, F.T., Jr. (1988). Cueing thinking in the classroom: The promise of theory-embedded tools. *Educational Leadership, 45*(7), 18–24.

Power Notes

Say you are in the market for a new automobile. Your mind immediately begins to sort and categorize information relevant to your decision. As you consider vehicles you would like to own, the first mental sorting divides vehicles into "cars you can afford" and "cars you cannot afford." Next you might group the affordable cars into subcategories, perhaps, based on vehicle size or fuel efficiency. Finally, within these clusters, you might list the makes of vehicles that are potential purchases.

Classifying and subdividing information is a natural mental activity and an essential process in classroom learning. As a proficient reader, you can "separate the wheat from the chaff." For example, as you peruse the daily newspaper, you delve into a complex article about the stock market that is full of market terms: *the Dow, drop of 32 points, day traders, NASDAQ, corporate downsizing, Federal Reserve Board, outsourcing, Internet overvaluing, yen, prime rate.* As you read, however, you dwell less on specific details and organize your thinking around main ideas, such as causes of current global economic shifts and the possible impact on consumers.

Many students struggle with perceiving integral relationships in their reading. As a result they have difficulty distinguishing attributes, examples, and details from main ideas. Power Notes (Santa, 1988; Santa, Havens, & Valdes, 2004) provides a systematic way to help students organize information for their reading, writing, and studying.

Using the Strategies

The Power Notes strategy is a streamlined form of outlining that is easy to introduce to students. Power Notes can also combined with Concept Mapping (see page 107 in the K-W-L Plus strategy) and Pattern Puzzles to further enhance students' comprehension and learning.

Power Notes involves assigning various components of a reading a different "power rating," which helps students differentiate more global concepts from specific information. Main ideas or categories are assigned a power 1 rating. Attributes, details, or examples are assigned power 2, 3, or 4 ratings. Using this strategy involves the following steps:

1 Start by modeling Power Notes using categories familiar to students. Point out how the powers relate to each other. For example, power 1 is a main idea or concept, like Fruit. Power 2s are examples or elaborations of power 1, in this case, bananas, peaches, grapes, pears, and apples. Power 3s are examples or elaboration of a power 2. For example, some power 3 examples for apples (power 2) would be varieties such as Macintosh, Yellow Delicious, and Winesap. For power 4s, students might offer characteristics, such as *red-skinned, great for pies,* and *keeps a long time.*

2 Provide students with practice using Power Notes to categorize information and relationships found in factual material. Select a number of power 1, 2, and 3 terms from a unit of study. Write them on separate index cards. Distribute sets of cards to students working in cooperative groups. As students group the cards, have them determine what power each term represents and then arrange the cards according to powers and corresponding relationships. For example, cards for a U.S. history unit on the Age of Reform would include a power 1, *reformers*; power 2s, *populists, unions,* and *progressives*; and power 3s, *NAACP, Farmer's Alliance,* and others. Students might arrange the cards as follows:

1. Reformers
   2. Populists
      3. National Grange
      3. Farmer's Alliance
      3. Populist Party
   2. Unions
      3. The Knights of Labor
      3. American Federation of Labor
      3. IWW
   2. Progressives
      3. Muckrakers
      3. NAACP
      3. Progressive Party

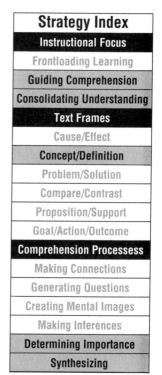

Strategy Index
Instructional Focus
Frontloading Learning
Guiding Comprehension
Consolidating Understanding
Text Frames
Cause/Effect
Concept/Definition
Problem/Solution
Compare/Contrast
Proposition/Support
Goal/Action/Outcome
Comprehension Processess
Making Connections
Generating Questions
Creating Mental Images
Making Inferences
Determining Importance
Synthesizing

Power Notes Concept Map of the Role of Fat in Human Diets

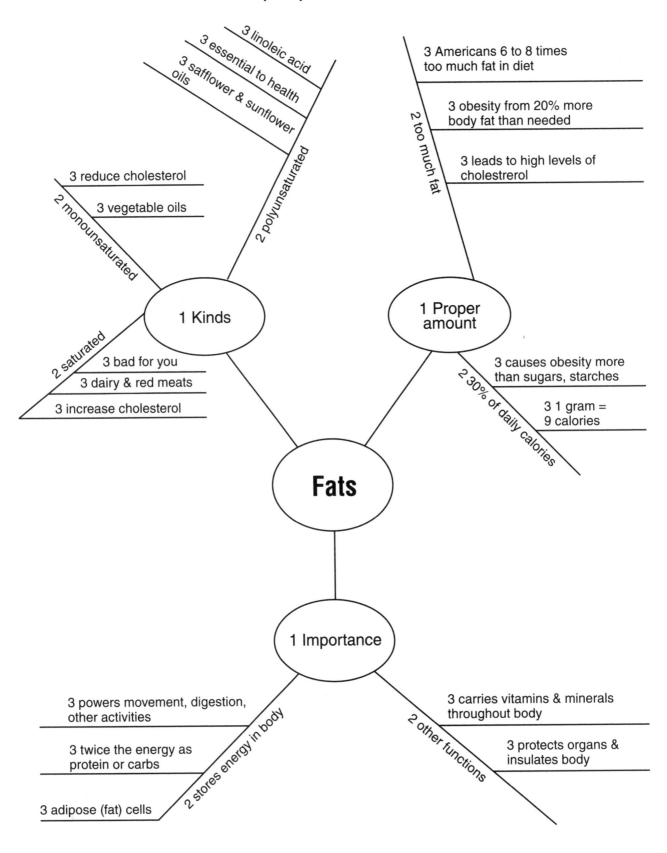

Source: Foss Science. (2005). *Food and nutrition* (pp. 1–4). Berkeley, CA: Delta Education.

This activity is an excellent review exercise. As an additional study technique, provide students with blank cards so they can add power 4 information to power 3 cards or add other items to the outline.

3 To help students organize their writing, have them use a simple 1-2-2-2 outline to construct a well-organized paragraph, such as in the following example:

1. Healthy methods to lose weight

    2. Set realistic goals

    2. Eat fewer calories

    2. Develop regular exercise program

> You should follow healthy methods if you want to lose weight. First, you should set realistic weight-loss goals. Next, you should plan a diet that involves eating fewer calories. Finally, you should develop a regular program of exercise in addition to your diet.

Students can further elaborate each point by adding power 3 and 4 details to their outline. Power Notes gives students a means to analyze their writing in terms of structure and development of ideas.

Power Notes and Concept Maps

After students understand the concept of Power Notes, the strategy can be expanded to enhance comprehension and learning. Power Notes work well with Concept Mapping activities (see the Concept Map example on page 107 in the K-W-L Plus strategy). Concept Maps, visual webs of information that illustrate important relationships within material, are sometimes constructed by students without a sense of superordinate and subordinate information. Their maps may be only a mishmash of facts. Combining Power Notes and Concept Maps involves the following steps:

1 Model Concept Mapping using Power Notes with students. Reserve the center of the map for the topic being developed. Stress that only power 1 ideas can emanate from the center. Each power 1 idea is further defined with power 2s, and power 3s elaborate on the power 2s on the map. For example, students reading a textbook segment about the role of fat in our diets determine three power 1s: importance of fat to our diet, kinds of fats, and proper amounts of fat in our diet (see the Power Notes Concept Map of the Role of Fat in Human Diets example). Each category is developed with power 2 and 3 details. The completed map is a strong visual representation of key information with corresponding relationships clearly defined.

2 Have students work with partners to create Concept Maps from a new selection. One option is to provide transparency film that can be displayed

Pattern Puzzle for Biology

1 Angiosperms are the most diverse and widespread of all plants.

  2 At one time, biologists divided the angiosperms into two classes: monocots and dicots.

  2 Monocots and dicots differ in the structures of their leaves, flowers, seeds, roots, and vascular tissues.

    3 For example, monocots generally have leaves with veins that run parallel to each other.

    3 Most dicots have branched veins. In addition, monocots usually have floral parts in multiples of three.

    3 Most dicots have floral parts in multiples of four or five.

  2 Recent research has added more branches to the evolutionary tree.

    3 Some flowering plants descended from ancestors that evolved earlier than the oldest monocot or dicot ancestor.

    3 Thus, these plants cannot be classified as either monocots or dicots.

Source: Campbell, N.A., Williamson, B., & Heyden, R. (2006). *Biology: Exploring life* (p. 436). Boston: Pearson/Prentice Hall.

on an overhead projector, giving students the option of sharing their maps with the entire class.

Power Notes and Pattern Puzzles

A second application of Power Notes is the Pattern Puzzle strategy (Santa, Havens, & Valdes, 2004). Pattern Puzzles prompt students to notice topic sentences, transition words, and paragraph structure as they read. This activity also models how to write well-organized paragraphs and essays. Using this strategy involves the following steps:

1 Choose a well-organized paragraph and segment it into individual sentences. Separate the sentences on slips of paper, each containing one sentence. Have students work in cooperative groups to arrange the sentences into a paragraph that reads smoothly and makes sense. To accomplish this task, students will have to attend to the power 1, 2, 3, or 4 information in the sentence, and they will also have to be sensitive to transition language that helps ideas flow from sentence to sentence.

For example, students in a biology class are provided with a pattern puzzle about angiosperms from a passage in their textbook. As they examine the individual sentences, they look first for a main idea statement, in this case the sentence talking about angiosperms as the most diverse and widespread of all plants. Further examination leads to three power 2 statements that offer elaboration on that main idea, each which are fleshed out with some power 3 detail sentences (see the Pattern Puzzle for Biology example).

2 Pattern Puzzles can be used in a variety of ways. For example, have students assemble a paragraph that represents a sequence or series of steps, such as the directions for conducting an experiment, so that they carefully analyze why order is important in the procedure. Math word problems or poetry are also excellent sources for developing Pattern Puzzle activities. As part of the process, students may discover that multiple solutions are possible for arranging sentences into paragraphs. In some cases, students may find their configurations of sentences from a passage preferable to those in the original text.

Advantages

- Students become aware of text structure as they read and write.

- Power Notes offer an easy-to-understand strategy for classifying information.

- Students learn to read actively and to prioritize main ideas from supportive details as they study.

- Students are prompted to look for relationships within material they are studying.

- Power relationships can guide students in taking coherent notes from textbooks or classroom presentations.

- Power Notes can be integrated with a number of other strategies to help students perceive how information is interconnected.

References

Campbell, N.A., Williamson, B., & Heyden, R. (2006). *Biology: Exploring life.* Boston: Pearson/Prentice Hall.

Foss Science. (2005). *Food and nutrition.* Berkeley, CA: Delta Education.

Santa, C. (with Havens, L., Nelson, M., Danner, M., Scalf, L., & Scalf, J.) (1988). *Content reading including study systems: Reading, writing and studying across the curriculum.* Dubuque, IA: Kendall/Hunt.

Santa, C.M., Havens, L., & Valdes, B. (2004). *Project CRISS: Creating independence through student-owned strategies.* Dubuque, IA: Kendall/Hunt.

Problematic Situations

How did the Egyptians build the pyramids? What did people use for medicines before there were commercial drugs? What would happen if you put too much yeast in a bread recipe? What would you expect the countryside to look like after a glacier has melted? How did Stone Age hunters kill large animals, such as woolly mammoths? What would you do if someone threatened to beat you up after school?

Children are never at a loss for questions, and from a young age many of these queries focus on *how* or *what*. Tapping into this natural curiosity is an excellent way to prepare students for reading material that deals with problems and solutions. Problematic Situations (Vacca & Vacca, 2007) is a strategy that presents students with a circumstance that is subsequently developed or explained in a reading selection.

Before reading the passage, students first brainstorm possible solutions to or results of the problematic situation. This process activates what students already know about the situation and helps them focus attention on key elements of the text as they read. Problematic Situations also increases motivation for reading, as students want to find out whether their solutions will be confirmed by the author.

Using the Strategy

Problematic Situations can be used to frontload instruction for any type of text that deals with a problem/solution relationship. Using this strategy involves the following steps:

1 Examine a reading assignment and develop a problematic situation for students to consider. Provide students with enough relevant information about the situation so that they are able to identify key ideas in the passage as they read. It is especially important that the context of the problem be clearly defined. The following Problematic Situation is created from the suspenseful short story "The Most Dangerous Game" by Richard Connell, first published in 1924:

> A man is trapped on a small island covered with jungle vegetation. He has a 3-hour start on someone who is trying to kill him. The killer is well armed, but the man has only a knife. The killer will be pursuing the man

with trained hunting dogs. What can this man do to try to save himself?

Students who will read a passage on nutrition and how different nutrients affect the body are given the following Problematic Situation:

> You are the conditioning coach for a national Olympics team. Two athletes come to you for advice about what foods they should be eating to stay in the best performing condition. One is a 180-pound sprinter, the other is a huge 275-pound heavyweight wrestler. What training suggestions would you give each athlete?

Another example relates to a history selection about the Puritan settlers in New England and their religious beliefs. Students decide what course of action might work best for the following Problematic Situation:

> A group of very religious people is living in a country where they cannot worship freely. They feel that the laws of the country and the government discriminate against them. Other people in this country attack their beliefs and this religious group feels persecuted. What can they do to solve their problem?

2 Pose the Problematic Situation to the students in cooperative groups. Have them generate possible results or solutions. Have each group record responses as they are discussed. Have them discuss each response and explain why each is appropriate or would be successful.

For example, students with the nutrition Problematic Situation might list foods like the following for the sprinter: steak, potatoes, vegetables, pasta, milk. Their reasoning might be that the sprinter needs to be strong but also fast, and will burn up a lot of energy on the field. The students realize that the wrestler is in

Strategy Index
Instructional Focus
Frontloading Learning
Guiding Comprehension
Consolidating Understanding
Text Frames
Cause/Effect
Concept/Definition
Problem/Solution
Compare/Contrast
Proposition/Support
Goal/Action/Outcome
Comprehension Processes
Making Connections
Generating Questions
Creating Mental Images
Making Inferences
Determining Importance
Synthesizing

danger of eating himself out of the competition. He needs to watch his weight, so they decide he should eat more vegetables, salads, and fruits and avoid fatty foods such as pizza or french fries.

3 Have each group decide on the most promising result or solution. As part of the deliberations, have groups develop justifications for their decision. For example, students discussing possible solutions for "The Most Dangerous Game" Problematic Situation will consider planning various ambushes and setting a variety of traps as the most conceivable and likely choices. Some solutions will be too improbable or take too much time to devise. Have groups present their solutions to the entire class for discussion.

4 Have students test their solutions by reading the selection. Instruct students to add to or modify solutions as they gain more information from the text. Students reading the nutrition selection may realize that the 275-pound wrestler also could eat lean meats as part of his diet but should watch how many carbohydrates he consumes. Students reading "The Most Dangerous Game" may discover that the hunted man, Rainsford, unsuccessfully tries some of their ideas as he struggles to outwit his adversary. Students reading about the Puritans may discover that the Puritans attempted several of the students' solutions before embarking for North American to create their new society.

5 Have students compare predictions with information provided in the text. Revisit the original Problematic Situation and solicit any revisions, additions, or further comments students may have now that they have read the selection. Open a discussion to consider whether some of the students' solutions might be better than those of the author.

Advantages

- Problematic Situations help students to successfully analyze material that deals with *how* or *what* relationships.
- Students have an opportunity to take stock of background knowledge that relates to ideas in a reading.
- Students' curiosity is piqued, and they are more motivated to tackle a reading that will answer their questions.
- Students anticipate the problem-solving frame of mind that they will need to assume when reading.
- Students consciously connect new information to their questions about problematic situations.

Reference

Vacca, R.T., & Vacca, J.L. (2007). *Content area reading: Literacy and learning across the curriculum* (8th ed.). Boston: Pearson/Allyn & Bacon.

Pyramid Diagram

Visualize the following setting: the conference room of a major company with a table surrounded by executives, each responsible for delivering a report. What follows is a parade of statistics, an array of colorful charts and computer graphics, and a pile of data. Clearly, the point of the meeting is to understand the implications of the information so that important decisions can be made. But what sense is to be made from all this information?

As a critical part of their daily reading demands, students also need to sort through information to draw conclusions and make generalizations. Yet many state and national assessments consistently indicate that students have much more difficulty making inferences and drawing generalizations than identifying facts. The Pyramid Diagram (Solon, 1980) guides students in selecting appropriate information from a reading to be analyzed and helps them consider possible implications of this material.

Using the Strategy

The Pyramid Diagram engages students in both reading and writing activities. Using this strategy involves the following steps:

1 Provide students with a focusing question that will help them select relevant information from a reading. For example, a focusing question for students reading a selection about Benjamin Franklin might be, What were Franklin's most significant accomplishments? A focusing question for students reading a passage on tropical storms might be, What are the problems caused by tropical storms?

2 Distribute index cards to the students and have them read a selection. As they read, they should record on the cards information that deals with the focusing question. One piece of information is recorded on each card. Students looking for Franklin's achievements might write, "invented the lightning rod" on one card, and "was ambassador to France" on a second card. Students continue making cards until they finish reading the passage.

3 Model the process of categorizing the selected information from the reading by soliciting student responses from their cards. Write each response on an index card and line the cards along the chalkboard tray in the order given. Next, ask students if any of the cards can be grouped together. Allow discussion and recognize disagreements as students determine how the cards might be categorized. Move the cards to reflect the class consensus, thus forming the foundation layer of the Pyramid Diagram.

4 Ask students to brainstorm category headings for each grouping of cards. Again, allow discussion and help the class reach a consensus. Write the headings selected for each group on new cards and tape them to the pyramid as a second layer above the corresponding categories. For example, students might decide on *statesman*, *politician*, or *leader* for cards detailing Franklin's roles as delegate to the Constitutional Convention and diplomat to France (see the Pyramid Diagram for Benjamin Franklin example). Several of Franklin's other accomplishments could fall under the categories of *inventor*, *writer*, or *scientist* after students consider the information on the other cards.

5 Draw on the chalkboard two rectangles representing the top two layers of the pyramid. Ask students to determine an appropriate title for the pyramid. The title should reflect the overall topic area of the selection and is placed in the top rectangle. *Benjamin Franklin's Accomplishments* might be offered as a potential title for the social studies example on Benjamin Franklin. Then, using the title, category labels, and details from the reading, have each student write a one-sentence statement that summarizes the information represented in the pyramid. For example, after constructing a Ben Franklin pyramid, students might conclude the following:

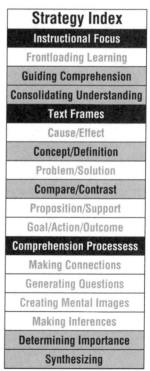

Strategy Index

Instructional Focus
Frontloading Learning
Guiding Comprehension
Consolidating Understanding
Text Frames
Cause/Effect
Concept/Definition
Problem/Solution
Compare/Contrast
Proposition/Support
Goal/Action/Outcome
Comprehension Processess
Making Connections
Generating Questions
Creating Mental Images
Making Inferences
Determining Importance
Synthesizing

Pyramid Diagram for Benjamin Franklin

Benjamin Franklin's Accomplishments							
Ben Franklin's accomplishments in writing, science, and government show that he was a man of many talents and interests.							
Writer		Inventor		Scientist		Statesman	
Published *Poor Richard's Almanack*	Wrote an autobiography	Invented the lightning rod	Devised the Franklin stove	Conducted experiments on electricity	Studied weather patterns	Delegate to the Constitutional Convention	Diplomat to France during the Revolutionary War

Source: Buehl, D. (1995). *Classroom strategies for interactive learning* (p. 85). Madison: Wisconsin State Reading Association.

Ben Franklin's accomplishments in writing, science, and government show that he was a man of many talents and interests.

6 Students now write a one-paragraph conclusion that addresses the focusing question. The second layer of the pyramid provides them with a topic sentence. The third layer suggests subsequent sentences that will expand on the topic sentence. The bottom layer identifies appropriate details that may be used to illustrate each of these examples. The following paragraph illustrates how students might combine the information in each layer of the Pyramid Diagram:

> Benjamin Franklin's accomplishments in writing, science, and government show that he was a man of many talents and interests. Franklin was a well-known writer who published the popular *Poor Richard's Almanack* and wrote an autobiography. He was an inventor, bringing us the lightning rod and Franklin stove. He also was a scientist who conducted experiments on electricity and studied weather patterns. Finally, Franklin was an important statesman who served as a delegate to the Constitutional Convention and as a diplomat to France during the Revolutionary War.

Once students have become comfortable with using Pyramid Diagrams, these steps may be accomplished in cooperative groups. Students first read the selection and complete their cards and then meet to construct the rest of the pyramid as a group. Students could then write their one-paragraph conclusions as individuals or as a group.

Advantages

- Students construct a visual representation of how important details are used to draw conclusions and make observations.

- Students are directive in their reading so that they actively search for appropriate information from a selection.

- Students gain practice in writing well-organized summaries of text.

References

Buehl, D. (1995). *Classroom strategies for interactive learning*. Madison: Wisconsin State Reading Association.
Solon, C. (1980). The pyramid diagram: A college study skills tool. *Journal of Reading, 23*(7), 594–597.

Suggested Reading

Kinkead, D., Thompson, R., Wright, C., & Gutierrez, C. (1992). Pyramiding: Reading and writing to learn social studies. *The Exchange. Newsletter of the International Reading Association Secondary Reading Special Interest Group, 5*(2), 3.

Question–Answer Relationships

wonder. I wonder how much rain these threatening clouds are promising. I wonder what response my proposal will elicit. I wonder why these tomato plants seem so droopy. I wonder if this traffic delay will cause me to arrive late. I wonder whether it makes any difference if I substitute honey for sugar in this recipe. I wonder where I misplaced my car keys again. When we wonder, we are posing questions to ourselves.

Questions provide the scripts of our daily internal dialogues with ourselves. We ask questions to speculate and to guide us. We ask questions to kindle our curiosity and to clarify our confusions. We realize that self-questioning is an essential component of critical thinking, decision making, problem solving, and constructing sense from our experiences. Self-questioning is also a hallmark of comprehension. Studies of proficient readers reveal that they spontaneously formulate their own questions before, during, and after reading a piece of text. Questioning helps readers focus, make inferences, read critically, and draw conclusions.

However, self-questioning is a reading strategy that many of our students employ sporadically or unsuccessfully. Self-questioning assumes an inquisitiveness about a text, an expectation that something in a passage will connect to a reader's experiences and background knowledge, an optimism that the act of reading will result in meaningful ends. Instead, many of our students appear programmed to routinely answer only questions provided to them by someone else. They become overly dependent on textbook editors, on worksheet activities, and on teacher-led discussions for discovering relevant questions that can be asked about a specific text. As a result, students may skim paragraphs searching for answers rather than engage in the more in-depth questioning process that is the core of reading comprehension. Invariably, teachers then hear, "I can't find the answer to this question!"

Understanding Question–Answer Relationships (QARs) is a critical component of learning. Many students are unaware of the different levels of thinking their questions may elicit. As a result, they follow a literal approach to answering questions—seeking direct statements from the text to answer questions—and feel betrayed or even give up when this strategy does not work. Other students pay only cursory attention to their reading; instead, they rely solely on what they already know to obtain answers, regardless of what is in the text. For them, answering questions becomes an exercise in using common sense rather than a thoughtful consideration of new information encountered in print.

Using the Strategy

QAR (Raphael, 1982, 1986) is a classic strategy for analyzing and understanding questions. QARs help students to recognize the kind of thinking they need when they respond to questions—their own as well as those posed by others. Using this strategy involves the following steps:

1 Introduce QARs with a example that clearly distinguishes between *in-the-book* and *in-my-head* QARs (see the Where's the Answer? chart). For example, a history teacher might select a short excerpt from a text on Lewis and Clark to illustrate these different question types. First, model clarifying questions that double-check something directly stated in the passage such as, What river did Lewis and Clark follow in the spring of 1804? (see the QARs for Lewis and Clark example). As students provide the answer (the Missouri River), have them locate the place in the text that provides the information for the answer. Then model a question that requires background information in addition to the text in order to answer. An in-my-head question could be, I wonder why Lewis and Clark found communicating with American Indians a difficult process? To construct an answer, students must draw from their background knowledge—that European settlers and American Indians spoke different languages—as well as clues from the author.

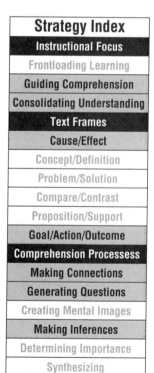

Strategy Index

Instructional Focus

Frontloading Learning

Guiding Comprehension

Consolidating Understanding

Text Frames

Cause/Effect

Concept/Definition

Problem/Solution

Compare/Contrast

Proposition/Support

Goal/Action/Outcome

Comprehension Processess

Making Connections

Generating Questions

Creating Mental Images

Making Inferences

Determining Importance

Synthesizing

2 Discuss with students how some answers can be found explicitly in the text and others require additional information based on what the reader already knows. Students are now ready for a more sophisticated analysis of QARs. Again, using the sample passage, point out that some in-the-book questions require more thinking than others. For example, the question "I wonder how long it took Lewis and Clark to complete their explorations?" requires students to put information together from more than one part of the passage. The answer, about 2½ years, can be obtained only after putting two pieces of information together—the dates mentioned in the first and last sentences.

Share with students that there are two types of in-the-book QARs: *right-there questions* (the river they followed), and *putting-it-together questions* (the length of their trip). The author provides sufficient information for both answers, but putting-it-together questions involve constructing answers using several pieces of information. Putting-it-together questions mandate the examination of more than one sentence in order to connect facts and draw conclusions. Another way to describe these two QARs is that right-there questions are already preassembled, waiting for you to find them, while putting-it-together questions have all the necessary pieces in the text but the reader has to locate each piece and assemble the pieces to create the answer.

3 Demonstrate that in-my-head QARs also can be of two types: *author-and-me* and *on-my-own*. The question concerning the explorers' difficulty communicating with American Indians can be answered using clues from the author (e.g., noticing that American Indian terms appeared in the journals) and general background knowledge (e.g., realizing that these peoples spoke different languages). This question is an author-and-me QAR, because answers are developed partly from hints from the author and partly from the reader's personal knowledge base. Another example is, I wonder who sent Lewis and Clark on their expedition? The author does not directly address this question, but an answer is implied: the explorers reported to President Jefferson when they returned. Student experiences may tell them that people who complete a mission usually report what happened to whoever sent them on that mission. Therefore, students would infer that Jefferson authorized this expedition.

The second type of in-my-head QAR—on-my-own—relies almost solely on the reader's personal knowledge. A question such as, I wonder why Lewis and Clark used American Indian terms for many of the plants and animals they encountered? cannot be answered based on the information in the passage. Students will have to hypothesize answers based on what they know. Students might offer that because North America contained many plants and animals unfamiliar to European settlers, it was natural for them to adopt American Indian terms.

On-my-own QARs often can be answered without reading the passage, which may lead to a variety of plausible responses. An on-my-own question such as, I wonder how American Indians reacted to the Lewis and Clark expedition? could lead to important discussions regarding the changing dynamic in the American West, but very little in the passage would contribute to this discussion.

4 Provide students with opportunities for classifying their own questions according to these four categories. Emphasize that recognizing the question type

---

Where's the Answer?

"In-the-Book" QARs

"In-My-Head" QARs

1. "Right-There"— Explicit Answer

(Answer is directly stated in text)

2. "Putting-It-Together"— Constructed Answer

(Answer involves combining text information from 2 or more sentences)

3. "Author-and-Me"— Implicit Answer

(Answer inferred using clues from text & background knowledge)

4. "On-My-Own"— Schema Answer

(Answer based solely on background knowledge)

Note: Adapted from Raphael, T.E. (1986). Teaching question answer relationships, revisited. *The Reading Teacher*, *39*(6), 516–522.

QAR for Lewis and Clark

Lewis and Clark followed the Missouri River for several hundred miles as they moved westward in the spring of 1804. Along with their goal of mapping the new territory, the two explorers were also instructed to keep careful records of their journey. As they traveled, the explorers gained a great deal of information through the difficult process of trying to communicate with the American Indians they met. Their journals were filled with words, such as *skunk, hickory, squash, raccoon, and opossum*, which are American Indian terms for plants and animals. After their return in September 1806, Lewis and Clark reported to President Jefferson and their journals were eventually published.

Right-there:

1. What river did Lewis and Clark follow in the spring of 1804?

2. What was the goal of Lewis and Clark's journey?

Putting-it-together:

3. How long did it take Lewis and Clark to complete their explorations?

4. Why did the explorers keep journals during their travels?

Author-and-me:

5. Who sent Lewis and Clark on their expedition?

6. Why was trying to communicate with American Indians a difficult process for Lewis and Clark?

On-my-own:

7. Why did Lewis and Clark use American Indian terms for many of the plants and animals they encountered?

8. How do you think American Indians felt about the Lewis and Clark expedition?

Source: Buehl, D. (2001). *Classroom strategies for interactive learning* (2nd ed., p. 107). Newark, DE: International Reading Association.

QARs Before/During/After Reading

QARs Before Reading

On-My-Own:
What do I already know that can connect me to this text?

Author-and-Me:
Based on the topic, title, and illustrations, what might this text be about?

QARs During Reading

Author-and-Me:
What do I think the author will tell me next?

Putting-It-Together:
What are the important ideas/information/details?

Right-There:
How does the author describe (the character, the setting, the event...)?
What is the main topic of this paragraph?

QARs After Reading

Author-and-Me:
What is the author's message?
What is the theme and how is it connected to the world beyond the story?
How can I synthesize the information with what I know from other sources?
How well does the author make his/her argument?
How is the author using particular language to influence our beliefs?

Putting-It-Together:
What evidence in the text can be found to support an argument?

Note: Adapted from Raphael, T.E., Highfield, D., & Au, K. (2006). *QAR now: Question answer relationships: A powerful and practical framework that develops comprehension and higher-level thinking in all students.* New York: Scholastic.

---

is an essential first step toward deciding an appropriate answer. Ask students to work in pairs or small groups to label questions as well as answer them. This activity is an effective way to develop the ability to handle questions that require inferential thinking and examining several parts of a passage—the putting-it-together and author-and-me QARs.

5 As students become comfortable with identifying types of questions, have them exchange questions with classmates, who then answer and classify the student-produced questions. In addition, Raphael, Highfield, and Au (2006) suggest prototypical questions that students might pose to themselves before, during, and after reading (see QARs Before/During/

After Reading). Emphasize that these are questions students should be in the habit of asking themselves as readers.

Advantages

- Students are encouraged to adopt an inquiring approach to their reading.

- Students begin to perceive that a variety of strategies are needed to answer questions.

- Students are guided in understanding that valuable responses to reading can range from the literal identification of basic information to very open-ended discussions that have no set, correct answer.

- Students are prompted to constantly tap into their own knowledge base as they encounter new information in reading.

- Teachers have a framework for analyzing comprehension gaps due to lack of adequate background knowledge rather than from an inability to answer in-the-book QARs.

References

Raphael, T.E. (1982). Question-answering strategies for children. *The Reading Teacher, 36*(2), 186–190.

Raphael, T.E. (1986). Teaching question answer relationships, revisited. *The Reading Teacher, 39*(6), 516–522.

Raphael, T.E., Highfield, D., & Au, K.H., (2006). *QAR now: Question answer relationships: A powerful and practical framework that develops comprehension and higher-level thinking in all students.* New York: Scholastic.

Questioning the Author

"Are you talking to me?" We exist as individuals in the midst of a daily buzz of language, and much of this linguistic hum may seem impersonal—generic jabbering, indiscriminately targeted, everyone talking to everyone else. Yet at times it becomes apparent that a speaker is singling you out as an audience. A flow of discourse, directed toward you personally—a joke, a comment, a criticism, a threat, a compliment, a confidence, a sharing, a solicitation. Someone wants *your* attention. Someone is talking to you.

In our daily lives, we are ever aware of others talking to us. In print, these communications assume a variety of forms: a set of directives delivered in a memo at our workplace, an editorial in the newspaper, an appeal mailed to our home, a request appearing on a computer screen via e-mail, a speech by a political leader televised in our living room. But we also tune into other voices reaching out to us: a novelist, perhaps dead for a century or more, speaking to us through a work of literature; a reporter, from across the globe, chronicling events in a distant land; a historian, looking back on a lifetime of study, constructing an analysis of a past civilization; or a scientist, steeped in research data, describing new insights on some physical phenomenon. As mature readers, we recognize that every time we pick up a piece of print, someone is talking to us.

This ability to perceive the person behind the message is a hallmark of proficient reading, a prerequisite for critical thinking. For many of our students, however, the voice of an author becomes lost behind a din of words. In particular, texts that students read in school may seem particularly "author-less." Students may become so immersed in grappling with information that they lose sight of the writer, thereby bypassing an author's intentions, viewpoints, assumptions, and perspectives. They read "just to get the facts" and miss the larger scope of a piece of text. They read as if no one is talking to them.

Beck and her associates (1997) argue that a mental posture of "questioning the author" is an especially powerful strategy to help students adopt an inquiring orientation to texts. Questioning the Author (QtA) focuses on a series of questions that one might naturally pose about any message we might receive, in any form. Who is talking to me? Why are you telling me this? What is the point of your message? What do you expect of me, as a reader of your message? What do you think I can (or should) do with your message? These are questions we would ask another human being, this time directed to the author.

Using the Strategies

In contrast to most of the questions that typify student experience, a QtA disposition moves students beyond merely identifying information and instead engages them in considering the person writing to them and what that person has attempted to offer them. An extension to this activity, Elaborative Interrogation, can help deepen comprehension even further.

Teaching this strategy to students requires frequent modeling during the classroom routine. Using this strategy involves the following steps:

1 Initially, QtA involves a subtle but significant shift in classroom language. Rather than talking about "what the book says" or "what it said in the story," recalibrate the classroom discourse to focus on authorship: "what did the author say." Emphasize that "books don't talk, authors do." This underscores that reading is an act of communication between an author and readers. Have students "personalize" the authors by identifying these individuals by name and locating available biographical information that provides insight on who they are. What perspective do they bring to the book?

Select a passage from classroom materials and model examination of the authorship with students. What does the author expect students to already know? What could the authors add or change to

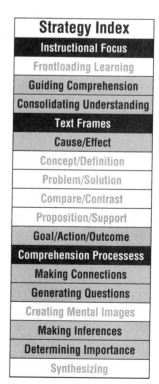

<table>
<tr><td colspan="1">Strategy Index</td></tr>
<tr><td>Instructional Focus</td></tr>
<tr><td>Frontloading Learning</td></tr>
<tr><td>Guiding Comprehension</td></tr>
<tr><td>Consolidating Understanding</td></tr>
<tr><td>Text Frames</td></tr>
<tr><td>Cause/Effect</td></tr>
<tr><td>Concept/Definition</td></tr>
<tr><td>Problem/Solution</td></tr>
<tr><td>Compare/Contrast</td></tr>
<tr><td>Proposition/Support</td></tr>
<tr><td>Goal/Action/Outcome</td></tr>
<tr><td>Comprehension Processess</td></tr>
<tr><td>Making Connections</td></tr>
<tr><td>Generating Questions</td></tr>
<tr><td>Creating Mental Images</td></tr>
<tr><td>Making Inferences</td></tr>
<tr><td>Determining Importance</td></tr>
<tr><td>Synthesizing</td></tr>
</table>

QtA Queries

- What is the author telling you?

- What does the author assume you already know?

- Why is the author telling you this?

- What is the point of the author's message?

- What does the author apparently think is most important?

- How does the author signal this?

- Does this follow with what the author told you before?

- How does this connect with information the author has already provided?

- Did the author explain this clearly?

- What could the author have done to clarify this?

- Why do you think the author tells you this information now?

- Does the author tell us why?

---

make the passage more understandable? Emphasize that authors have opinions and make decisions about what to put in their writing. And, although authors may be very knowledgeable about the material, sometimes they may not express their ideas in ways that are clear to all readers.

Note that the intent of the modeling is not to condemn classroom texts as poorly written but to underscore the natural tension that occurs between readers and writers. Writers have a responsibility to clearly communicate their ideas to the target audience. Readers have a responsibility to size up what an author provides and what they must do to make sense of a text. (As mentioned in Chapter 1, some texts are more considerate of readers than others in the way they present information and ideas.)

2 Preview a selection that will be assigned for reading. Decide what is most important for students to understand from this material. In addition, identify any segments that may present difficulties for students. Choose places in the text where you will stop students and initiate discussion to clarify key points. Unlike most textbook lessons that involve discussion before or after reading, a QtA activity has the teacher lead discussion *during* reading, at predetermined breaks in the text. Students might read a paragraph or two before a discussion break, or you might wish to follow a pivotal single sentence with discussion. For example,

the following earth science passage is deceptively difficult:

> An earthquake is a shaking of Earth's crust caused by a release of energy. Earthquakes can occur for many reasons. The ground may shake as a result of the eruption of a volcano, the collapse of a cavern, or even the impact of a meteor. The cause of most major earthquakes is the strain that builds up along faults at or near boundaries between lithospheric plates. A fault is a break in the lithosphere along which movement has occurred. (Spaulding & Namowitz, 2003, p. 214)

A key QtA here is, What do the authors assume readers already know? This question immediately cues students to make connections to prior knowledge. The authors assume that students are aware of giant underground caverns, although why these should collapse and how often they do so is not explained. The authors also assume that students know about meteors and that these objects sometimes collide with the earth, which is implied in the paragraph, although the frequency with which this occurs also is not discussed. Finally, the authors tap into assumed previous learning about volcanoes and lithospheric plates. The end of this paragraph is an excellent place to "pause" the reading and clarify information with students.

3 Focus discussion during pauses on *author queries*, questions that are not about the information but rather about the author's intentions: What is the author trying to say? What is the author's message? Did the author explain clearly? How does this connect with what the author has told us before? (See QtA Queries.) Model for students how a proficient reader endeavors to make sense of sometimes confusing or inadequate text. Discuss what the author is trying to communicate and continually focus student attention on the text to verify what the author has provided for readers. At times you will need to rectify mismatches between the author and your students by interjecting additional information that fills in gaps in prior knowledge. The strength of QtA discussions is derived from the modeling of appropriate problem-solving questions that help readers think about their comprehension as they read.

4 As students become comfortable responding to QtA queries, ask them to generate their own for a selection. With a partner, ask them to lightly pencil in an asterisk or mark with a small sticky note a few places in the text where they believe a reader should stop and ponder. Have them select one or more of the queries from the QtA Queries (listed on a classroom poster or on an individual copy, such as a bookmark), which a reader might ask at each of these junctures. For added practice, group two sets of partners together and have them pose their queries to one another.

Questioning the Author makes the previously overlooked actions of the author more visible to students as they attempt to learn from textbooks.

Elaborative Interrogation

Asking *why* is especially significant for deepening comprehension. Elaborative Interrogation (Pressley et al., 1988, 1990) prompts students to ask probing "why" questions of the author, which help them elaborate on text material in two ways:

1. By looking for hints from the author that connect information
2. By activating relevant prior knowledge that might help to explain why

Using this strategy involves the following steps:

1 Model for students appropriate *why* questions about the material the class is studying. Initially, it might be helpful to provide students with important factual statements from the material or story, which will guide them on the types of information worthy of consideration. For example, the following excerpt from a history textbook dealing with the invention of the printing press could be modeled as an Elaborative Interrogation exercise:

> The European invention of printing appears to have been independent of the Chinese process. Scholars believe that in about 1450, Johannes Gutenberg of Mainz, Germany, became the first European to use movable type to print books. Gutenberg used his printing press to print copies of the Bible. Not all Europeans were enthusiastic about Gutenberg's invention. Some complained that books printed on paper would not last long. Others noted that hand-copied manuscripts were far more beautiful than printed books. Scribes, who made a living by hand-copying manuscripts, realized that the printing press threatened their profession. The impact of Gutenberg's work was economical as well as social and technological. (*World History*, 2003, p. 359)

After students review the statements, ask a series of why questions that will focus student attention on implied cause-and-effect relationships in the material, such as, Why would the Chinese and European developments be independent of each other? Why would the author say "scholars believe" Gutenberg was the first? Why would Gutenberg start with printing the Bible? Why were some not enthusiastic about this invention? Why would the author say the impact was economical, social, and technological? And so forth. As students ponder possible responses, emphasize that the author may give hints to the answers, but that they must also "use their heads" and consider things they already know (see Question–Answer Relationships beginning

on page 133). Clearly, this passage contains a great deal of "hidden knowledge" (see Chapter 2).

Students may express frustration that they do not know enough or are not told enough to come up with plausible answers to some of these why questions. Reassure them that they will not always be able to determine unambiguous or exact answers to why questions they might pose. The strength of the Elaborative Interrogation strategy lies in the process of analyzing what an author says for possible relationships. By asking, Why? students are engaged in a much deeper level of processing than if they merely read the material; they are making connections and drawing possible conclusions.

2 As students study new information, have them work with partners to generate "why" questions about the material and to brainstorm possible responses to their questions. When students become practiced in asking good why questions, they can create their own why questions for their classmates. Pair students and have them create a series of why questions for one section of a passage. Then have them exchange their questions with those of another student pair, who developed questions on a different section. Each pair will then reread the appropriate sections to hypothesize answers to their classmates' questions. The Elaborative Interrogation strategy can work just as successfully with fiction as with nonfiction.

Advantages

- Students are engaged in a more active form of questioning, which goes beyond questions that target a literal level of understanding.
- Students are less likely to be frustrated by difficult text as they realize that part of the responsibility for a passage making sense belongs to the author.
- Students are taught to be metacognitive—readers who actively monitor their comprehension during reading.
- Students become deeply engaged with reading, as issues and problems are addressed while they learn, rather than afterward.
- Students learn to internalize a self-questioning process that proficient readers use to monitor and enhance their comprehension.
- QtA discussions can be used to introduce selections that students will read independently, perhaps as homework. They are especially helpful when students may need some assistance coping with difficult but important segments of a chapter.
- QtA discussions are valuable as a comprehension-building strategy for struggling readers.

- QtA lessons may be developed in all content areas and can be tailored for young students as well as adolescent learners.

References

Beck, I.L., McKeown, M.G., Hamilton, R.L., & Kucan, L. (1997). *Questioning the author: An approach for enhancing student engagement with text*. Newark, DE: International Reading Association.

Pressley, M., Symons, S., McDaniel, M.A., Snyder, B.L., & Turnure, J.E. (1988). Elaborative interrogation facilitates acquisition of confusing facts. *Journal of Educational Psychology, 80*(3), 268–278.

Spaulding, N.E., & Namowitz, S.N. (2003). *Earth science*. Evanston, IL: McDougal Littell.

World history: The human journey. (2003). Austin, TX: Holt, Rinehart and Winston.

Suggested Reading

Wood, E., Pressley, M., & Winne, P.H. (1990). Elaborative interrogation effects on children's learning of factual content. *Journal of Educational Psychology, 82*(4), 741–748.

Quick Writes

"Could you run that by me again?" Sometimes, once is not quite enough when we are trying to understand. Often we will interject, "Wait! Did I hear you say...?" as we listen to a speaker, rephrasing the message to ensure that it makes sense to us. Or we reach for the replay button on our remote as we view a video, needing to absorb a scene a second time and mull over what we saw. And most especially, as we read, we periodically need to pause, a thumb holding our place in the book, while we ponder and consider, perhaps sneaking another look at a crucial passage to verify what we think.

As learners, we frequently discover that we need opportunities for further deliberation, to double-check our understandings and to clarify our thinking. This essential component of comprehension—synthesizing—involves processing a message so that it has personal meaning. Students need ongoing practice in reformulating what they learn into their own words. Expressing their understandings in writing is particularly important.

Quick Writes, advocated by Linda Rief (1998), are planned interludes during class for students to respond to their learning. As they express their thoughts and understandings in these rapidly written brief reflections, students make personal connections to a text and become increasingly comfortable integrating new vocabulary into their "talk" about key ideas and concepts.

Using the Strategies

With Quick Writes, students are allocated a prescribed period of time to quickly gather their thoughts about some aspect of a course of study. Learning Logs (Fulwiler, 1980) are an extension of Quick Writes, in which students record their thoughts and ideas while learning as a way to explore and evaluate what they have learned. An additional extension of Quick Writes is Admit and Exit Slips, which also encourages students to reflect on their learning.

Quick Writes represent informal writing, not polished or edited composition. Using this strategy involves the following steps:

1 Establish with students the purpose of this strategy in your curriculum. Quick Writes might be collected as a part of a class learning log or included as classroom journal entries. The ground rules for a Quick Write are as follows:

- Students are informed of time parameters (a one-minute write, for example).
- Students are expected to begin writing immediately and use the entire (albeit short) time period.
- Students quickly jot down the thoughts that occur to them as they respond to the writing prompt.
- Students should not be overly concerned about writing form (the intent of a Quick Write is fluency of expression rather than careful writing).
- Students may be asked to share their Quick Writes with a partner.

A timer with a buzzer is an especially useful tool during Quick Writes, to reinforce that students need to transition directly into their thinking and that extended writing is not an expectation. An appropriate time reserved for a Quick Write depends on the students and the nature of the topic. Rief (1998) frequently uses one-minute writes to involve students very quickly in casual thinking about a topic. With a short period of time to work in, students cannot ponder and procrastinate before they commence writing. Instead, when they hear, "Go!" everybody goes, and "says something" in their writing.

2 Consider appropriate prompts to stimulate a Quick Write. Prompts are an essential element of a Quick Write. A prompt is intended to jump-start student thinking about some important aspect of a unit of study and to provide some focus for their personal musings. Prompts do not need to be lengthy; a read-aloud of a minute or two may suffice in guiding

Strategy Index
Instructional Focus
Frontloading Learning
Guiding Comprehension
Consolidating Understanding
Text Frames
Cause/Effect
Concept/Definition
Problem/Solution
Compare/Contrast
Proposition/Support
Goal/Action/Outcome
Comprehension Processess
Making Connections
Generating Questions
Creating Mental Images
Making Inferences
Determining Importance
Synthesizing

student thinking about a topic. A striking quote or a read-aloud from a portion of a class text can be a highly effective Quick Write prompt.

As students listen, they have a chance to rehearse their thinking about the material. For example, students studying the Vietnam War protests in the 1960s listen to the teacher read a couple of paragraphs from the history textbook describing student demonstrations on college campuses. Then students produce a one-minute Quick Write about what they were thinking, such as in the following example:

> I was wondering if the protests about Iraq today are anything like the 1960s. It seems that the anti–Vietnam War protests were happening all over the country and they were frequently violent. I wonder if I would have been involved if I had been in a college like Kent State.

Quick Write prompts are also an excellent place to bring in quality short passages outside the required text material. The prompt below excerpted from *National Geographic* magazine provides science students learning about volcanoes with vivid mental imagery of these destructive natural forces:

> In the first seconds of the eruption, the collapsing north face of St. Helens sends juggernauts of ice tumbling down into the hot ash. Quickly the ice melts, and an estimated 46 billion gallons of water create the combination of mudflow and flood that geologists had feared.... Like a science-fiction monster, the debris eats the river, the roads, the downed trees, the logging trucks, a few cars and campers. (Findley, 1981, p. 35)

3 A Quick Write may, of course, be open-ended, allowing students to pen whatever is on their minds as they respond to a prompt. However, Quick Writes can also be constructed to elicit specific types of thinking. In addition to providing a prompt, teachers can also indicate a stem that students can use to frame their thinking, such as the following:

- "This reminds me of..." (to emphasize making connections between the curriculum and personal knowledge and experiences)

- "I wonder what..., if..., why..., whether..." and so on (to stimulate questions that occur to students about the topic)

- "What seems especially important to me..." (to help students narrow into key concepts and ideas)

- "I was interested in..." or "I feel that..." (to engage students in examining personal responses to a topic)

- "I think that..." (to encourage conclusions or generalizations about the material)

4 Quick Writes can be expanded or applied in additional ways to take students deeper into their learning of course content. Quick Writes provide an excellent opportunity for students to explore new vocabulary. For example, students in a geometry class could be asked to "write down what comes to mind when you hear the term *symmetrical*," or students in a science class may be asked to use the terms *precipitation*, *evaporation*, and *transpiration* for a Quick Write summarizing the water cycle. Students may also use Quick Writes to summarize their reading. A seven-minute write, for example, allows students to talk about what they have read, describe what they found interesting or important, and interject other personal sentiments about the material.

Learning Logs

Learning Logs are a systematic way to integrate more extended informal reflective writing in the curriculum (Fulwiler, 1980). These Logs can become a journal component of a class notebook assignment. Using this strategy involves the following steps:

1 Emphasize to students that Learning Logs are a mechanism for recording thoughts and ideas while learning, which is also a time for evaluating learning. Ask your students to reserve a separate section of their class notebook for a Learning Log. In some cases it may make more sense to follow a thematic approach and have students integrate their reflections along with other homework and assignments recorded in their notebooks.

Establish with students the role this strategy will play in monitoring their learning. Learning Logs can have a number of applications in the classroom (Santa & Havens, 1991). This strategy can be especially useful as an introductory exercise to initiate class or cooperative-group discussions. Learning Logs provide students with the opportunity to explore their thinking before being called on to communicate their ideas to others. Other applications include

- Reflecting on a unit of study to prepare for exams

- Predicting results of experiments or situations

- Expressing personal opinions related to what is being studied

- Explaining why something happened

- Summarizing understandings of a previous lesson

- Clarifying points of confusion and raising questions about material that is not yet clearly understood

- Recording observations, such as during a science experiment or the viewing of a video

- Comparing how ideas have changed after learning, or how misconceptions have been corrected

2 Highlight the importance of Learning Logs in the classroom because they tend to be most effective if students use them frequently—two or three times a week is ideal. Students may be given 2 to 10 minutes to record entries. Establish that Learning Logs are informal writing—the recording of reflections—not polished, edited writing, and that the focus is more on thinking and less on writing form. Note that entries will be collected periodically, read, and perhaps responded to by the teacher, thus creating a written dialogue between teacher and students.

3 Use Learning Logs as an integral part of the routine for learning in your classroom. You might have students write an entry to prepare for learning new material. For example, before a group of fifth graders reads a science passage on glaciers, ask them to write about some of the things they already know about this topic, such as in the following example:

> Glaciers are made of ice. I know we had them in Canada, because of a camping trip our family took. We hiked along hills the glacier made. All these glaciers must have melted, but I don't know why.

Reflective writing is also appropriate after students have read a selection; for example, the following is an entry by a ninth grader reading a U.S. history passage on the Progressive Era:

> I was especially upset that the Progressives were doing these reforms and they were ignoring African Americans. I agree that they did a lot of good things like the child labor laws, but they mostly left racism alone. I didn't know that the NAACP was started then, but I can see that the NAACP were the Progressives who wanted to fight racism.

Admit and Exit Slips

Admit and Exit Slips is an additional Quick Write strategy that encourages summarizing and personal reflection. Students jot down thoughts, questions, confusions, or key ideas on index cards or small slips of paper, which are collected as they enter the room at the beginning of class, or as they leave at the end of a period. Using this strategy involves the following steps:

1 Admit Slips can be assigned as a homework component, which students need to hand the teacher when they arrive in class (the slip acts as a ticket to enter the room). Exit Slips are perfect for the last few minutes of class to ask students to engage in some synthesizing when ideas are still fresh (this time the slip serves as a ticket to leave the room). Students might be provided with a variety of prompts that encourage revisiting their learning:

- Write one significant thing you learned today on the front of the card and one question you have about the material on the back.
- If you shared one thing you learned in our class today, what would it be and why does it strike you as that important?
- Write one: "I didn't know that..." on the card and briefly describe what it is.
- Write one thing in particular about today' reading or lesson that you think might be confusing to a lot of people (even yourself) and comment on what might make it confusing.
- Select a quote from your reading that you feel is worthy of some discussion and, on the back of the card, briefly mention why.

2 Admit and Exit Slips also provide the teacher with feedback on points needing further clarification or discussion. The teacher can read from selected cards to start a class period and refocus the previous day's learning. At times you may wish to have the slips be anonymous, to encourage honest responses to confusions or questions that remain, and at other times you may decide to have the students include their names on their slips.

Advantages

- Students are encouraged to reflect on their learning and they receive practice in using writing to internalize what they are studying.
- Students come to realize that learning does not happen all in one step, but that they need to return several times to new material to continue to explore it.
- Students receive regular prompts to express their learning in their own words.
- Students receive continued practice in reducing what they are learning to meaningful summaries, which emphasize key ideas rather than merely an accumulation of information.
- Teachers are provided with direct feedback and insight on how their students are understanding their curriculum and what difficulties are being encountered.

References

Findley, R. (1981). In the path of destruction. *National Geographic, 159*(1), 35–49.

Fulwiler, T. (1980). Journals across the disciplines. *The English Journal, 69*(9), 14–19.

Rief, L. (1998). *Vision & voice: Expanding the literacy spectrum.* Portsmouth, NH: Heinemann.

Santa, C.M., & Havens, L.T. (1991). Learning through writing. In C.M. Santa & D.E. Alvermann (Eds.), *Science learning: Processes and applications* (pp. 122–133). Newark, DE: International Reading Association.

RAFT
(Role/Audience/Format/Topic)

Who do you imagine yourself to be as you read? As you drift through a novel, F. Scott Fitzgerald's *The Great Gatsby*, for example, who are you? Do you identify with the tragic Jay Gatsby? Or the unhappy Daisy? Maybe Tom, the aggrieved but inadequate husband? Or the narrator, Nick Carraway, observing the unfolding story as an increasingly involved outsider? Or perhaps Daisy's friend, Jordan Baker? As you become engaged in the story and emotionally attached to the characters, you splice yourself into the action. You indulge yourself in the delicious experience of living other people's lives, vicariously, through print.

The ability to interject ourselves into our reading deepens our comprehension and broadens our learning as we begin to develop empathy for the situations of others and perceive perspectives that are not necessarily our own. Encouraging students to adopt this mental role-playing frame of mind can help them improve their reading of classroom materials and provide focus to writing assignments.

We know, in particular, that writing is an effective way to help students synthesize their understandings. But often teachers are frustrated with the quality of writing completed by students—writing that is too brief, lacking in detail, poorly organized, bereft of imagination, and carelessly thrown together. Students tend to view writing as a laborious task in which they have no personal investment. As a result, the purpose of using writing as a tool for learning is sometimes defeated.

The RAFT strategy (Santa, 1988; Santa, Havens, & Valdes, 2004) addresses these teacher concerns with student writing. A RAFT activity infuses a writing assignment with imagination, creativity, and motivation. The strategy involves writing from a viewpoint other than that of a student, to an audience other than the teacher, and in a form other than a standard assignment or written answers to questions.

Using the Strategy

RAFT is an acronym for

R—Role of the writer ("Who are you?")

A—Audience for the writer ("To whom are you writing?")

F—Format of the writing ("What form will your writing assume?")

T—Topic to be addressed in the writing ("What are you writing about?")

Using this strategy involves the following steps:

1 Analyze the important ideas or information that you want students to learn from a story, a textbook passage, or other classroom material. Consider how a writing assignment will help to consolidate this learning. How might writing help students remember the stages of the digestive system? Or understand the frustrations of North American colonists? Or empathize with the emotions of a character in a story? This establishes the topic for the writing.

2 Brainstorm possible roles students could assume in their writing (see the Examples of RAFT Assignments). For example, students studying the colonial period in a U.S. history class could assume the role of a colonist upset with the lack of self-government. Students reading Roald Dahl's book *James and the Giant Peach* in a language arts class could assume the role of James, who needs to tell somebody about how his malevolent aunts are treating him. Students in a science class could personify a french fry, describing the physical changes experienced during each stage of the digestive process.

Decide who the audience will be for this communication and determine the format for the writing. For example, the colonist could be writing in the form of a petition intended for other outraged colonists. James could be writing a letter to state adoption authorities complaining of his ill treatment. The french fry could be writing in the format of a travel journal, to

Strategy Index
Instructional Focus
Frontloading Learning
Guiding Comprehension
Consolidating Understanding
Text Frames
Cause/Effect
Concept/Definition
Problem/Solution
Compare/Contrast
Proposition/Support
Goal/Action/Outcome
Comprehension Processess
Making Connections
Generating Questions
Creating Mental Images
Making Inferences
Determining Importance
Synthesizing

Examples of RAFT Assignments

Role	Audience	Format	Topic
Newspaper reporter	Readers in the 1870s	Obituary	Qualities of Crazy Horse
Lawyer	U.S. Supreme Court	Appeal speech	Dred Scott Decision
Abraham Lincoln	Dear Abby	Advice column	How to deal with slavery
Oprah	Television public	Talk show	Women's suffrage in early 20th century
Frontier woman	Self	Diary	Hardships in 1700s America
Constituent	U.S. senator	Letter	Need for civil rights legislation in 1950s
Public relations agent	Public	News release	Coal being formed
Chemist	Chemical company	Instructions	Dangerous combinations to avoid
Astronaut	Future travelers	Travel guide	Surface of Jupiter
Plant	Sun	Thank-you note	Sun's role in plant's growth
Scientist	General public	Memo	Need to correct misconception
Square root	Whole number	Love letter	Explain relationship
Repeating decimal	Set of rational numbers	Petition	Prove you belong to this set
Chef	Other chefs	Recipe	Revolution
Tour guide	Museum visitors	Script	Understanding Impressionism
Doctor's association	Future parents	Web page	Proper prenatal nutrition
Advertiser	TV audience	Public service announcement	Fruits & vegetables in diet
Lungs	Cigarettes	Complaint	Effects of smoking
Huck Finn	Jim	Telephone conversation	What I learned on the raft
Joseph Stalin	George Orwell	Book review	Reactions to *Animal Farm*
Comma	Ninth-grade students	Job description	Use in sentences
Trout	Environmental Protection Agency	E-mail	Global warming effects on lake
Mozart	Prospective employer	Résumé	Qualifications as a composer

be read by other french fries headed toward the digestive system.

3 After students complete the reading assignment, write RAFT on the chalkboard and list the role, audience, format, and topic for their writing. You can assign all students the same role for the writing, or offer several different roles from which students can choose. For instance, after reading a passage on soil erosion, students could write from the perspective of a farmer, a fish in a nearby stream, a corn plant, or a worm in the topsoil. Students could be given the choice of several characters from a story to represent their role for writing.

Before students begin writing the RAFT, engage them in developing a deeper understanding of their roles (Shearer, 1998). Some students will be confused and uncertain about how they should react to the topic in their role. Place students with the same role in a cooperative group, and have them brainstorm critical elements of that role. Suggest the following questions for the group to consider:

- What perspective would I, in my role, have on the assigned topic?
- Why do I care about this particular topic?
- Where would I look to find out more about this perspective?
- What information (or parts of the story) do I need to examine carefully for my role?

- What should I be particularly concerned about within this topic?
- What emotions might I be feeling as I think about this topic?
- Is this a role that might lead me to be in favor of or against something related to this topic?
- Could a person in my role have a choice of several viewpoints on this topic? Which viewpoint might appeal to me the most?
- How can I give my role some personality?
- How can I ensure that what I say about the topic in my role is accurate?

To provide a visual framework for this brainstorming phase, provide each student with a three-column chart, which will prompt them to write down pertinent thoughts as they probe their role in their groups (see the Appendix for a reproducible version of the Role Definition Chart). The chart can serve as a guide for their writing. For example, students in a music performance class can use the chart to brainstorm the role "12 Bar Blues," in order to create a Facebook website page for this "individual" (see the RAFT Role Definition Chart on 12 Bar Blues). The chart guides them into exploring more deeply their knowledge of this form of music.

4 Make available sample authentic examples for a specific RAFT project for students to consult as they plan their writing. For example, if they are

RAFT Role Definition Chart on 12 Bar Blues

Personality—Who am I and what are some aspects of my character?	Attitude—What are my feelings, beliefs, ideas, concerns?	Information—What do I know that I need to share in my writing?
I am a type of music, a specific form of "the blues"	Sometimes I'm really down in the dumps	Got started in the South and moved all over the world
Jazz is my first cousin	My music helps me get by	Has African American roots
I like to take my time; I can be pretty laid back	There's comfort and security in my repetition	Basic pattern can be found in wide range of music, including rock
I can also be spontaneous sometimes	My predictability makes it possible to risk improvising	Examples include some Delta Blues and Chicago Blues
I repeat myself a lot	I'm flattered that so many writers use me in their music	Is a repeating chord progression
(I need to tell people how I'm feeling)	I'm proud to be an American	(Uses only 3 chords: I, IV, V)
I'm very predictable		Blue Notes: lower 3rd, 5th, & 7th of the scale

creating a television script, supply examples to help them visualize what to include in their versions. By consulting actual examples, students can rely on a measure of reality to give them ideas for how to proceed with their personal RAFTs. As students become comfortable with writing in the guise of various roles, they eventually can be expected to define their own RAFT assignments. Students can devise an appropriate role for a unit of study, designate a relevant audience, and consider possible formats for communicating their thoughts.

Advantages

- Students offer more thoughtful and often more extensive written responses as they demonstrate their learning.

- Students are actively involved in processing information rather than merely writing out answers to questions.

- Students are given a clear structure for their writing—they know what point of view to assume and they are provided with an organizational scheme. Furthermore, the purpose of the writing is outlined clearly.

- Students are more motivated to undertake a writing assignment because the task involves them personally and allows for more creative responses to learning the material.

- Students are encouraged to examine material from perspectives other than their own and to gain insights on concepts and ideas that may not have occurred to them during the initial reading of an assignment.

- RAFT is a strategy adaptable to all content areas, including science, social studies, and math.

References

Santa, C.M. (1988). *Content reading including study systems.* Dubuque, IA: Kendall/Hunt.

Santa, C., Havens, L.T., & Valdes, B.J. (2004). *Project CRISS: Creating independence through student-owned strategies.* Dubuque, IA: Kendall/Hunt.

Shearer, B. (1998, February). *Student directed and focused inquiry.* Paper presented at the Wisconsin State Reading Association Conference, Milwaukee.

Role-Playing as Readers

"What do you think about...?" We live in an age when people's points of view are being solicited almost continuously. Public opinion polls, radio call-in shows, newspaper sound-off columns, man-in-the-street interviews, telephone surveys, blogs—all are attempts to find out what we think.

Role-Playing strategies capitalize on this interest in examining the perspectives of others. Students read a selection—not as themselves—but while imagining they were a character involved in the events being described. The process of reading becomes more personalized as students bring insights related to a role into their understanding of the text.

Using the Strategies

Role-Playing as Readers can be constructed for a wide variety of material, including literature, social studies, and science selections. Two variations of this strategy are included: Point-of-View Study Guides and Readers Theatre.

Point-of-View Study Guides

The Point-of-View Study Guide (Wood, 1988) follows an interview format and encourages students to respond in their own words to the ideas and information in the reading. Using this strategy involves the following steps:

1 Identify an appropriate role or character from a selection that students have already read. Model the strategy for students by assuming this role yourself. Ask students to interview you by having them generate meaningful questions that could be answered by information in the text. For example, following the reading of a textbook passage about explorers in the Americas, you could be interviewed as an Aztec farmer of that time. Or following a selection on endangered species, you could be interviewed as a whale. Slip into a character during your modeling, showing how your reading of the material is affected by the perspective you bring. Demonstrate that your attitudes might diverge from the point of view of the author in the textbook or novel. Students will notice that you are connected to the material more emotionally than they are, because you are talking about things that affect you and that you really care about.

2 Choose a role or character from a new selection. Create a series of interview questions that will help students focus on the important elements of the text. Distribute these questions as the study guide for the selection. For example, students reading the novel *Bridge to Terabithia* by Katherine Paterson could be asked to comment on events at the end of the book from the perspective of Leslie, the girl who had died. In another example, students reading a history passage on immigration could be asked to read from the perspective of a specific immigrant (see the Point-of-View Study Guide for Social Studies example). Students reading a biology selection on roots could answer interview questions from the perspective of a taproot (see the Point-of-View Study Guide for Science example).

3 As students read, have them look for information that will enable them to respond to interview questions. Interview responses should be written in the first person and should elaborate on material from the reading. The responses should read as dialogue, not as typical answers to questions in the text. For example, the following is a student response to a question asked of an Italian immigrant regarding the difficulties of life in the United States:

> We have not been accepted by many Americans. We have encountered prejudice because of our different languages and customs. We also have had to work in jobs with long hours and low wages, and some of us have experienced acts of violence. Some of us are accused of being anarchists or socialists, and are treated as if we are a threat to the government.

Strategy Index
Instructional Focus
Frontloading Learning
Guiding Comprehension
Consolidating Understanding
Text Frames
Cause/Effect
Concept/Definition
Problem/Solution
Compare/Contrast
Proposition/Support
Goal/Action/Outcome
Comprehension Processess
Making Connections
Generating Questions
Creating Mental Images
Making Inferences
Determining Importance
Synthesizing

Point-of-View Study Guide for Social Studies

Chapter 5: The Age of Industry

You are about to be interviewed as if you were a person living in the United States in the latter half of the 1800s. Respond to the following interview questions as if you were an Italian immigrant.

1. During what time period did most of your fellow Italian immigrants come to the United States?

2. What made you decide to leave Italy?

3. When you landed in New York, you met immigrants from many other countries. What countries were they from and what were some of their reasons for coming to the United States?

4. What types of employment did you have to choose from when you came to the United States?

5. Why do some immigrants object to the process of assimilation?

6. Have you encountered any difficulties being an immigrant in the United States? What kinds of problems have you and your fellow immigrants experienced?

7. As an immigrant, what are your feelings toward legislation to limit immigration? Would you support or oppose such legislation?

Source: Buehl, D. (1995). *Classroom strategies for interactive learning* (p. 71). Madison: Wisconsin State Reading Association.

Point-of-View Study Guide for Science

Chapter 23: Roots and Stems

You are about to be interviewed as if you were a part of a plant. Respond to the following questions as if you were a taproot.

1. What plant are you a taproot for? What other plants have taproots?

2. We notice that some plants have fibrous root systems. How are you different from these roots?

3. Not to get personal, but all you roots seem rather hairy. Why do you roots have those hairy growths?

4. Could you take a couple of moments and describe how you grow?

5. Roots must need to be tough for growing through the soil. What enables you to push through the soil?

Source: Buehl, D. (1995). *Classroom strategies for interactive learning* (p. 72). Madison: Wisconsin State Reading Association.

An even more intriguing use of Point-of-View Guides involves assigning groups of students different characters with different sets of questions relevant to each role. For example, in addition to being interviewed as an Italian immigrant, students might assume the role of a native-born factory worker, an African American sharecropper, a U.S. Senator, or a New York City social activist. After reading, have each group conduct their interview for the entire class. The multiplicity of viewpoints will significantly enhance students' understanding of and insight into the material.

4 As the students become familiar with Point-of-View Guides, have them create their own interview questions. Assign a role, and have students work in pairs. Have one student read the selection as the character, and have their partner read as the interviewer. The interviewer's task is to formulate questions to be posed to the character. Following the reading, have students participate in a mock interview, or have them answer the questions as a writing exercise.

Readers Theatre

Reformatting a text segment into a Readers Theatre script is another option for engaging students in role-playing as readers. Using this strategy involves the following steps:

1 Preview materials to identify passages that could be modified for Readers Theatre with little editing. Create a script for a group of four or five students who can take turns reading lines. If necessary, rework any material to fit the Readers Theatre format and change the language from third person to first person (e.g., *he* and *they* become *I* and *we*). Therefore, a descriptive passage becomes a personal narrative when delivered by the Readers Theatre group. For example, a United States history textbook passage describing a pivotal event during the Progressive Era provides an excellent framework for a quick reworking into a readers script (see the Readers Theatre for Social Studies example).

3 Students read their parts as if they were assuming these roles. Readers Theatre read-alouds need not be elaborate productions. However, allow students sufficient time to review their lines so that they can be read with polish for the entire class.

4 Students can be asked to work with partners to create their own Readers Theatre excerpts from a classroom text.

Readers Theatre for Social Studies

The Triangle Fire

(Readers A & B—News reporters; Readers C & D—Immigrant workers; Reader E—Rose Schneiderman)

A: A gruesome disaster in New York in 1911 galvanized Progressives to fight for safety in the workplace.

B: About 500 young women,

A: most of them young Jewish or Italian immigrant women,

B: worked for New York City's Triangle Shirtwaist Company, a high-rise factory that made women's blouses.

A: One Saturday, just as these young workers were ending their six-day workweek

C: A fire erupted, probably from a discarded match.

D: Within moments the eighth floor was ablaze, and the fire quickly spread to two other floors.

C: Escape was nearly impossible.

D: Many doors were locked to prevent theft.

C: The flimsy fire escape broke under the weight of us panic-stricken people

D: Sending us victims tumbling to our deaths.

C: With flames at our backs, dozens of us workers leaped from the windows.

D: More than 140 of us men and women died in the Triangle Shirtwaist Company fire.

A: Union organizer Rose Schneiderman commented on the senseless tragedy.

E: This is not the only time girls have been burned alive in the city. Each week I must learn of the untimely death of one of my sister workers. Every year thousands of us are maimed. The lives of men and women are so cheap and property is so sacred. There are so many of us for one job it matters little if 143 of us are burned to death.

B: The Triangle Shirtwaist fire was a turning point for reform.

A: With the efforts of Schneiderman and others

B: New York State passed the toughest fire-safety laws in the country.

Source: Ayers, E., Schulzinger, R., de la Teja, J., & White, D. (2007). *The American anthem*. Austin, TX: Holt, Rinehart and Winston.

Advantages

- Students use their imaginations to become more personally engaged in their reading, which helps bring material to life.

- Students gain practice in translating the language of text into their own words and are involved in a more in-depth synthesis of the material.

- Students are encouraged to draw from their own experiences to understand events in text and are asked to elaborate on information in a meaningful way.

- Students develop sensitivity to different perspectives of events and ideas.

- Role-Playing as Readers can be used effectively with materials in all content areas and is especially effective with social studies and literature.

References

Ayers, E., Schulzinger, R., de la Teja, J., & White, D. (2007). *The American anthem*. Austin, TX: Holt, Rinehart and Winston.

Buehl, D. (1995). *Classroom strategies for interactive learning*. Madison: Wisconsin State Reading Association.

Wood, K.D. (1988). Guiding students through informational text. *The Reading Teacher, 41*(9), 912–920.

Suggested Reading

Wood, K.D., Lapp, D., Flood, J., & Taylor, D.B. (2008). *Guiding readers through text: Strategy guides for new times* (2nd ed.). Newark, DE: International Reading Association.

Flynn, R.M. (2007). *Dramatizing the content with curriculum-based Readers Theatre, grades 6–12*. Newark, DE: International Reading Association.

Save the Last Word for Me

Think back on various point–counterpoint news programs that you have watched. Sometimes you witness a verbal free-for-all, with a news correspondent desperately mediating between two or more individuals who have diverging viewpoints they are eager to express. Each wants to capture air time to tell you, the public, what "it really means." And each wants the last word.

Wouldn't it be refreshing if your students also wanted the last word about what they are learning in class? Instead, usually only a handful of students venture thoughts about what they found interesting in class reading assignments. The rest of the class is often hard-pressed to verbalize what the reading really means to them.

For many students, *reading* translates to a quick, superficial trip through a text for the sole purpose of answering assigned questions. Unfortunately, these students often never achieve more than a cursory, literal idea of what they have read. Classroom discussions that encourage students to think about their reading tend to sputter as a result because students do not engage in reflective reading behavior.

Activities that stimulate students to reflect on what they read help to develop active and thoughtful readers. One effective strategy for developing readers who are thinkers is Save the Last Word for Me (Burke & Harste, described in Vaughan & Estes, 1986). Save the Last Word for Me prompts students to actively engage with the text and provides a cooperative group format for the subsequent class discussion.

Using the Strategy

Save the Last Word for Me is an excellent strategy to use with material that may elicit differing opinions or multiple interpretations. The strategy's discussion format is controlled by the students rather than directed by the teacher (see the Save the Last Word for Me Instructions). The small-group setting is more inviting to students who are reluctant to talk in front of an entire class, and in addition, gives them time to rehearse their comments by writing their thoughts on index cards. Using this strategy involves the following steps:

1 Assign a story, selection, or passage to be read. Have students locate five statements that they find interesting or would like to comment on—statements with which they agree or disagree or that contradict something they thought they knew. They could be statements that particularly surprised, excited, or intrigued them. When reading literature, students also could select revealing statements or actions made by characters in a story. Have students place a light pencil mark or affix a small sticky note next to their five chosen statements.

2 Distribute five index cards to each student, a card for each selected statement. Have students write one statement on the front side of a card. On the reverse side, have them write comments about the statement. For example, a student reading a selection about wolves as an endangered species might select the following statement for the front of a card: "Wolves are sometimes illegally shot by ranchers who fear that their livestock will be attacked." On the reverse side, the student may write the following comment: "Ranchers ought to have a right to protect their animals from dangerous predators like wolves."

3 Divide the class into small groups of four or five members. Display the Save the Last Word For Me instructions on an overhead transparency. All students in each group take turns sharing one of their five text statements with their group members. The first student reads a statement to the group and helps members locate the statement in the text. However, the student is not allowed to make any comments on the statement until all other members of the group give their reactions or responses. In effect, the student gets "the last word" in the discussion of the statement. For example, a student might share the following statement: "Wolves

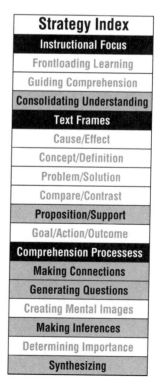

Strategy Index
Instructional Focus
Frontloading Learning
Guiding Comprehension
Consolidating Understanding
Text Frames
Cause/Effect
Concept/Definition
Problem/Solution
Compare/Contrast
Proposition/Support
Goal/Action/Outcome
Comprehension Processess
Making Connections
Generating Questions
Creating Mental Images
Making Inferences
Determining Importance
Synthesizing

Save the Last Word for Me Instructions

1. As you read, make a light check mark (✓) in pencil or place a sticky note next to five statements that you

   - agree or disagree with

   - already know something about

   - are wondering something about

   - found interesting

   - want to say something about

2. After you finish reading, write each statement on the front of a separate index card.

3. On the back of each card, write the comment you would like to share with your group about each statement.

4. When you meet in your group, take the following steps:

   - Select a group member to go first.

   - The selected member reads the statement from the front of one of his or her cards, but is *not* allowed to make any comment.

   - All other group member talk about the statement and make comments.

   - When everyone is done commenting, the member who wrote the statement makes comments.

   - A second group member is selected, and the process is repeated until all cards are shared.

naturally try to avoid contact with humans." But the student does not discuss her comments—that people's fears of wolves are exaggerated, especially because of the way wolves are treated in fairy tales—until other group members have commented about the statement. The attitude during this phase is: Here is a statement that interested me. You tell me what you think, and then I will tell you what I think.

4 Have students continue the process until everyone in the group has shared one statement and has provided the "last word" in the discussion. Begin another round with students sharing another of their cards.

Advantages

- Students are given an opportunity to adopt a more reflective stance as they read.

- Students are encouraged to talk about things in the reading that they personally connect to, and they all have an opportunity to participate in the class discussion on the reading.

- Students are able to hear classmates' views before offering their own, giving them the chance to adjust their comments and reflect on ideas before expressing them to others.

Reference

Vaughan, J.L., & Estes, T.H. (1986). *Reading and reasoning beyond the primary grades.* Boston: Allyn & Bacon.

Science Connection Overview

How does the world around us work? What is in a match head that makes it burst into flame when scratched? Where do rainbows come from? Why do cats purr? How does electricity move through wires? What does aspirin do to your body to make it feel better? Why does our hair turn gray as we become older? Questions—all part of the process of making sense of the world we live in and making sense of ourselves. We are born into this world observing the phenomena around us, and we spend a lifetime trying to understand it. Humans, as a species, seem determined to know.

This natural curiosity about the workings of the world should form a strong foundation for student learning in science classrooms. Yet for many students, science does not necessarily appear to be connected to their questions about "real-life" processes. Instead, science looms as a formidable body of difficult technical information that intimidates and frustrates. For these students, reading science materials is like reading a foreign language. Consider the following biology example:

> Humans as well as most animals are vertebrates. Vertebrates are chordates that have a vertebral column. The first vertebrates evolved from the class of jawless fishes known as agnathans. Agnathans today include the lampreys, whose skeleton is composed mostly of cartilage. Lampreys have a notochord, which functions as their major support column. The gills of these creatures are contained in pouches that branch out from the pharynx. Many lampreys live as external parasites and cause great damage to the host populations of fish.

Whew! Students reading science materials may encounter an avalanche of unfamiliar words that have precise meanings in the language of science. Many of these new terms are seen only rarely outside a science context. Students soon become bogged down in this detailed information and lose sight of possible relationships between the science in their books and their understandings of the world around them.

Using the Strategy

The Science Connection Overview (Buehl, 1992) is a frontloading strategy that guides students into making connections to their lives and experiences as they study topics in science. The strategy involves previewing a science chapter or article before reading to link the content with what students already know or have experienced. Before students become immersed in the details of the reading, they gain an overview of "the big picture" of a chapter and how it relates to the world around them. Using this strategy involves the following steps:

1 Introduce the exercise by discussing with students how science helps them understand aspects of their lives or world. Select several examples of science material and elicit from the class how each can be connected to their lives; for example, a passage on cold and warm fronts and the resulting rain might connect to student questions about why rain occurs when it does or why it is often colder after it rains. For a chapter on microorganisms that live in water, students might connect by reflecting on why it is unsafe to drink lake or river water. For an article on endangered plants and animals, students might connect to news stories about the Amazon jungle or dolphins captured in tuna nets.

2 Distribute a blank Science Connection Overview (see the Appendix for a reproducible version of the Science Connection Overview) to students and model its use on an overhead projector. Tell students to follow along as you skim a portion of a science text and think aloud about things mentioned in the text that you recognize or with which you are familiar. Intentionally ignore technical terms or information that seems unfamiliar. For example, modeling an overview of a biology chapter on fungi, you would pass over terms like *basidiomycota*, *multinucleate*, and *zygospore*. Instead you would focus

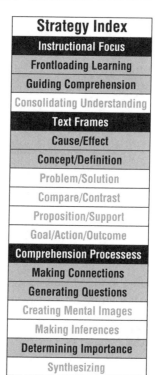

Strategy Index
Instructional Focus
Frontloading Learning
Guiding Comprehension
Consolidating Understanding
Text Frames
Cause/Effect
Concept/Definition
Problem/Solution
Compare/Contrast
Proposition/Support
Goal/Action/Outcome
Comprehension Processess
Making Connections
Generating Questions
Creating Mental Images
Making Inferences
Determining Importance
Synthesizing

Science Connection Overview for Fungi

What's familiar?

> What's the connection? Skim and survey the chapter for things that are familiar and that connect with your life or world. List them below:
> - mushrooms
> - mold on spoiled food
> - spores
> - yeasts
> - plant rusts
> - fungi on rotting plants
> - lichens
> - penicillin
> - Dutch Elm disease

What topics are covered?

> Read the summary. What topic areas seem to be the most important?
> - how they look or are structured
> - how they reproduce
> - how they feed and stay alive

What are you wondering?

> Questions of interest. What questions do you have about this material that may be answered in the chapter?
> - Why do mushrooms grow in damp places?
> - Why does food get moldy when it spoils?
> - Why do they put yeast in bread doughs?
> - Why are some mushrooms poisonous?
> - How can you tell which mushrooms are poisonous and which are safe?
> - What do fungi eat?
> - Does the medicine penicillin come from a fungus?

What will the author tell you?

> Chapter organization: What categories of information are provided in this chapter?
> - structure of fungi
> - nutrition
> - reproduction
> - variety of fungi: molds
>   imperfect
>   yeasts
>   mushrooms
>   lichens

Read and translate

> Use index cards for vocabulary.

Source: Buehl, D. (1992). The connection overview: A strategy for learning in science. *WSRA Journal, 36(2)*, 21–30.

on familiar terms, such as *mushrooms, bread mold, yeast,* and *Dutch Elm disease.*

3 Have students work with partners to survey the remainder of the chapter. First they complete the "What's Familiar" section of the Connection Overview. Emphasize that only familiar, nontechnical information

should be gleaned from their survey and skimming of the chapter. Encourage them to use the pictures and graphics in the chapter to assist them in making connections. For example, students doing an overview of the chapter on fungi would likely discover that even though the text contains a heavy load of terminology, there is much that connects to their lives and experiences (see the Science Connection Overview for Fungi example). Most students would recognize many of the mushrooms, lichens, and molds featured in chapter photographs. They can begin to weave this chapter's materials into their life's experiences. In addition, some textbook authors include features that are intended to help students make personal connections to the material. Make sure students notice where these features are placed in a chapter.

4 If the chapter has a summary, direct students to read it as the next phase of the overview. Ask them to identify key topics that seem to be the focus of the chapter. Although summaries are typically placed at the end of a chapter, students should develop the habit of consulting this study feature *before* becoming immersed in the new information. For example, the summary of the fungi chapter indicates that three general areas appear to be addressed: how fungi are structured, how they reproduce, and how they feed. These items are entered in the "What topics are covered?" section of the overview.

5 Ask students to generate personal questions about the material. Working with partners, encourage them to think about what they know in this topic area and what they might be wondering. These are entered in the "What are you wondering?" section. Initially, you

will need to model the kinds of questions that people normally have about science—questions typically not featured in textbooks, which instead tend to emphasize factual details. Pose more general questions about the material that naturally inquisitive people might raise. For example, questions generated about fungi might be, Why do mushrooms grow where they do? Why are some mushrooms poisonous? Why do they put yeast in bread? Why does food get moldy? Are there spores in the air in this room? What happens when you breathe them in? How do we get medicine from fungi?

6 Will students receive answers to their questions in the reading? Have students complete the "What will the author tell you?" portion of the Science Connection Overview by outlining the chapter organization. Categories on information are usually signaled by headings or section titles. For example, the fungi chapter was organized into four sections: structure, nutrition, reproduction, and variety. Students now have taken an aggressive and directive survey of the chapter. They have focused on making connections with the material rather than allowing themselves to become overwhelmed by a mass of challenging new vocabulary.

7 Ask students to read the first section of the chapter, having their Connection Overview available to consult as they encounter technical terminology

---

Card for Science Vocabulary

Front
of
card

rhizoid
(rye bread)

Back
of
Card

Little fibers that grow out of a mold spore.

They are like roots and they hook the mold onto the bread or other food.

Source: Buehl, D. (1995). *Classroom strategies for interactive learning* (p. 95). Madison: Wisconsin State Reading Association.

and detailed information. As students read, have them use index cards (or a vocabulary section of their notebooks) to translate technical science terms (see the Card for Science Vocabulary example). Science terms (referred to as Tier 3 words on page 175 in the Student-Friendly Vocabulary Explanations strategy) usually are featured in easily identifiable ways within the text. Students are adept at locating the definitions and writing them down as answers to questions; however, they may not really understand what the terms mean. Encourage students to treat science vocabulary as they would foreign language vocabulary: by translating it into English. Have students use the index cards for the same purpose—to translate science terms into more understandable language.

8 Integrating memory clues on index cards is an especially effective technique for helping students become conversant with the new vocabulary (Levin, 1983). A memory clue helps students associate the word with its meaning or explanation (see the Vocabulary Overview Guide beginning on page 183). For example, the memory clue *rye bread* for the term *rhizoid* may trigger remembering that rhizoids are the little hooks that attach mold to what it's growing on. The clue is suggested by the pronunciation of the word, which triggers a connection between rhizoids and their later appearance on a slice of rye bread. Encourage students to use their imaginations when developing these memory clues for different vocabulary.

Advantages

- Students make meaningful connections with science texts before they are asked to comprehend unfamiliar information.

- Students see how the information fits together and they build a mental construct for making sense of what they read.

- Students are provided with a structure for translating academic vocabulary into meaningful understandings.

References

Buehl, D. (1995). *Classroom strategies for interactive learning.* Madison: Wisconsin State Reading Association.

Buehl, D. (1992). The connection overview: A strategy for learning in science. *WSRA Journal, 36*(2), 21–30.

Levin, J. (1983). Pictorial strategies for school learning: Practical illustrations. In M. Pressley & J.R. Levin (Eds.), *Cognitive strategy research: Educational applications* (pp. 213–237). New York: Springer-Verlag.

Self-Questioning Taxonomy

*G*rover *Cleveland*. The answer is, *Grover Cleveland*. But what is the question? Students have become well conditioned to answering questions, especially those that feature expected responses like *Grover Cleveland*. The questions may vary: Who was the only U.S. President whose two terms in office were not consecutive? or Who was the only Democrat to serve as President in the over 50 years between the American Civil War and World War I? or even Who was one of the pudgiest fellows to occupy the highest office in the United States?

Students know how such questions "work." Often, they merely need to undertake minimal surface sampling of a text in order to derive an acceptable answer. Questions like these are rarely much of a challenge. Students can answer them rather quickly, and even struggling readers can frequently get through them with little assistance. But literal, fact-level questions—like the ones outlined above—have little to do with the comprehension of written texts. Researchers have long cautioned us that these questions can in many cases be answered even if a student is confused about a text's meaning. In other words, questions asked ostensibly to help students "get the facts" rarely help students to construct an understanding of an author's message. Students can find answers, but they miss the important questions—the questions they should pose to themselves to guide their reading and learning.

Instead of searching for answers, students need to be able to find the questions. The answer, in fact, is not *Grover Cleveland*. *Grover Cleveland* is the *question*. Grover Cleveland? Why Grover Cleveland? What's the significance of his Presidency? What is it about Grover Cleveland that is important to know? In what ways did his actions change the United States? How did Cleveland's solutions to the country's problems compare with those of other Presidents? What are we to conclude about Cleveland—is he worthy of extended study or should he be relegated to a cursory glance before we move on to more compelling topics?

Of course, the questions in the previous paragraph sound very much like the questions history teachers ask themselves as they grapple with setting priorities for instructional emphasis. Okay, the textbook has a section on Cleveland. Do the students need to read it? And for what purpose? Why is it truly worth their time as learners to zero in on this President? These are excellent questions, too good to be asked solely by teachers. Students also need to be asking *themselves* such questions, and attempting to answer them.

Using the Strategies

Most educators are well familiar with Bloom's Taxonomy of Educational Objectives, which argued that teachers need to prompt more complex thinking from their students (Bloom, Englehart, Furst, Hill, & Krathwohl, 1956). Often the taxonomy is employed to help teachers ask better and deeper questions, but the other side of this dynamic is for teachers to model self-questioning strategies so that students themselves begin to generate increasingly more sophisticated questions as they engage with written texts. Bloom's Taxonomy, updated by Anderson and Krathwohl in 2001, presents an excellent framework for guiding comprehension instruction as students read and learn during classroom lessons (see Bloom's Taxonomy, Revised). To illustrate a more extended application of this strategy, the Self-Questioning Taxonomy for Literary Fiction is presented to guide comprehension instruction when working with fiction texts specifically.

Using this strategy involves the following steps:

1 Walk students through the different levels of thinking in the revised taxonomy. Notice that the revised version emphasizes strong verbs as cues for thinking: *remembering, understanding, applying, analyzing, evaluating,* and *creating*. Model as a think-aloud how these different levels of thinking influence your comprehension. For example, the following think-aloud based on an article on the Great Wall of China demonstrates these different levels of thinking:

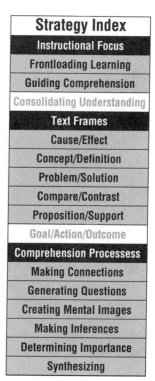

Strategy Index

Instructional Focus

Frontloading Learning

Guiding Comprehension

Consolidating Understanding

Text Frames

Cause/Effect

Concept/Definition

Problem/Solution

Compare/Contrast

Proposition/Support

Goal/Action/Outcome

Comprehension Processes

Making Connections

Generating Questions

Creating Mental Images

Making Inferences

Determining Importance

Synthesizing

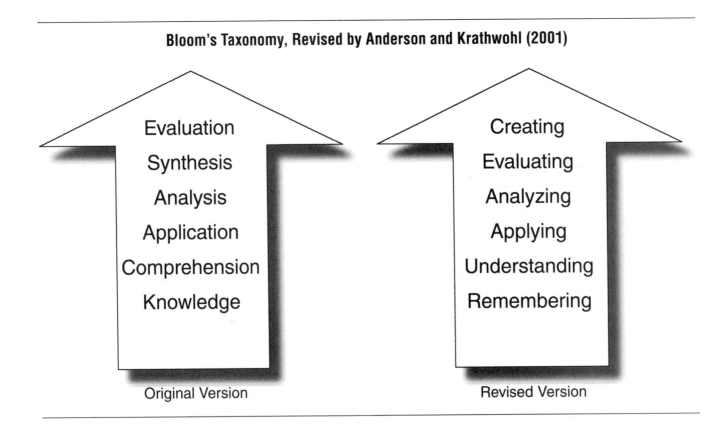

Bloom's Taxonomy, Revised by Anderson and Krathwohl (2001)

Original Version

Evaluation
Synthesis
Analysis
Application
Comprehension
Knowledge

Revised Version

Creating
Evaluating
Analyzing
Applying
Understanding
Remembering

Hmmm. What does this author want me to understand about the Great Wall? Large sections are being eroded by sandstorms. Why does the author argue this is happening? Let's see…farming practices that have drained underwater reservoirs have led to ecological change, leading to sandstorms, which cause the wall to crumble. What crucial information should I remember? Predictions are that parts of the wall will disappear in only 20 years. How can I use this knowledge? Perhaps we need to be more careful in how we use natural resources, or we may suffer similar climate changes that can destroy features that have lasted for centuries? Does this information seem reliable? The author supports these conclusions with lots of convincing data and quotes an esteemed museum director. How has my understanding changed? I realize that even long-standing treasures like the Great Wall can quickly fall victim to climatic change.

2 Introduce the Taxonomy of Self-Questioning Chart (Buehl, 2007, September). Relate each level of thinking to a statement a reader can make to assess comprehension of a text (see the Taxonomy of Self-Questioning Chart). Emphasize that a deep comprehension—rather than surface-level comprehension—will include understanding at all six of these levels. For example, *evaluating* asks a reader to view a text through a critical lens: "I can critically examine this author's message." Each statement reflects an expectation of a level of thinking that a reader should factor in to construct an in-depth comprehension of

a text. In addition, walk students through how the comprehension strategies of proficient readers are also cued by the thinking at each level.

3 Each statement of the taxonomy is aligned with a focus question. Emphasize that proficient readers constantly check their comprehension through self-questioning. For example, when readers ask themselves, "How has the author's perspective influenced what he or she tells me?" they are *evaluating* a message. These focus questions should be modeled extensively with a variety of materials so that they become a "habit of mind" for students as readers. Developing a wall poster or bookmarks of the Taxonomy of Self-Questioning Chart can serve as a daily reminder of this array of questions to guide comprehension.

4 As students become practiced with eliciting focusing questions on their own, they can be provided with additional examples. *Analyzing* could also include questions like, How does the author support these ideas? Companion questions for *Evaluating* might be, Does the author adequately support the viewpoints or conclusions? Is the argument convincing? Did the author omit or overlook other possible arguments or evidence?

Self-Questioning for Literary Fiction

Our students encounter stories as an ongoing facet of their education. From their earliest years in school, as

Taxonomy of Self-Questioning Chart

Level of thinking	Comprehension self-assessment	Focusing question	Comprehension process
Creating	I have created new knowledge.	How has this author changed what I understand?	Synthesizing
Evaluating	I can critically examine this author's message.	How has the author's perspective influenced what he or she tells me?	Inferring
Analyzing	I can take my understanding to a deeper level.	How is this similar to (or different from) other material I've read?	Making connections Determining importance
Applying	I can use my understanding in some meaningful way.	How can I connect what this author is telling me to understand something better?	Making connections Inferring
Understanding	I can understand what the author is telling me.	What does this author want me to understand?	Determining importance Inferring Creating visual/sensory images
Remembering	I can recall specific details, information, and ideas from this text.	What do I need to remember to make sense of this text?	Determining importance

Source: Buehl, D. (2007, September). Modeling self-questioning on Bloom's Taxonomy. *OnWEAC*. Retrieved from www.weac.org/News/2007-08/sept07/readingroom.htm

beginning readers, through high school and beyond, students transition into reading longer and more complex works of literature. And while they are often held accountable for relating what exactly transpired in a story, many times students scratch their heads and think to themselves, Why are you telling me this? What are we to make of this story? What does this story mean to its author? And what might this story mean to us? What's the point of this story? Providing students with tools that help them use questions such as these to "crack open" literary prose is essential for improving comprehension of this genre of written text. The Self-Questioning Taxonomy for Literary Fiction (Buehl, 2007, November) guides students into building meaningful interpretations of fictional works. Using this strategy involves the following steps:

1 Begin by differentiating between stories that are narrative nonfiction and stories that are literary fiction. Narrative nonfiction—such as biographies, autobiographies, and historical recountings—share many elements with literary fiction: characters, actions, a flow of events. However, narrative nonfiction generally presents a straightforward storyline, perhaps interspersed with author commentary, interpretation, and conclusions. Literary fiction, in contrast, may feature storylines that are less open and obvious. Authors of literary fiction tend to rely on the reader to make interpretations and draw conclusions, to construct a meaning of their message that is more implicit rather than explicitly stated.

A key difference, then, is author intent. Authors of narrative nonfiction usually attempt to directly tell what happened in a clearly outlined narration, often in order to support an interpretation of what these events mean to them. Authors of literary fiction create stories from their imagination that can help readers reflect upon and understand their lives in some way. But authors of literary fiction typically do not reveal everything; readers may need to infer some of what is going on in the story. As a result, readers are expected to develop their own interpretations of what a story might mean, both to an author and especially to themselves.

Taxonomy Self-Questioning Chart for Literary Fiction

Level of thinking	Comprehension self-assessment	Focusing questions
Creating	I have developed an interpretation of what this story means.	Why is the author telling me this story? What theme or idea might the author be exploring in this story? What does this story mean to me?
Evaluating	I can critically examine this author's story.	Who is the author and how has author perspective influenced the telling of this story? What does the author's choice of words indicate about what the author might be thinking? What emotions is the author eliciting? Does the author have an "attitude," and if so, about what?
Analyzing	I can take my understanding to a deeper level.	What literary devices does the author use? What seems to be the purpose for using these literary devices?
Applying	I can use my understanding in some meaningful way.	How can I connect this story to my life and experiences? Why might the author have the characters say or do this? What point might the author be making about the characters' actions? Why might the author place the story in this setting?
Understanding	I can understand what the author is telling me.	How does the author have the characters interact with one another? How do the characters feel about one another? How do character feelings and interactions change? How does the author use conflict in this story? How does the author resolve this conflict?
Remembering	I can follow what happens in this story.	Who are the characters? Where does the story take place? What are the major events of the story? What is the sequence of these events? What event initiates the action of the story?

Source: Buehl, D. (2007, November). Questioning literary fiction. *OnWEAC*. Retrieved from www.weac.org/News/2007-08/nov07/reading room.htm

2 Introduce the focusing questions to be used for guiding the students' understanding of short stories, novels, and other works of fiction (see the Taxonomy of Self-Questioning for Literary Fiction). Comprehension of literary works begins with a series of questions readers ask to monitor if they have grasped the basic story grammar of a fictional work: characters, setting, and plot (see Story Mapping beginning on page 166).

Because authors of literary fiction may place demands on readers to infer some of the key elements of a story, initially students need to check whether they can follow what is occurring in the story. These focusing questions correspond to the level of *remembering*.

3 In addition, literary fiction will examine conflict of some dimension: within a character, between characters, and in conjunction with larger forces, such as a struggle against some aspect of nature. Understanding literary fiction necessitates tracking how these conflicts unfold and are resolved. Furthermore, the dynamics between characters are very important for readers to perceive: how the characters feel about one another and how they interact, and whether these feelings and interactions change in any way. These focusing questions are represented on the level of *understanding*.

4 As students clarify the basic story components, they transition to posing questions that help them interpret a fictional work as a form of communication. Focusing questions at the *applying* level let students delve into using their own life experiences to connect to the work and to speculate why an author chooses to have characters behave in a certain way. At the *analyzing* level, students are encouraged to notice the author's craft and to ponder how the author's use of literary devices—such as symbolism, an unreliable narrator, or figurative language—provides clues to what the story means to the author.

5 As students consider author "moves" in writing this story, students are cued to factor in author identity at the *evaluating* level. Who is telling them this story, and are there any indicators embedded in the text that suggest the perspective the author may be bringing to the work? In particular, sensitivity to emotional content

of the selection is important, especially if the author signals personal attitudes about topics and events mentioned in the story (see Reading With Attitude on page 64).

6 Finally, the culminating questions at the *creating* level emphasize the following: What is the point of this story? Why is the author telling me this? and What sense can I make of this story?

Advantages

- Students use focusing questions that cue them to use increasingly more complex thinking as they become more sophisticated readers and learners.

- Students expect to generate their own questions about literary works rather than respond to questions developed by someone else.

- Students' comprehension of a text factors in both their "read" of what an author is saying, as well as their personal interpretations of the meaning of a work.

References

Anderson, L.W., & Krathwohl, D.R. (Eds.). (2001). *A taxonomy for learning, teaching, and assessing: A revision of Bloom's Taxonomy of educational objectives*. New York: Longman.

Bloom, B., Englehart, M., Furst, E., Hill, W., & Krathwohl, D.R. (1956). *Taxonomy of educational objectives: The classification of educational goals. Handbook 1: Cognitive domain*. New York: Longman.

Buehl, D. (2007, September). Modeling self-questioning on Bloom's Taxonomy. *OnWEAC*. Retrieved from www.weac.org/News/2007-08/sept07/readingroom.htm

Buehl, D. (2007, November). Questioning literary fiction. *OnWEAC*. Retrieved from www.weac.org/News/2007-08/nov07/readingroom.htm

Story Impressions

Teen athletes...concussions...soccer, football, volleyball...susceptible...head injury...62,800...headaches, sleep disorders...high risk...learning disabilities.

Can you piece together the storyline implied by the preceding chain of keywords excerpted from a recent newspaper article? In all likelihood, by connecting these terms and drawing from what you already know about them, you can successfully infer the focus of this public health report.

As you probably surmised, the article raises cautions about concussions suffered by teen athletes, especially those participating in sports such as soccer, football, and volleyball. Adolescents are more susceptible to head injury from concussions, and a recent study estimated that 62,800 adolescents receive at least mild sports-related concussions each year. Symptoms of a concussion include headaches and sleep disorders, and students with learning disabilities are especially at risk for lingering brain injury resulting from concussions.

The chain of keywords that was provided prompted you to access what you know about sports concussions, and perhaps your curiosity was piqued about what the article said concerning dangers for teen athletes. You were able to form an impression of the text before you actually read it.

Using the Strategy

Story Impressions (McGinley & Denner, 1987) is a strategy that introduces significant terms and concepts to students before they encounter them in an assignment. Using this strategy involves the following steps:

1 Preview a text section or story, and identify a series of terms or two- to three-word phrases related to significant information or plot events. List the terms or phrases in the order students will encounter them while reading the text. Include both familiar words and terms that will reflect new learning for many students. This vocabulary listing cues students about the sequence of events or cause/effect relationships. Create a student worksheet with the terms arranged in a vertical column, connected by arrows to indicate order. For example, to prepare students for a science textbook passage on geysers, select a chain of terms and phrases that emphasize how volcanic activity leads to the heating of groundwater, which can sometimes create geysers (see the Story Impressions for Earth Science example).

2 Have students work with partners to brainstorm possible connections to the chain of clues on their worksheets. Using what they might know about some of the terms, encourage them to make predictions about both the content of the text and the meanings of unfamiliar keywords. In the earth science example, students can tap their knowledge of how volcanic activity generates heat and brainstorm possible connections to geysers. Some students will realize that heated water builds up pressure, which explains the phenomena of geysers such as Old Faithful in Yellowstone National Park, Wyoming, USA. Students may also need to form conjectures of the meanings of terms such as *igneous*, *fissure*, and *constricted* as they work on their predictions.

3 Have the partners draft their own impression of what a text might contain. First, inform them of the context for the terms—textbook passage, short story, newspaper article, or biographical excerpt. Ask students to create a possible version of this text, based on their knowledge of the key terms and their hunches about unknown items. In the box adjacent to the word chains, have students write a paragraph representing their prediction of the text in the appropriate style of the original material (textbook passage, story, newspaper article, web page, and so forth). All terms from the chain must be used in this paragraph, and students should integrate them with their writing in the order that they appear on the list. Have partners share

| **Strategy Index** |
| Instructional Focus |
| Frontloading Learning |
| Guiding Comprehension |
| Consolidating Understanding |
| Text Frames |
| Cause/Effect |
| Concept/Definition |
| Problem/Solution |
| Compare/Contrast |
| Proposition/Support |
| Goal/Action/Outcome |
| Comprehension Processess |
| Making Connections |
| Generating Questions |
| Creating Mental Images |
| Making Inferences |
| Determining Importance |
| Synthesizing |

their prediction summaries with the entire class. For example, a pair of earth science students might use their partial knowledge of terms to record the following impression:

> Volcanic activity pushes igneous rocks out of the center of the earth. The high temperature there heats groundwater to the boiling point, and it becomes steam. This steam has pent-up pressure which causes it to fissure and then change to hot springs. The hot springs come out of the ground in a constricted tube with an

eruption. This is called a geyser, like Old Faithful in Yellowstone.

4 Now that students have encountered key terms and concepts, activated relevant prior knowledge, and entertained predictions about the material, have them test their impressions by reading a text selection or story. As they read, have them check off the terms in the chain that they used accurately in their prediction summaries. To solidify new learning, have students write a second paragraph, again using all the terms

---

Story Impressions for Earth Science

Chain of events

Your version of what the textbook might say: Write a paragraph using the chain words in order.

volcanic activity
↓
igneous rock
↓
temperature
↓
groundwater
↓
boiling
↓
steam
↓
pent-up pressure
↓
fissure
↓
hot springs
↓
constricted tube
↓
eruption
↓
geyser
↓
Old Faithful

Source: Buehl, D. (2001). *Classroom strategies for interactive learning* (2nd ed., p. 133). Newark, DE: International Reading Association.

in the order they are represented in the chain, which summarizes what they've read and corrects their predictions. Our earth science students will discover that some of their original story impression was confirmed by the text but other parts now need to be revised to be accurate.

As another example, students studying early 20th-century U.S. history were given a story impression for a textbook section on Theodore Roosevelt's presidency. After reading the passage, students revisited key terms, added new terms deemed significant to the

time period, and developed a summary paragraph that demonstrated their understanding of the passage (see the Story Impressions for History example).

A Story Impressions chain makes an excellent prompt for essay exams. Students can be asked to synthesize their learning by linking together key information into a meaningful summary statement of the material from a unit of study. Furthermore, students use important new academic vocabulary in a meaningful discussion of their understandings, rather than

Story Impressions for History

Roosevelt Era

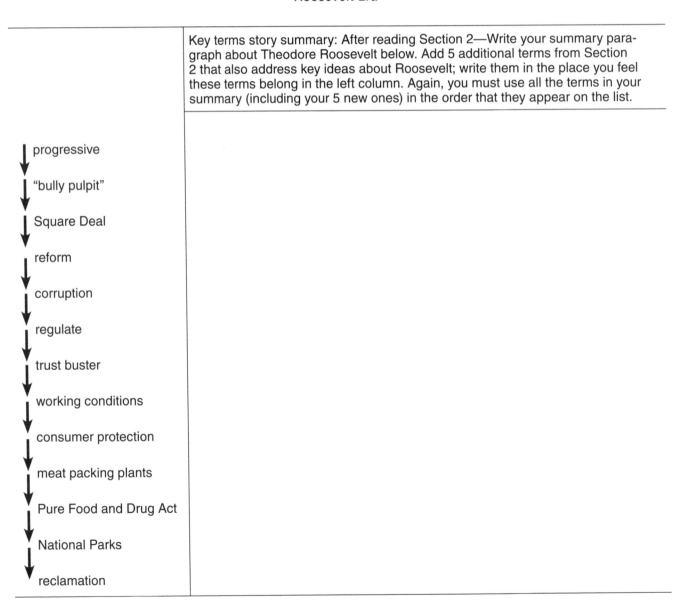

Key terms story summary: After reading Section 2—Write your summary paragraph about Theodore Roosevelt below. Add 5 additional terms from Section 2 that also address key ideas about Roosevelt; write them in the place you feel these terms belong in the left column. Again, you must use all the terms in your summary (including your 5 new ones) in the order that they appear on the list.

progressive

"bully pulpit"

Square Deal

reform

corruption

regulate

trust buster

working conditions

consumer protection

meat packing plants

Pure Food and Drug Act

National Parks

reclamation

Source: Buehl, D. (2001). *Classroom strategies for interactive learning* (2nd ed., p. 134). Newark, DE: International Reading Association.

merely respond to isolated facts in multiple-choice or matching items.

Advantages

- Students are introduced to essential terminology and information before they become immersed in reading.
- Students marshal what they know about a topic and brainstorm possible connections to the new material.
- Students receive guidance in two comprehension tasks that are often difficult: determining importance and summarizing.

- Students have an opportunity to verbalize their learning in writing and can contrast what they knew before reading with what they know now.
- After sufficient practice, students can be asked to create their own chains of key terms—as a comprehension activity and for use as story impressions to prepare their classmates for a new selection.

References

Buehl, D. (2001). *Classroom strategies for interactive learning* (2nd ed.). Newark, DE: International Reading Association.

McGinley, W.J., & Denner, P.R. (1987). Story impressions: A prereading/writing activity. *Journal of Reading, 31*(3), 248–253.

Story Mapping

"What's the point of this story?" We have all been afflicted with the tedious experience of being ensnared by a rambling storyteller who persists with trudging us through a wearisome litany of events and details that apparently have no guiding focus, and ultimately, no real meaning for us: "Then she said...and he couldn't find...so the two of them...just yesterday...they decided to..." and so on. Usually we listen politely, resolving to quickly change the subject when the opportunity presents itself, or perhaps even positioning ourselves for a quick exit. All the time we are thinking, Why are you telling me this? Students have similar experiences with stories they read in school; events unfold but the point of the story remains elusive.

Stories—we grew up hearing them as children. We read them throughout our schooling. We relax while enjoying them in novels we read for pleasure. We experience them on television and in movie theaters, and we tell them to our friends. Much of the way we view the world around us is organized into stories. But in addition, stories are also a timeless method of sharing ideas, insights, and understandings with one another. A well-told story can illustrate a truth, prompt reflection and introspection, challenge our preconceptions, stimulate discussion and refinement of our thinking, inspire us and move us to action, or change the way we understand ourselves and our world. Stories are a powerful way of communicating to us things we need to know. But stories are also predominately an indirect method of delivering messages—as listeners and readers, it is often up to *us* to figure out just what a story is saying.

Children encounter narrative text very early in their lives, and they begin to internalize the common elements found in most stories. Story Mapping (Beck & McKeown, 1981) helps students track their knowledge of narrative structure to analyze stories. Story Maps feature graphic representations of key story elements to help students build a coherent framework for understanding and remembering a story.

Using the Strategy

Story Maps can be created for both short stories and longer works of fiction, such as novels. Using this strategy involves the following steps:

1 Reinforce with students the key elements of a story. For example, introduce story structure by telling students, "I'm going to read you a story. What would you want to know about this story?" Students would likely comment that they want to know who the story is about, what happens in the story, where the story takes place, and how the story ends. These common elements of narrative structure can be presented as a Story Star on an overhead transparency (see the Story Star). Note how each of the above questions can be reworded to reflect the basic elements of a story: *Who?* refers to characters, *Where?* and *When?* involve setting and mood, *What happened?* details events of the plot, and *How did it end?* involves the resolution of the story's conflict. *Why* questions get at possible themes or ideas explored by an author.

2 Select a story for its clear illustration of story structure. When students have read the story, hand out blank Story Maps (see the Appendix for reproducible versions of the Story Map). Have them fill in the key information from the story as you model this process on an overhead transparency sheet. Emphasize the recording of only major events—those that move the plot along—and establish the initiating event that sets the story into motion. (Instruct students to circle the number of this event on their maps.) Students expect a story to feature some sort of conflict, and how that conflict gets resolved is what makes a story interesting. As part of

Strategy Index
Instructional Focus
Frontloading Learning
Guiding Comprehension
Consolidating Understanding
Text Frames
Cause/Effect
Concept/Definition
Problem/Solution
Compare/Contrast
Proposition/Support
Goal/Action/Outcome
Comprehension Processess
Making Connections
Generating Questions
Creating Mental Images
Making Inferences
Determining Importance
Synthesizing

Story Star

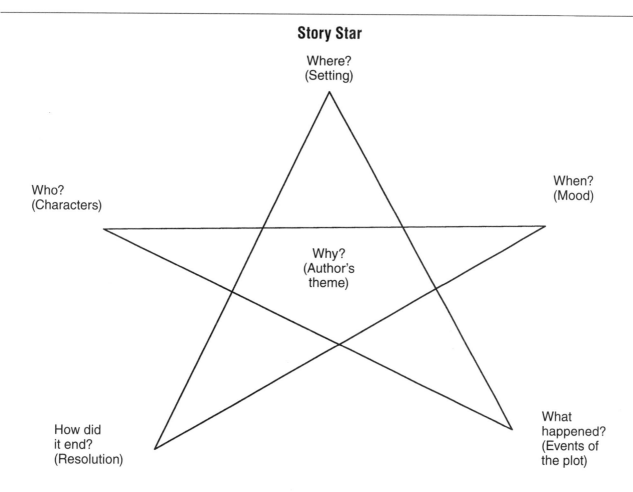

Where?
(Setting)

Who?
(Characters)

When?
(Mood)

Why?
(Author's
theme)

How did
it end?
(Resolution)

What
happened?
(Events of
the plot)

Source: Buehl, D. (1995). *Classroom strategies for interactive learning* (p. 103). Madison: Wisconsin State Reading Association.

the modeling, review the basic kinds of conflict inherent in fictional literature:

- **Within a person**—A character is struggling within him or herself, trying to figure out what to do.

- **Between people**—A character has some sort of problem with others that needs to be addressed.

- **Between people and nature**—A character is presented with a difficult natural situation that he or she must overcome—threatening animals, treacherous weather, a dangerous environment, or a disaster such as a fire.

For example, eighth graders reading the short story version of Daniel Keyes's classic *Flowers for Algernon* encounter a narrative told through diary form, which means they have to extrapolate the story structure from the progression of entries. First they identify the characters (Charlie, the doctors, Miss Kinnian, factory workers) and the setting (a laboratory in the 1950s). They note that the action is initiated by Charlie's acceptance for the experimental operation, and they

record the other major events leading to the climax—such as when the mouse Algernon becomes violent and loses his intelligence. Subsequent action includes Charlie's desperate attempt to use his intelligence to forestall a similar fate, and then his eventual reversion to the character met at the beginning of the story. Students identify the conflict as "Charlie vs. nature," as he confronts changes in his own nature as a person, and observe that this conflict is resolved with Charlie losing his intelligence and becoming again the person he used to be (see the Story Map for "Flowers for Algernon" example).

3 Model with students how to use the organized information in the Story Map to develop an interpretation of author's theme. Emphasize that the conflict and the way it is resolved provide a great deal of insight on possible points the author may have wished to communicate through the story. Students will recognize in "Flowers for Algernon" that a good-faith action, an experiment to improve one's intelligence, has unintended consequences and ends up hurting people.

4 Demonstrate how significant questions that can be asked about a story conform to the structure displayed in the Story Map. Significant questions should relate to the setting, character development, events of the plot, the conflict and its resolution, and the author's possible themes. Questions may also focus on the author's craft, such as the use of language and literary devices used in developing the story's components. For example, questions for "Flowers for Algernon" might highlight the irony of a formerly cognitively disabled person becoming smarter than the scientists and actually becoming engaged in investigating his own experimental procedure. Students may raise questions whether it is "right" to manipulate a person like this for scientific knowledge and the ethics of experimenting with human subjects, especially those who do not understand what will transpire. They may ponder whether Charlie was better off having been granted superior intelligence, even if he lost it eventually.

Story Map for "Flowers for Algernon"

Title: Flowers for Algernon

Climax: Algernon becomes violent & loses intelligence.

Events: Rising Action

10. Learns several languages, reads challenging book, becomes a genius.

9. Dinner with Miss Kinnian and realizes he loves her.

8. Figures out improvements for factory, but quits because of petition to fire him.

7. Realizes workers have been making fun of him.

6. Charlie beats Algernon & resumes lessons with Miss Kinnian.

5. Listens to TV while sleeping to build intelligence.

4. Has operation and still loses to Algernon.

3. Accepted for operation & warned may not be permanent.

2. Charles races Algernon and loses.

1. Charlie starts diary, fails ink blot test.

Falling Action

11. Charlie researches his experiment and writes report that it is a failure.

12. Algernon dies.

13. Charlie realizes he is losing his intelligence.

14. Charlie goes back to old life in factory.

Major Characters: Charlie, Miss Kinnian, Dr. Strauss

Minor Characters: Dr. Nemur, Joe, Frank

Conflict: Charlie vs. nature (Charlie's own nature changes from operation)

Resolution: Operation fails and Charlie becomes again who he was before.

Setting: Research laboratory in the 1950s

Author's theme: Sometimes good-intentioned acts go wrong; we should not experiment with people's lives.

5 Have students use the Story Map to analyze a short story that they read independently. After reading, have the students work with a partner to complete a new Story Map. Solicit possible statements from the whole group about the author's theme, and discuss the rationale for each statement based on information from the story.

Advantages

- Students are provided with a visual framework for understanding and analyzing stories, and their knowledge of story structure is reinforced as a foundation for the successful reading of narrative text.

- Questions for guiding and discussing stories that are derived from the elements of story structure lead to more coherent and integrated comprehension from students. Students improve their ability to predict probable questions for a particular story.

- Students become practiced in using story structure as a basis for the creation of their own stories. Students also have a clear model for the writing of summaries and other reactions to the stories they read.

- This strategy is appropriate for most narrative text. It can be modified for use with some types of expository material, such as biographies and autobiographies.

References

Beck, I.L., & McKeown, M.G. (1981). Developing questions that promote comprehension: The story map. *Language Arts*, *58*(8), 913–918.

Buehl, D. (1995). *Classroom strategies for interactive learning*. Madison: Wisconsin State Reading Association.

Structured Note-Taking

A workshop on how to set up a webpage. A genealogical investigation of vital records at a county courthouse. Your grandmother's recipe for au gratin potatoes. The directions to a track meet in a neighboring city. A plan of action being developed by the school literacy committee.

What do all of the above situations have in common? They all involve note-taking. As you recall instances when you have taken notes recently, you too will probably notice that your note-taking had a very pragmatic emphasis. You took notes because you needed a written record of information that you could refer to and use. Sometimes your notes serve a particular function and are then discarded. Other notes are kept as a reference for years.

Yet teachers are frequently disappointed with the results of student note-taking. "Make sure you take notes on this!" is an oft-heard directive delivered by teachers almost daily to students. Teachers know that note-taking is a prerequisite for remembering and learning, and that it is an essential study strategy. But student notes often are disorganized and lack important information. Students are frequently confused as to what to write down and what to leave out. Some students associate note-taking with mindlessly copying material verbatim from a book, the chalkboard, or from an overhead transparency display. The result may be a notebook that contains quite a bit of writing but is ineffective as a resource for understanding.

Structured Note-Taking (Smith & Tompkins, 1988) is a strategy that guides students toward taking more effective notes. The strategy makes use of graphic organizers, a powerful means of representing ideas and information. Graphic organizers provide students with a visual framework for making decisions about what should be included in their notes and impose a structure on student notes that makes them useful for future deliberations. Structured Note-Taking is an excellent strategy to use in all aspects of classroom learning in which note-taking is desirable—whether from print materials, video, web-based inquiries, teacher presentations, or class or group discussions. Proposition/Support Outlines, a variation of Structured Note-Taking, are also discussed.

Using the Strategies

Structured Note-Taking provides an effective alternative to worksheets and provides students with a well-organized visual display of important information. This strategy engages students in the crucial comprehension processes of determining importance and synthesizing understanding.

Using this strategy involves the following steps:

1 Preview the content students will be learning and identify the organizational structure that is best represented in the material. The following six text frames address common ways that information is organized (see Text Frames in Chapter 3): Problem/Solution, Compare/Contrast, Cause/Effect, Proposition/Support, Goal/Action/Outcome, and Concept/Definition.

2 Create a graphic organizer using boxes, circles, arrows, and other visual structures that emphasize a particular text frame (or frames). It is essential to label the graphic with frame language, such as causes/effects, similarities/differences, or problem/causes of problem/possible solutions. Distribute this graphic organizer to students as a note-taking study guide. They will take notes by recording relevant information in the appropriate spaces in the graphic outline. Highlight the type of text frame being used each time you provide structured notes so that students recognize the various types of text frames and internalize their use. Students need to be aware that boxes and circles are not randomly placed on a page, but that each graphic organizer is devised to help them perceive meaningful connections.

For example, a selection for a science class about endangered animals may adhere to a problem/solution text frame. A science

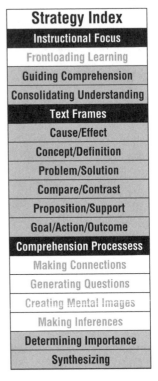

Strategy Index

- Instructional Focus
- Frontloading Learning
- Guiding Comprehension
- Consolidating Understanding
- **Text Frames**
- Cause/Effect
- Concept/Definition
- Problem/Solution
- Compare/Contrast
- Proposition/Support
- Goal/Action/Outcome
- **Comprehension Processess**
- Making Connections
- Generating Questions
- Creating Mental Images
- Making Inferences
- Determining Importance
- Synthesizing

Structured Note-Taking for Science on Endangered Animals

What kind of problem is this animal having?

Dolphins are being caught in underwater tuna nets and are being killed.

Who or what is causing the problem?

Commercial fisheries who use this type of underwater net to catch tuna.

Write the name of an endangered animal here:

Dolphin

Where does this animal live?

Dolphins live in deep sea waters in the Atlantic Ocean and Mediterranean Sea.

What can be done to help this animal?

We can buy tuna that is marked "dolphin-safe."

We can write letters to government leaders for international fishing controls.

Source: Buehl, D. (1995). *Classroom strategies for interactive learning* (p. 107). Madison: Wisconsin State Reading Association.

teacher provides students with graphic outlines for their notes from the reading on endangered animals (see the Structured Note-Taking for Science on Endangered Animals example). The first endangered animal in the selection is the dolphin. As they read, students select information that fits into the four boxes in the graphic: that dolphins get caught in underwater tuna nets, commercial fisheries are causing the problem, we can buy tuna with the "dolphin-safe" designation, and we can lobby for international fishing regulations. Students then continue reading and complete a second graphic organizer for the next endangered animal.

3 Structured Note-Taking provides a number of opportunities for students to collaborate. When introducing the strategy, have students work in pairs while reading a passage and justify to their partners their decisions on what to select and where to place it in the graphic outline. For example, history students

viewing a video program on the decisions of African Americans to move from the rural, southern United States to northern cities in the early 20th century are provided with a graphic organizer that presents both cause/effect and compare/contrast text frames (see the Structured Notes for History Video example). Students first individually record information that describes life in the rural South and the contrasting life in Chicago, Illinois. Students also are cued to seek the causal factors that encouraged African Americans to relocate to northern urban areas. The teacher periodically pauses the video for "think time" and advises students to write quickly and not to worry about legibility and completeness.

When the video is over, students work in pairs or small groups on a second blank copy of the graphic organizer. Students compare notes from the video with their classmates to develop a more thorough set

Structured Notes for History Video

Life in the South before migration North

- Many lived in shacks
- Poor food
- Segregation
- Low wages
- Few jobs
- Sharecropping
- Jim Crow laws
- KKK harassment
- Poor schools
- Second-class status
- Discrimination
- Boll Weevil ruined cotton
- Racial violence
- Lack of protection from courts and law

Factors that encouraged African Americans to move North to Chicago

- Recruited to North by factories needing laborers
- Were protected with free transportation (railroads)
- Agents sent South encouraged African Americans to come North
- World War I caused need for workers and brought about new jobs and new factories
- New laws restricted immigration from other countries
- The *Chicago Defender* newspaper spoke to African Americans
- Violence and lynchings were increasing in the South

Life in Chicago for African Americans

- Last hired, first fired
- Had jobs but little money
- Postwar depression put people out of work
- Created neighborhoods for all African Americans
- Housing shortages
- Culture flourished—music, food, churches
- African American city leaders and business leaders emerged
- Competed for jobs with returning WWI soldiers
- Race riots, bombs, killings

Source: Buehl, D. (1995). *Classroom strategies for interactive learning* (p. 108). Madison: Wisconsin State Reading Association.

of Structured Notes. The final exemplary notes are collected and photocopied for each member of the group.

4 Ask students to use their Structured Notes as a guide for verbalizing their understandings. Although much of what is contained in the notes will be forgotten (see the Fact Pyramid discussion in Chapter 4), the notes should prove invaluable in "holding" information so students can synthesize their understandings—summarize key ideas, draw conclusions, and make generalizations. Structured notes are especially useful for written syntheses of new learning.

5 As students gain practice using Structured Notes, they will begin to develop their own graphic organizers to structure their notes (Jones, Pierce, & Hunter, 1988/1989). At first, help students to identify the most appropriate text frame for student-created notes, a task that they will become increasingly able to accomplish independently.

Proposition/Support Outlines

Proposition/Support Outlines (Buehl, 1992) are a variation of Structured Note-Taking for material that presents viewpoints, opinions, debatable assertions, theories, or hypotheses. Proposition/Support Outlines supply students with a framework for analyzing the types of justification an author uses to support a conclusion or generalization.

1 Initiate a discussion with students about the differences between facts and opinions. Brainstorm with students to create definitions of each and generate a list of examples. "The Earth's rain forests are shrinking" is a fact statement. "The loss of rain forests will lead to an environmental disaster" is an opinion—in this case a hypothesis—that may or may not be supported by facts. Emphasize that fact statements can be proven right or wrong, but opinion statements cannot. Clearly, some opinion statements are more defensible than others because they are well supported by known facts. Opinions that have little basis in fact are termed *unfounded*.

2 Introduce the term *proposition*—a statement that can be argued as true. Provide students with several possible propositions such as the following:

- Today's movies are too violent.
- Drug testing is necessary for all professional athletes.

- Dogs make the best pets.

Divide students into cooperative groups and assign each group the task of generating several arguments that could support one of these propositions. Introduce a blank Proposition/Support Outline on an overhead transparency sheet (see the Appendix for a reproducible version of the Proposition/Support Outline), and model with students how various supports for a

---

Proposition/Support Outline for Rain Forests

Proposition:

> The loss of rain forests will lead to an environmental disaster.

Support:

1. Facts
   - Rain forests use carbon dioxide.
   - There is increased carbon dioxide in the earth's atmosphere.
   - The rain forests contain many endangered plant and animal species.
   - Deforestation leads to widespread soil erosion in many areas.
   - The burning of fossil fuels puts carbon dioxide into the environment.

2. Statistics
   - The 1990s were the "hottest" decade in the last 100 years.
   - One acre of rain forest disappears every second.
   - Four million acres (larger than the state of Connecticut) disappear every year.
   - Fifty to 100 species are destroyed with each acre of forest cleared.
   - If present trends continue, half the rain forests of Honduras and Nicaragua will disappear in the early 21st century.

3. Examples
   - India has almost no remaining rain forest.
   - Current plans target eliminating much of the Congo's rain forest.
   - Run-off from deforestation in Indonesia threatens their coral reefs and diminishes the fish population.
   - Cutting of rain forests in Bangladesh and the Philippines has led to killer floods.

4. Expert authority
   - Computers predict doubling of carbon dioxide in the 21st century, raising temperatures by 3 to 9 degrees.
   - National Center for Atmospheric Research believes increased carbon dioxide will lead to the Greenhouse Effect and global warming.
   - Nobel Prize–winner Al Gore calls the Greenhouse Effect our most serious threat ever.

5. Logic and reasoning
   - Warmer temperatures will harm crops and increase energy costs.
   - More people will starve because of less food and increased population growth.
   - The polar glaciers will melt and raise the sea level, flooding coastlines.
   - Many species useful to humans will disappear.
   - More sections of the world will become uninhabitable deserts due to soil loss, erosion, overgrazing, and overcultivation.

Source: Buehl, D. (1992). Outline helps students analyze credibility of author's premise. *WEAC News & Views, 28*(1), 8.

proposition can be categorized in five ways—as facts, statistics, examples, expert authority, or logic and reasoning.

3 Assign students a Proposition/Support selection and have them work with partners to complete the outline as they analyze the author's arguments. Select for students a text that features a clear proposition. For example, students in a social studies class read an article detailing how the loss of the world's rain forests portends global environmental disaster. After ascertaining this proposition, they complete the outline in order to categorize arguments supporting the global-catastrophe scenario. In this case, the rain forest article contained information and arguments reflected in all five support categories (see the Proposition/Support Outline for Rain Forests example).

4 Analyze with students the type of support presented. How convincing is it? Does the author rely solely on logic, reasoning, and examples, neglecting to use statistics or other facts? Is only a single expert authority cited? How reliable are the statistics? (For example, public survey results are statistics but are volatile and change frequently.) Do the examples seem to be typical or atypical? Has important counteracting information been omitted from the discussion? As the rain forest outline is discussed, students will make a judgment about the case presented by the author—whether to accept or reject the author's proposition.

The Proposition/Support Outline is also an excellent guide for independent inquiry, as it provides students with a framework for scrutinizing websites and reference materials for relevant information and arguments. For example, students assigned the task of writing a position paper on a topic or preparing for a debate will find the strategy to be an excellent prompt for examining sources and organizing writing.

Advantages

- Students are able to see relationships between ideas as they take notes—they realize that note-taking is more than writing down isolated pieces of information.

- Students are able to take notes that are coherent and easy to use for synthesizing their understandings in subsequent discussions and writing activities.

- Structured notes emphasize visual representation of information, which facilitates memory of the material.

- Proposition/support outlines provide students with practice in developing critical reading skills as they become adept at noticing an author's viewpoint.

References

Buehl, D. (1992). Outline helps students analyze credibility of author's premise. *WEAC News & Views*, *28*(1), 8.

Buehl, D. (1995). *Classroom strategies for interactive learning.* Madison: Wisconsin State Reading Association.

Jones, B.F., Pierce, J., & Hunter, B. (1988/1989). Teaching students to construct graphic representations. *Educational Leadership*, *46*(4), 20–25.

Smith, P.L., & Tompkins, G.E. (1988). Structured note-taking: A new strategy for content area readers. *Journal of Reading*, *32*(1), 46–53.

Suggested Reading

Armbruster, B.B., & Anderson, T.H. (1982). *Idea-mapping: The technique and its use in the classroom, or simulating the "ups" and "downs" of reading.* (Reading Education Report No. 36). Urbana: University of Illinois, Center for the Study of Reading.

Student-Friendly Vocabulary Explanations

How comfortable are you with the following words: *inclined, abnormal, privy, unsought, feigned, preoccupation, levity, intimate, revelation, quivering, horizon, plagiaristic, marred, suppressions, infinite, snobbishly, fundamental, parceled?*

Very likely, some of these words surface occasionally in your speech and writing. Others are easily recognizable as words you can confidently understand when you are reading or listening. Perhaps there is even a word or two on this list that you are not necessarily sure of. What do these words have in common? Each word on this list is an example of a Tier 2 word—a word encountered predominantly through written texts but heard less frequently in spoken language (Beck, McKeown, & Kucan, 2002). In addition to being Tier 2 words, each of the above words share another similarity. Imagine these words appearing together in a paragraph. What might this paragraph be about? How might these words be related to each other? Each word can be sighted in the third paragraph of the opening page of F. Scott Fitzgerald's classic novel *The Great Gatsby.* Like many authors, Fitzgerald expected his readers to be able to navigate prose packed with vocabulary that extends beyond the normal discourse of spoken language.

As teachers, we are frequently asked what a word "means." What students are generally expecting from us is a definition, a word or short phrase that can be conveniently inserted as a substitution for the unknown word. Yet researchers are pessimistic about the effectiveness of definitions in building knowledge about vocabulary. Various studies have shown that about two thirds of the sentences created by students to use new words based on definitions did not make sense. Without truly having a feel for the new word, students tend to swap unknown words into familiar contexts, resulting in sentences that are awkward, odd, or nonsensical.

Using the Strategy

Concerned that students equate copying definitions from a dictionary with vocabulary development, Beck, McKeown, and Kucan (2002) recommend Student-Friendly Vocabulary Explanations, a strategy for constructing word knowledge as networks of personal connections and useful associations. To gain facility with a new word, students learn multiple facets of the word's meaning, practice using the word in a variety of acceptable contexts, and integrate the word and their existing background knowledge. Using this strategy involves the following steps:

1 Determine which words are most worthy of instructional time by considering three levels of utility. Beck and her associates (2002) categorize words as falling into three tiers (see the Three Tiers of Vocabulary). Words targeted for instruction will include a mix of Tier 2 and Tier 3 words.

Feldman and Kinsella (2004) caution, however, that many words highlighted in textbooks or listed in the teacher's manual do not deserve instructional attention, and other mainline and essential words are left for students to infer a meaning. They offer the following types of words to serve as guidelines for teachers who want to select high-utility words for instruction:

- **Big Idea words**—Tier 3 words that are the core of the academic language of a content discipline. These would include key conceptual science terms, social studies terms, math terms, language arts terms, and so forth. Words such as *seismic, feudalism, equation,* and *verb* fall under the category of Big Idea words.

- **Academic Tool Kit words**—Tier 2 words that students will meet again and again, across academic disciplines. Words such as *contrast, function, environment* and *perspective* pop up continually in written texts, yet these words are typically not taught, and as a result students develop hazy or imprecise meanings of highly crucial and recurring vocabulary.

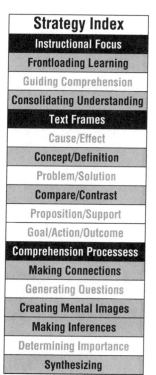

Strategy Index

Instructional Focus
Frontloading Learning
Guiding Comprehension
Consolidating Understanding
Text Frames
Cause/Effect
Concept/Definition
Problem/Solution
Compare/Contrast
Proposition/Support
Goal/Action/Outcome
Comprehension Processess
Making Connections
Generating Questions
Creating Mental Images
Making Inferences
Determining Importance
Synthesizing

Three Tiers of Vocabulary

Tier 1 Words	Tier 2 Words	Tier 3 Words
Basic words that commonly appear in spoken language.	The more sophisticated vocabulary of written texts.	Words central to building knowledge and conceptual understanding within the various academic disciplines and which are integral to instruction of content.
Because they are heard frequently, in numerous contexts, and in consort with a great deal of nonverbal communication, Tier 1 words rarely require explicit instruction in school. English-language learners, of course, must first develop this conversational language as a foundation for further vocabulary growth.	Mature language users employ such words with regularity, but students encounter them less frequently as listeners. As a result, these words are unknown to many of our learners. Because of their lack of redundancy in oral language, Tier 2 words present challenges to students who primarily meet them in print.	Medical terms, legal terms, biology terms, and mathematics terms are all examples of Tier 3 words. These words surface relatively rarely in general vocabulary usage, but students must master them as they study the various content disciplines. All content areas feature their own distinct Tier 3 words that need explicit instruction.

- **Disciplinary Tool Kit words**—Tier 2 words common to the study of an academic discipline that are used frequently in the discourse of an subject area. Terms like *alliance* and *policy* in social studies, or *hypothesis* and *dilute* in science are words that students may have to figure out totally on their own, and as a result accrue only indistinct meanings for them.

- **Polysemous words**—words that have multiple meanings, and often very specific meanings in an academic discipline. *Matter* has a distinct meaning in science that contrasts a great deal from its general usage; *mean* in mathematics does not *mean* anything close to the second usage of the word in this sentence. In these examples, both *matter* and *mean* qualify as Tier 3 words that should receive explicit instruction.

For example, a history teacher might chose Big Idea words like *segregation, integration,* and *Jim Crow laws* when studying the U.S. Civil Rights movement of the 1950s and 60s. But Academic Tool Kit words, such as those related to argumentation—*contention, proposition,* and *counteract*—would also be useful to discussions of people's beliefs and justifications for actions. Disciplinary Tool Kit words might include *discriminate, boycott,* and *martyr.*

2 Model for students how to "explain" a word rather than seeking a definition. A Student-Friendly Explanation should include the following components:

- The word is described in everyday language, rather than "dictionary-speak."

- The word is explained in connected language, not with isolated single word or short phrase definitions.

- The explanation exemplifies multiple contexts that feature the word in action.

- The explanation includes "you," "something," and "someone" to help students to ground the new word in familiar situations.

For example, a teacher modeling an explanation of the word *belligerent* might say, "If you are *belligerent* with someone, you are showing a lot of hostility to that person. Someone who is *belligerent* with you is threatening to you, and you feel like you are being attacked. Someone who has a *belligerent* attitude will likely get into a lot of fights. Two countries that are at war are called *belligerents*." Notice how an explanation reaches far beyond the provision of a simple one-word definition or synonym.

3 Solicit students to provide their own examples of the word in action. Students need guided opportunities to playfully experiment with contexts that might feature the new word. Usually, the individual in the classroom who gets the most practice saying a keyword is the teacher; instead students need to begin the process of moving the word into their spoken vocabulary: "My cat is very *belligerent* to other cats; it always snarls and hisses at them." "The Al-Qaeda terrorists have been extremely *belligerent* toward the United States." As students explore appropriate usages of the word, encourage them to continue to refine their understanding by venturing into possible uses that do

Word Study Guide

Word	Explanation	Examples	Visual image
Boycott **Found in this sentence:** The Montgomery bus boycott in 1955 protested the practice of racial segregation in the public transit system.	When you boycott something, you avoid having anything to do with it.	My sister had an argument with our parents and now she boycotts family gatherings. Because the store owner is rude to young people, all the kids now boycott shopping there.	(Students draw a visual representation of the word here.)

not exactly parallel your examples. As a result, students are less likely to narrowly "trap" the word into the original context where they first encountered it.

This experimentation phase can also clear up misunderstandings or misconceptions about a word's usage. For example, the student who offers "The approaching thunderstorm was very *belligerent* to me" has overgeneralized the connection between *belligerent* and *threatening*. A clarification that *belligerent* is a threatening attitude shown by people or animals can be added to the explanation at this time.

4 Prompt students to consider "Who would use this word?" Ask students to imagine the kinds of people who would likely be regular users of the new word and to create sentences that reflect what these people might say, such as the following:

- A police officer: "The violence in the community was caused by a *belligerent* confrontation between two gangs."
- A school principal: "If you don't stop being *belligerent* to those boys, you will be suspended!"

Be conscious of regular modeling of Tier 2 and Tier 3 words in your oral language. Students will incrementally gain a grasp of a new word as a result of these ongoing repetitions in a variety of appropriate contexts.

5 Have students keep records in their class notebooks of the new words you devote to explicit instruction. Feldman and Kinsella (2004) recommend a word study guide that features a graphic organizer that tracks facets of a word's meaning (see the Word Study

Guide example). Students record the initial context for where the word was sighted; this offers students an appropriate model for its usage. They then fashion their student-friendly explanation of the word and practice "putting it in play" themselves with an example or two. Visual representations of a new word can be especially powerful. Ask students to quickly sketch an image that crystallizes their understanding of the word, or some key aspect of it. Students can be expected to add words that they are taught as an integral class assignment.

Advantages

- Students receive assistance in how to meld understandings of new words with their existing background knowledge.
- Students learn many facets about a new word instead of fixating on a single definition.
- Students associate vocabulary learning with practicing using new words in their speaking and writing rather than as merely "memory" work.
- Students gradually build their academic vocabulary, making them better prepared to learn academic subjects.
- This strategy may be used with students from elementary through secondary levels.

References

Beck, I.L., McKeown, M.G., & Kucan, L. (2002). *Bringing words to life: Robust vocabulary instruction*. New York: Guilford.

Feldman, K., & Kinsella, K. (2004). *Narrowing the language gap: The case for explicit vocabulary instruction* (Scholastic Professional Paper). New York: Scholastic.

Template Frames

Dear Grandma, thank you for the T-shirt you got me on your trip to Alaska. I really like the funny picture of the grizzly bear on it, and red is my favorite color. I have been wearing my shirt to school and all my friends are asking when I went to Alaska! Thanks for remembering me on your vacation.

Think about assisting a child who is writing a thank-you note. You might find yourself prompting the child on what a good thank-you note should include. In addition to thanking someone, the note should identify the gift, express appreciation, and perhaps comment on how the gift is being used. A conclusion usually recognizes the gift-giver for his or her thoughtfulness.

Clearly there is an internal structure to this specific communication—the thank-you note—which you are teaching to this child. In effect, you have in your mind a template for a thank-you note that can be adapted to other written communications: a sympathy note, an invitation, a letter of complaint, a mail-order purchase, and others. Each mandates a different structure or template that you have internalized for use as the situation dictates.

Using the Strategy

A template is an outline or a pattern used to re-create something. Templates are used in quilting, woodworking projects, genealogy charts, computer applications, and of course, writing. However, because templates for writing are mental structures, many students never figure them out. Their writing lacks coherence, with information randomly stated and key parts missing. Teachers can use templates as a strategy to develop students' ability to handle a variety of classroom writing tasks. Templates are especially valuable in helping students cope with essay exams. Using this strategy involves the following steps:

1 Share with students exemplary models (either created or collected) of the kind of writing you expect. Well-written examples will exhibit a clear text-frame organization, such as cause/effect, compare/contrast, proposition/support, problem/solution, or concept/definition. To reveal the structure of the template, underline key elements of the writing, such as

topic sentence, text-frame language, transitions, and summary or conclusion. This will make the template explicit for students. For example, the following essay illustrates a cause/effect template for students studying weathering in science:

Explain the causes of mechanical weathering and describe its effects on rocks.

Mechanical weathering is caused by water, by plants, and by animals. First, water causes weathering in two ways: by freezing and by wetting and drying. Freezing water forms ice in cracks of rocks, which splits them apart. Water also causes weathering because when some rocks get wet they expand and when they dry they shrink. This leads to rocks breaking up. Secondly, plants cause weathering when their roots grow into cracks in rocks and then break them up. Thirdly, animals dig holes in the ground, which expose rocks to water, which weathers them. As a result of mechanical weathering, rocks are broken into smaller pieces but keep their same chemical composition.

2 Provide students with a template containing the key elements of a paragraph to use as an outline for a writing task. This will guide them in constructing an organized written response. Keywords that forecast the text organization of the paragraph are emphasized, as in the following examples:

- comparison (similarly, likewise, in like manner)

- contrast (but, yet, however, on the other hand, on the contrary)

- concept/definition (for example, furthermore, such as)

- problem/solution (for this reason, therefore, instead of)

- proposition/support (in conclusion, if, indicate, suggest)

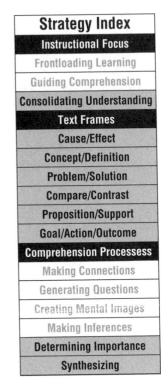

Strategy Index

Instructional Focus

Frontloading Learning

Guiding Comprehension

Consolidating Understanding

Text Frames

Cause/Effect

Concept/Definition

Problem/Solution

Compare/Contrast

Proposition/Support

Goal/Action/Outcome

Comprehension Processess

Making Connections

Generating Questions

Creating Mental Images

Making Inferences

Determining Importance

Synthesizing

- cause/effect (because, consequently, since, then, as a result)
- goal/action/outcome (steps, first, second, next, finally)

The following is a template frame for students responding to an essay question on a history test:

> Question: What problems did the women's suffrage movement encounter and what did they do to solve their problems?
>
> Answer: The women's suffrage movement encountered a number of problems that made winning voting rights very difficult. First _____. Another problem _____. _____ was a third challenge they had to face, because _____. One action followed by leaders of the suffrage movement was _____. They also _____. Finally, _____.

Emphasize to students not to treat the template frame as a fill-in-the-blank exercise. Instead, instruct them to use the cues provided in the template as a guide to rewriting answers in a paragraph format. Some students will customize the template to fit their ideas and writing style. Encourage them to expand their paragraphs with additional sentences and information. The purpose of the template is not to render students' writing as mechanical and formalistic, but to help them to construct a coherent, well-formed essay.

3 As students become practiced in using template frames, ask them to assume more responsibility for organizing their writing by doing the following:

- Have them work in cooperative groups to develop a template frame for a question to be answered
- Have the class choose the template they feel would work best for the essay
- Offer multiple template options

Advantages

- Students learn how to craft well-written responses that can be personalized as they become more sophisticated writers.
- Students are given an organized way of getting started when confronted with demanding writing tasks.
- Students learn to use key transition elements that reflect appropriate text frames, such as cause/effect or proposition/support.
- Template frames also can be used to structure the writing of lab reports in science, character analysis in language arts, book critiques, position papers, and other types of student writing.

Suggested Reading

Santa, C.M., Havens, L.T., & Valdes, B. (2004). *Project CRISS: Creating independence through student-owned strategies* (3rd ed.). Dubuque, IA: Kendall/Hunt.

Text Coding

You are lying in bed about to drift off to sleep after an eventful day jam-packed with activity. Your mind is still percolating with thoughts as you relax, and suddenly you realize that you have chanced upon an excellent idea for tomorrow's lesson. "I should click on the light and write this down," flickers through your consciousness, but instead, inevitably, you continue to relax and soon are fast asleep. And sure enough, the next morning you awaken with the knowledge that a great idea occurred to you the night before, but of course, you cannot recall it.

The above scenario is a frequent happening in our lives. As we are engaged in a variety of routines—driving a car, jogging, eating lunch—valuable thoughts pop into our minds, but because they are ephemeral, and our mind moves on to other territory, we soon lose them. We need a system for tracking our thinking.

This also holds true for reading comprehension. A text triggers a host of useful connections and associations as we read along, but if we have no system for processing them, these insights may not be available to us when we reflect back upon the passage and decide how to make sense of it. Struggling readers in particular have difficulty harnessing their thinking as they negotiate the terrain of a challenging text. As a result, they may conclude their reading with only a hazy outline of disjointed facts.

Proficient readers carry on an internal monologue while they read. It is as though proficient readers operate with a split personality. One personality is hard at work with the task at hand—reading a textbook chapter, for instance. The second personality works in the background, directing and evaluating all the cognitive activities needed to learn successfully—making meaningful connections, posing questions about the author's message, determining what is important in the chapter, and synthesizing understanding. This personality represents that inner voice that issues commands during reading: "Slow down! This is pretty tough going!" "Hold it here! This doesn't make any sense. Better reread." or "This stuff doesn't look very important. I'll just skim over it quickly and get into the next section." Proficient readers talk to themselves.

Researchers call this internal monologue *metacognition*—the ability to think about thinking and monitor comprehension (see discussion in Chapter 1).

Metacognition reflects an ability to switch gears and try something else when learning breaks down—such as when a reading passage is proving particularly difficult—rather than continuing to plow ahead even if nothing is making sense. All readers can be taught how to activate the control center in their minds that directs their learning.

Using the Strategy

Text Coding (Harvey & Goudvis, 2007; Tovani, 2000) represents an annotation system for students to track thinking while reading. As students "catch" themselves in the act of a specific comprehension process, they can apply the following codes to the texts they read:

R—"This reminds me of..." to signify a connection to background knowledge or experiences

V—"I can picture this..." to signify visualizing and creating mental images

E—"This makes me feel..." to signify an emotional response to the text

Q—"I wonder..." to signify a question that occurred during reading

I—"I figured out that..." to signify making an inference, such as a prediction or an interpretation

?—"I don't understand this..." to signify a segment that is confusing or doesn't make sense

!—"This is interesting..." to signify something that particularly intrigued you

Using this strategy involves the following steps:

1 Model how readers "talk to themselves" and "talk back to the author" with a text displayed on an overhead transparency sheet. Think aloud

Strategy Index
Instructional Focus
Frontloading Learning
Guiding Comprehension
Consolidating Understanding
Text Frames
Cause/Effect
Concept/Definition
Problem/Solution
Compare/Contrast
Proposition/Support
Goal/Action/Outcome
Comprehension Processess
Making Connections
Generating Questions
Creating Mental Images
Making Inferences
Determining Importance
Synthesizing

as you read, jotting comments in the margin and underlining key segments or terms. Select a short piece of challenging text and introduce the selection to the class by noting that even excellent readers occasionally encounter problematic texts. Short pieces that contain confusing segments, ambiguities, unfamiliar vocabulary, or technical subject matter make excellent choices for these think-alouds.

Read the passage out loud as the students follow along. Pause periodically to illustrate what you are thinking. For example, you can demonstrate predicting by saying, "I think this author is going to talk about...." and making connections by saying, "This reminds me of...." You can model creating images by saying, "I can picture what the author is describing...." and posing questions by saying, "I wonder (why, how, what, who, where)...." Clarifying can be demonstrated by saying, "This doesn't make sense to me. I think I should try...."

For example, the following short passage about rugby, a game unfamiliar to most students, could serve as an excellent think-aloud:

> Rugby is a type of football that is popular in the United Kingdom. Rugby matches consist of two 40-minute periods of play, with a 5-minute halftime break. A match begins with a kickoff, from the center of the halfway line, of an oval-shaped ball somewhat larger than a U.S. football. Each team, which consists of 8 forwards and 7 backs, attempts to ground the ball in the opposing team's goal area. Action is generally continuous, although after a penalty, play is resumed by a *scrummage*. In a tight scrummage, a player rolls the ball into a tunnel formed by the opposing team's forwards, who are linked together with their arms about each other's waists. As they push, both teams attempt to heel the ball.

Parts of this passage will probably make sense, but at other points a pause is needed so you can record a question mark to highlight material that needs clarification. After reading the entire passage, model to students how to paraphrase material in words that make sense to them. For example, you might say, "I wonder if in rugby the kickoff is like place kicking in American football, or if it is more like the goalie kicking the ball in soccer." In this case, you are demonstrating both self-questioning and making connections to your personal experiences and knowledge.

2 After students have experienced several teacher think-alouds, have them practice the process themselves with partners as they tackle potentially difficult class material. The partners take turns reading a segment out loud, pausing to share their thinking and strategies as they go along.

3 Prepare students to track their thinking through text coding. Coding a text involves two elements: highlighting or marking a spot in a paragraph, and then jotting a symbol in the margin to indicate the kind of thinking that was elicited at this point (see the list of Text Codes identified on page 180). Notice how these text codes parallel the comprehension processess outlined in Chapter 1.

As a variation for use with texts that cannot be marked, provide students with packs of small sticky notes, which can be affixed to the margin with a text code. In addition, Tovani (2000) recommends using Double-Entry Diaries (see Double-Entry Diaries beginning on page 79). The left side of the paper is reserved for phrases that are "lifted" from the text; on the right side, students place the code and jot down thoughts they had at that point in the reading.

4 Have students confer with partners and talk about places in the text where they have placed a code. Emphasize that these are particularly interesting spots, because they represent something the author said that triggered deeper thinking on their part as readers.

During partner shares, ask students to pay special attention to "?" codes, places where they experienced confusion or needed clarification. The Self-Monitoring Approach to Reading and Thinking (SMART) strategy (Vaughan & Estes, 1986) emphasizes problem-solving these glitches in understanding (see the SMART Strategy Steps). The steps to the SMART strategy could be displayed on a classroom chart or overhead transparency.

Ask partners to brainstorm what could be done to make sense of those parts. Observe that some question marks may have made sense after the entire passage is read. Partners should collaborate to specify the source of their problem (an unfamiliar word, an unclear sentence, or a need for more examples), and explain how they tried to resolve their lack of understanding.

5 Text Graffiti (Buehl, 2004) is a method of annotating a text that expands on text coding by including marginal commentary. As learners we all have highlighted, underlined, and annotated texts to impose our priorities on someone else's words. It is this conception of graffiti that can be employed as a classroom strategy—personalizing learning through activities that prompt students to put their face onto texts created by others.

Model and solicit from students their contributions for marginal graffiti. Emphasize that readers can begin to own a text by intertwining their ideas with those of an author's. Provide them with a photocopy of the text that allows wide margins on both right and left sides to facilitate their graffiti. An alternative is to provide

SMART Strategy Steps

1. Reread.

2. Self-translate. At the end of each section, stop and explain to yourself, in your own words, what you read. Look back at the text as you go over the material.

3. Troubleshoot. Go back to each "?"

   a. Reread the trouble spot to see if it now makes sense. If it still does not make sense:

   b. Pinpoint a problem by figuring out why you are having trouble:

      • Is it a difficult word or unfamiliar vocabulary?

      • Is it a difficult sentence or confusing language?

      • Does the author expect you to know something you do not know?

   c. Try a fix-up strategy:

      • Use vocabulary resources (glossary, dictionary).

      • Use visual information (pictures, other graphics).

      • Use other parts of the chapter (summary, review section, diagrams, or other features).

   d. Explain to yourself exactly what you do not understand or what confuses you.

   e. Collaborate and develop an interpretation of what the text might mean.

Source: Vaughan, J.L., & Estes, T.H. (1986). *Reading and reasoning beyond the primary grades*. Boston: Allyn & Bacon.

students with pads of sticky notes to affix their comments to a text that cannot be reproduced. Point out the usefulness of the following annotations:

• Enumerate ideas and information by writing numbers and keywords for each item in the margin (for example, three reasons for..., two results of..., or four events that...).

• List significant examples, both those presented in a text and those that occur to the reader.

• Integrate additional information on charts or other graphics to make them more understandable and to connect visual information to what is discussed in a passage.

• Create a marginal glossary of key terms and definitions.

• Use margins to posit possible meanings of key terms if definitions are not directly stated.

• Indicate areas of agreement (A) or disagreement (D) with the author or positives (+) and negatives (-), and briefly register reasons why.

• Jott down "gist" statements that sum up key segments in the reader's words, not the author's.

Color felt-tip pens are an excellent resource for annotating texts. Researchers estimate that consistent use of color for coding (for example, red for main points, blue for details or examples) can enhance memory of a text up to 20%. Students can achieve the same effect by using different colored pads of sticky notes if they are attaching their commentaries to a textbook chapter or to the pages of a novel. As students begin writing their graffiti on the text, reiterate that this activity asks them to go public with their thinking as they read, and allows them to place their personal stamp on an author's message.

Advantages

• Text Coding while reading is a powerful strategy that helps students retain their thinking and create a personal understanding of an author's message.

• Students come to realize that comprehension is the result of the interplay between an author's words and a reader's thinking.

• Students become accustomed to listening to their inner dialogue about a text as they read.

• Students are provided with a system to verbalize their problem solving through difficult texts, and are encouraged to attempt fix-up strategies rather than give up or accept partial comprehension of a passage.

• Students become involved in summarizing the material in their own words, thus helping them to remember as well as understand.

References

Buehl, D. (2004). Using graffiti as a reading tool. *OnWEAC In Print, 4*(8), 13.

Harvey, S., & Goudvis, A. (2007). *Strategies that work: Teaching comprehension for understanding and engagement* (2nd ed.). Portland, ME: Stenhouse.

Tovani, C. (2000). *I read it, but I don't get it: Comprehension strategies for adolescent readers*. Portland, ME: Stenhouse.

Vaughan, J.L., & Estes, T.H. (1986). *Reading and reasoning beyond the primary grades*. Boston: Allyn & Bacon.

Suggested Reading

Simpson, M.L., & Nist, S.L. (1990). Textbook annotation: An effective and efficient study strategy for college students. *Journal of Reading, 34*(2), 122–129.

Vocabulary Overview Guide

The vagaries of Andrew's life before he returned to Oregon and joined the family business are rarely mentioned these days.

Vagaries? Can you recollect seeing this word before? Could you offer a hunch as to its meaning? Would you feel confident using this word in your speaking and writing? For many people, a word such as *vagaries* lies on the periphery of their vocabularies. The word may be somewhat familiar, perhaps encountered infrequently during reading, but most people have never had the urge to look it up in a dictionary.

Instead, they develop an increasingly meaningful concept of this word through context. Initially, proficient readers would look at the word for possible etymological connections (Does *vagary* fit with *vague*, or is *vagrant* a better match? How about *vagabond*?). Then they would track subsequent sightings of vagary and begin to construct a working definition based on its appearance in multiple contexts, such as "The vagaries of government policy toward the homeless..." or "The vagaries of his jokes until they hit the punch line...." Eventually, readers would refine their understanding that vagary refers to aimless and unpredictable wandering or actions.

As teachers, we know that vocabulary development is a critical component of reading comprehension, but many of the activities we use with students to improve their vocabularies are not as successful as we would like them to be. Students who are given lists of words to look up and study admit that they forget most of them once the test is over. Instead, vocabulary study that is embedded in discussions of written texts is particularly valuable.

Using the Strategy

The Vocabulary Overview Guide (Carr, 1985) is a graphic organizer that includes a meaningful clue in addition to rich contextual information. This strategy conditions students to be sensitive to Tier 2 words (encountered predominately in written texts and frequently in spoken language) and Tier 3 words (words used to communicate key concepts in specific academic disciplines) as they read (see the Student-Friendly Vocabulary Explanations strategy beginning on page 175). The strategy also provides a system for studying words so that students are able to retain their meaning over time. Using this strategy involves the following steps:

1 Select vocabulary words from material students are reading in class, and be sure to select words that are connected to key themes or ideas in the text. Traditionally, teachers often identify difficult words from a text, ask students to ascertain the meanings of these words, and then quiz them in some fashion, perhaps asking for definitions and demonstration of usage in a sentence. However, Beck, McKeown, and Kucan (2002) caution against this practice. They argue that many students merely copy a simplistic definition from the dictionary, without really gaining a solid understanding for the new word.

Therefore, Tier 2 and 3 words that are related to key themes and ideas represent the most meaningful vocabulary to highlight for instruction, because they naturally coincide with class activities and discussions about the selection. As a result, these words become part of the discourse of learning while students explore a written text.

2 Rather than sending students to the dictionary, start with a knowledge rating activity. Ask students to evaluate their current level of knowledge about each selected word: *K*—I know it; *H*—I have a hunch what it means; *S*—I've seen it but I don't know it; and *N*—I've never seen it before today.

Next display from the selection the actual contexts for each of these target words. However, researchers argue that relying on context alone is often inadequate because students may misread contextual clues, or the specific context may be open to several

Strategy Index
Instructional Focus
Frontloading Learning
Guiding Comprehension
Consolidating Understanding
Text Frames
Cause/Effect
Concept/Definition
Problem/Solution
Compare/Contrast
Proposition/Support
Goal/Action/Outcome
Comprehension Processess
Making Connections
Generating Questions
Creating Mental Images
Making Inferences
Determining Importance
Synthesizing

varied interpretations of a word's possible meaning. Therefore, to help students react to a word in a variety of contexts, next provide multiple instances of the word in action. For example, students in a social studies class might initially see the word *chide* in a newspaper article that says, "Critics chided the government for the slow response to requests for disaster aid." In addition to this contextual example of *chide*, ask students to examine the following additional examples:

- Jeremy was tired of his parents constantly chiding him for the messy state of his room.
- Her friends chided Mandi into apologizing for the rude remark.
- The principal chided the students for their noisy behavior in the hallway.

Ask students to determine the tone of the context. Does it seem to be positive, negative, or neutral? Does *chide* seem like something you would like someone to do to you? Next, ask them to try to substitute a word or phrase that seems to work within the general parameters of the context. For example, what word might critics use to tell the government that it was responding too slowly to disaster aid requests? How about *criticized? Condemned? Blamed? Scolded?* Which word fits best in all contexts? As students explore each context, they will realize that although all their guesses might work with the first context, the subsequent sentences cause them to narrow and refine their working definitions and come up with the closest synonym (*scold*— to goad someone into action). They develop a much richer and more complex understanding of a useful word than if they had merely attempted to memorize a possibly obscure dictionary definition.

3 Students read the selection, again paying special attention to the broader contexts of the target words, as well as other unfamiliar words they encounter.

4 Now that students have taken stock of their own level of knowledge of the target words and have been provided with further information about each word with examples of usage, ask students to begin to explain each word in terms of what they know or think they might know. Emphasize that you are not seeking a tidy definition but instead are seeking to articulate useful associations and various facets of a word's meaning. In these discussions encourage students to verbalize hunches they had about the words and how these hunches were confirmed, or not confirmed, by the contextual information. What contexts do they associate with these words?

Distribute Vocabulary Overview Guides as a strategy for recording their developing understandings of these words (see the Appendix for a reproducible

version of the Vocabulary Overview Guide). For example, target words in the classic Shirley Jackson short story "Charles" might include *insolently, swagger, reformation, warily, incredulously,* and *haggard.* Discuss with students the main topic or theme of the selection, and note how the words selected connect to this topic or theme. Students enter these target words on the Guide (see the Vocabulary Overview Guide for "Charles" example).

Encourage students to develop a strong association between new words and mnemonic clues that trigger a sense of their meanings. These clues help link new words to background knowledge. For example, students may decide that *insolently* is acting in a way that one would find insulting. *Insult* becomes their meaningful clue for remembering this word. Or *beware* reminds students of their meaning for *warily*—to be very cautious about something. Encourage students to personalize their clues. A clue that works for one student may not connect with another. For example, some students might connect *swagger* to the way a particular actor walks in a movie; students who have not seen this movie will need a different clue to remember swagger. As students study new words on the Vocabulary Overview Guide, ask them to cover the definitions to see if their clues are sufficient to help them recall the word's meaning.

5 Embed these target words in classroom activities and purposefully interject them into ongoing discussions of the text so that students are hearing them as well as reading them. Provide students with multiple opportunities to test-drive these Tier 2 words as they talk about and write about the book, story, or selection. In particular, include them in assessments, not as separate vocabulary items, but instead to demonstrate word knowledge by using the words to discuss their understandings: "Describe why the word *insolently* would be a good way to describe the way the main character acts in his kindergarten classroom. What would be some examples of his insolence?"

6 Gradually move students toward accepting more responsibility for selecting and explaining words they deem important in a reading. Transition to assigning these tasks in small groups or with student pairs. Finally, have individual students construct their own Vocabulary Overview Guides based on a reading assignment.

Advantages

- Students come to regard vocabulary learning as more than looking up definitions in a dictionary, as they develop ownership of new words that they encounter and use.

Vocabulary Overview Guide for "Charles"

Topic: "Charles"

insolently

Clue:	insult
Explain:	someone who acts in a disrespectful manner
Use:	Laurie acted insolently toward his teacher.

swagger

Clue:	walk with "attitude"
Explain:	when you walk as if you think a lot of yourself
Use:	Laurie's swagger showed he thought he was grown up.

reformation

Clue:	reform
Explain:	something that changes for the better
Use:	The story is about the reformation of Laurie.

warily

Clue:	beware!
Explain:	you are very cautious about something
Use:	The teacher would have to warily watch Charles.

incredulously

Clue:	too incredible
Explain:	you really can't believe something
Use:	The parents were incredulous Charles could be that naughty.

haggard

Clue:	hag
Explain:	someone who looks worn out
Use:	Laurie's teacher looked haggard after all he did in class!

Note: Adapted from Carr, E.M. (1985). The vocabulary overview guide: A metacognitive strategy to improve vocabulary comprehension and retention. *Journal of Reading, 28*(8), 684–689.

- Students have the opportunity to incrementally build their knowledge of new words as they connect to ideas in their reading, and practice using them in their speaking and writing.

- Students are provided with a well-organized structure for keeping track of and studying important words.

- Students approach vocabulary learning thoughtfully and come to realize that word knowledge is gained gradually, through repeated exposures and uses in a variety of contexts.

- Students are more motivated to learn words that they have personally selected from a reading.

References

Beck, I.L., McKeown, M.G., & Kucan, L. (2002). *Bringing words to life: Robust vocabulary instruction*. New York: Guilford.

Carr, E.M. (1985). The vocabulary overview guide: A metacognitive strategy to improve vocabulary comprehension and retention. *Journal of Reading, 28*(8), 684–689.

Word Family Trees

Can you guess this word? It once referred to a scrap of food given to someone less fortunate. The word, initially a Latin term, was later adopted by the French in medieval times to signify a lump of bread or other leavings of a meal provided to a beggar. The English expanded the word's usage from "a gift begged" to "a present." Along the way, the word has taken on a decidedly negative connotation. The modern meaning is to offer a gift, sometimes substantial, to influence someone's behavior.

The word? *Bribe.* What an interesting etymological journey—from a small gesture of generosity to a calculating act of corruption. One can almost speculate the circumstances that led the word *bribe* to be associated today with a different type of beggar.

Clearly, a word such as *bribe* has a deep and involved meaning. We understand the word far beyond any terse dictionary definition. All sorts of connections may come to mind: a parent who offers a child candy to quell a tantrum; a favor from a sibling for keeping quiet about a family rule infraction; a payment made to a decision maker to influence the awarding of a contract; a campaign contribution handed to a politician to further a group's political (or financial) agenda. *Bribe* is a rich concept with many layers of meaning; it is not a mere vocabulary word.

Students, however, often view vocabulary learning in a very narrow sense. They look up a new word in a dictionary, perhaps obtaining only a foggy notion of its meaning or grasping quickly at a possible synonym. If they must master the word for a vocabulary quiz, they memorize it as an act of short-term learning, forgetting it soon after and never incorporating it into their speaking and writing. Students often attempt to learn vocabulary words as facts (definitions), not as concepts. Encouraging students to be word browsers, to become playfully engaged with new vocabulary, can help reinforce that true vocabulary acquisition involves more than quick trips to a dictionary.

Using the Strategy

The Word Family Tree (Buehl, 1999) is strategy that involves students in connecting a key term to its origins, to related words that share a common root, to words that serve a similar function, and to situations in which one might expect the word to be used. Using this strategy involves the following steps:

1 Introduce the Word Family Tree graphic organizer as a means of vocabulary study (see the Appendix for a reproducible version of the Word Family Tree). As an analogy, refer to genealogical "family trees" to prepare students for this activity. Family trees list an individual's ancestors, direct descendants, and other relatives, such as cousins, aunts, and uncles, while the Word Family Tree lists the "relatives" of a word.

2 Teaching vocabulary strategies that help students detect meaningful word parts is referred to as generative vocabulary instruction—students become skilled in generating possible meanings of a string of new words based on their knowledge of roots and affixes. Start with the basic premise that if you learn one word, you actually learn 10 (Templeton, 2008). When students learn the word *convert*, they have in effect also learned *converts, converted, converting, converter, converters,* and *unconverted,* a natural byproduct of their encountering these forms of the word in their reading. However, other less familiar forms may be overlooked by students and should also be displayed when students are learning a useful "base" word like *convert: convertible, convertibility, convertibleness, inconvertible, inconvertibility, unconvertible, reconvert, reconvertible.* If the teacher does not intentionally include these words in the conversations about *convert,* then many students will not notice their relationship to a word they have come to know. As a result, students are more likely to skip the word as "too hard" when they encounter *reconvert* in a text, even though they have constructed sufficient knowledge about the

Strategy Index
Instructional Focus
Frontloading Learning
Guiding Comprehension
Consolidating Understanding
Text Frames
Cause/Effect
Concept/Definition
Problem/Solution
Compare/Contrast
Proposition/Support
Goal/Action/Outcome
Comprehension Processess
Making Connections
Generating Questions
Creating Mental Images
Making Inferences
Determining Importance
Synthesizing

"base" word to successfully hypothesize a probable meaning.

As students examine the variations on how *convert* might appear in a larger word, ask them to apply knowledge of suffixes and prefixes to speculate on possible meanings of these more sophisticated forms. In addition, use the opportunity to teach the root in the base word—in this case *vert* which means "to turn." So if *convert* means to turn something into something else, then *convertible* can be explained as something that is capable of being turned into something else.

3 Introduce students to the Word Family Tree by using an important term taken from a classroom text. For example, *acquiesce* is a Tier 2 word (see the Student-Friendly Vocabulary Explanations strategy beginning on page 175 for more discussion on Tier words) encountered by students in a history text. Show how the word is linked to a meaningful root to help them gain insight on likely contexts where the word might appear (see the Word Family Tree for *Acquiesce* example).

4 Select a group of target Tier 2 and Tier 3 words for students to investigate. These could be pivotal words in a short story, key terms in a unit of study, or generally useful vocabulary words. For example, key terms in a biology unit might include *genetics, mutation, recessive, inherited,* and *dominant.* Although students will encounter other biological terminology, selected words should represent essential concepts to be learned. The history passage that included *acquiesce* might also feature words such as *imperialism, treaty,* and *colonialism.* Have students work with partners or in cooperative groups to complete Word Family Trees for target words, using appropriate resources including textbooks, a thesaurus, a dictionary, online vocabulary sites, or other vocabulary-rich sources. Part of the activity involves brainstorming to determine what kinds of people might be heard using the word and devising possible sentences for those contexts. Ask students to brainstorm possible mnemonic clues to help remember the meaning of the word. In the biology example, students investigating the Word Family Tree for *genetics* may uncover a rich array of relatives all derived from the same origin: *gene, genealogy, gender, genius,* and *generate.*

Allow time for students to share Word Family Trees with classmates to discover other related words, possible synonyms, and useful contexts where the word might make an appearance. For example, a music teacher may ask, "Can you remember the difference between a *sonata* and a *concerto?*" The word *concerto* is derived from the same Latin root *concertare*—to organize or arrange, as in *concert*—to act together, to work in harmony: It will take the *concerted* effort of our entire community to revitalize the downtown area. A *concerto* is a composition that requires the soloist(s) to work together with a symphony orchestra to produce music. Students creating a family tree for *sonata* will discover that the ancestor is the root *sonare*—to sound. Close relatives that share this origin are *sound, sonar, sonic, sonnet,* and *sonorous.* Similar words include *solo* and *recital.*

5 Next, take frequent opportunities to model vocabulary problem solving using knowledge of a key base word and root. Here is another example of a potentially difficult word for students: The negotiations finally were called to a halt because both sides proved to be *intractable.* Templeton (2008) recommends modeling a four-step analysis procedure for tackling new words like *intractable:*

- First, ask yourself if there are any prefixes or suffixes (parts added to the beginnings and ends of words). If you find some, take them off (erase *in* and *able*).

- Second, notice what is left. In this case, the long word is built around the root *tract.* Ask yourself what you know about this base word or root. Where have you seen it before?

- Third, think of a familiar keyword that contains that word part: *tract.* How about *tractor?* You know that a tractor "pulls things."

- Fourth, put the affixes back on—the suffix and the prefix. Develop your hunch about the word's meaning, and see if the sentence makes sense. Sometimes, you may need to study more than just the sentence—you may need to read over the entire paragraph or think about the topic or main idea of the whole passage. In this case *intractable* seems to be a word that has something to do with "not being pulled," which makes sense because the negotiations were stopped, so it seems that neither side could be "pulled" into an agreement.

As an integral component of generative vocabulary instruction, be constantly on the lookout for meaningful keywords, already known to students, to be used as automatic problem-solving prompts. For example, notice how the meaningful keyword *fracture* (to break) can be used as a tool to problem solve these more sophisticated forms: *fractionate, fractious, refraction, fracas, infraction.* Notice that Tier 3 words with meaningful parts appear as key vocabulary in a wide variety of subject areas. *Fractionate* (as in a country *fractionating*) may surface in social studies texts. *Refraction* is a science concept, *fraction* a math concept, *infraction* a physical education concept, and

Word Family Tree for *Acquiesce*

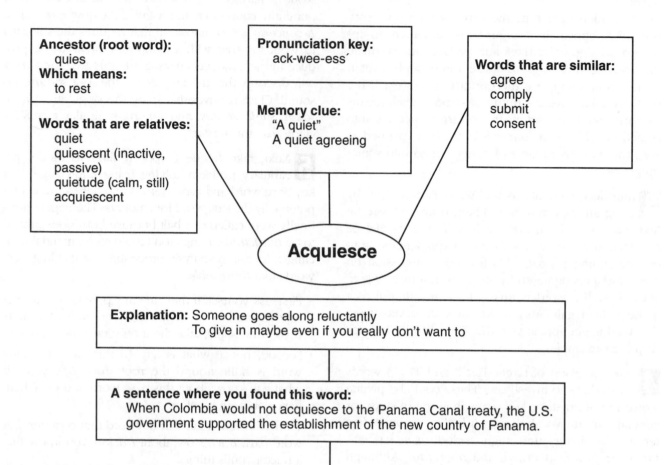

Ancestor (root word):
quies
Which means:
to rest

Words that are relatives:
quiet
quiescent (inactive, passive)
quietude (calm, still)
acquiescent

Pronunciation key:
ack-wee-ess´

Memory clue:
"A quiet"
A quiet agreeing

Words that are similar:
agree
comply
submit
consent

Acquiesce

Explanation: Someone goes along reluctantly
To give in maybe even if you really don't want to

A sentence where you found this word:
When Colombia would not acquiesce to the Panama Canal treaty, the U.S. government supported the establishment of the new country of Panama.

Who would say it? Pick three kinds of people who might say this word and write a sentence showing how they might use it.

Politician	Judge	Business person
After a few changes to the bill, the senator *acquiesced* and voted for it.	The judge told the jury that any dissenters had to *acquiesce* in reaching the verdict.	I will *acquiesce* and buy your computers, if you guarantee that they will work for my company.

Source: Buehl, D. (1999). Word family trees: Heritage sheds insight into words' meaning and use. *WEAC News & Views, 35*(2), 14.

fractious could be employed to describe a character in a short story or novel. It is therefore incumbent on all teachers to take advantage of the daily opportunities for generative vocabulary instruction in their curriculum.

Advantages

• Students develop a thorough understanding of important vocabulary.

• Students come to see the organic nature of vocabulary, as word meanings have grown and changed over the years.

• Students begin to identify useful word roots and notice connections among words derived from similar origins.

• Students are more likely to remember new words and feel confident in using them when they write and talk.

- Students are encouraged to raise questions of their own about possible word backgrounds, and to consult sources other than abridged dictionaries to enrich their vocabulary understanding.

References

Buehl, D. (1999). Word family trees: Heritage sheds insight into words' meaning and use. *WEAC News & Views, 35*(2), 14.

Templeton, S. (2008, February 8). *Revolutionizing vocabulary instruction, Grades 4–12*. Paper presented at the Wisconsin State Reading Association convention, Milwaukee, WI.

Suggested Reading

Klemp, R.M. (1994). Word storm: Connecting vocabulary to the student's database. *The Reading Teacher, 48*(3), 282.

Written Conversations

u k? sry 4gt 2 cal u lst nyt Can you decipher this message? Chances are, if you have become a devoted "text messenger," this is a quick read, which mandates an instant reply: *im gr8*.

The electronic age has updated the age-old practice of passing notes by combining modern equivalents of telegraphic brevity with a desire for immediate response. Could you decipher the opening message ("Are you okay? I'm sorry I forgot to call you last night.") and response ("I'm great.")? Computerized communication forms, such as text messaging, e-mail, chat rooms, and instant messenger, have made it easier to carry on a written conversation over a distance, whether it is a school desk away or across the continent. Classroom activities that capitalize on students' desire to talk to each other represent promising strategies for focused discussions around reading assignments. Daniels, Zemelman, and Steineke (2007) suggest planning written conversations, which engage students in shared writing with their classmates to pursue their thinking about classroom texts.

Written conversations are a variation of dialogue journaling and can be used with fiction or nonfiction texts. Unlike class discussions that feature one person talking while the rest of the students wait for a possible turn to add their comments, written conversations are silent, ongoing discussions that involve every student as a communicator in the entire process.

Using the Strategy

Written conversations can be configured in a number of ways, depending on the nature of the material and course objectives. Using this strategy involves the following steps:

1 Students complete their reading of a passage from a textbook, article, chapter, or story. Inform students that they will be participants in a silent conversation about topics and ideas in their reading. Outline the ground rules for a written conversation:

- All talking during a written conversation must be in writing; no oral communication is permitted. If you want to say something, put it in writing.

- The "no oral communication" rule also applies to transition periods when written conversations are passed on to the next student.

- A written conversation is a "quick write" (see the Quick Writes strategies beginning on page 141). In other words, the writing format is expected to be generally informal, as if students were chatting about the topic. Students need not be preoccupied with turning out clean, highly edited pieces. However, writing fluency practice is prized, so "text message shorthand" is also not intended here. Their writing needs to be readable as they quickly jot down what they are thinking. The rule is "just write!"

- A written entry must be focused on the task and the text; students need to avoid going off-topic in their responses.

- All responses need to respect the comments and ideas of your conversational partners. However, disagreeing with a viewpoint is a natural dynamic in many conversations, and students are encouraged to *respectfully* disagree and offer their own interpretations.

- Students are expected to fill their allotted writing time. When students inquire, "How much am I supposed to write?" underscore the expectation that they will write as much as they can until told to pass the paper. At this juncture, conversations are forwarded to the next student and the process is continued.

- Finally, their writing is personal. They are writing to their partners or classmates and are responding to what their fellow students are thinking, as well as offering their own comments.

Strategy Index
Instructional Focus
Frontloading Learning
Guiding Comprehension
Consolidating Understanding
Text Frames
Cause/Effect
Concept/Definition
Problem/Solution
Compare/Contrast
Proposition/Support
Goal/Action/Outcome
Comprehension Processess
Making Connections
Generating Questions
Creating Mental Images
Making Inferences
Determining Importance
Synthesizing

2 Decide upon an organization for the written conversation. For example, students can be assigned a partner, and their conversation will represent thoughts that pass back and forth between the two of them. Or students can work in groups of four, and pass the paper to the left each time, until the conversation they started returns to them.

In addition, the format of the conversation can vary. Each student can begin by writing the initial entry on a sheet of paper or on a page in their class journals. These papers are then swapped, and partners write their thoughts in response to these first entries. The papers move back and forth for continued conversation. Another method is to use large sticky notes that are affixed to the text students are responding to. One partner may be using yellow notes, the other green. The text with the sticky note comments is then passed between partners.

3 Provide a focus for the written conversation. Of course, students can be instructed to write about anything in the text that they want to talk about. But many students will benefit from a prompt that offers some specific directions for targeting their thinking.

Possible writing prompts for fiction include the following:

- I made a connection to...
- I know the feeling...
- I love the way...
- I don't really understand...
- I can't believe...
- I realized...
- I wonder why...
- I noticed...
- I was surprised...
- I think...
- If I were...
- I'm not sure...

Possible writing prompts for nonfiction include the following:

- I learned...
- I was surprised to learn...
- I already knew that...
- I was wrong to think...
- I wonder why...
- I still don't know...
- I found it interesting that...
- I thought it was especially important...
- I would tell someone...

- I found it confusing when...
- This helped me explain...

4 Decide upon an appropriate amount of time for each individual written entry. A range of 1 to 3 minutes per round will provide students with just enough time to record some of their thoughts before passing the conversation on. Then start the written conversations. Emphasize that these are simultaneous responses; all students are writing. When the allotted writing time has expired, say "pass." Provide students with a brief period to read their partner's response. Then say "start" to cue students to comment on their partner's thoughts.

With partners, allow opportunities for three to four exchanges, pausing each time to grant some reading time before continuing with the written conversation. With the "Write Around" variation, which expands the conversation to groups of four, every student responds to ideas initiated by three classmates. The fourth exchange lands the conversation back where it started, so the final entry features feedback from three classmates, and allows each initiating student the "final word" on that series of comments.

5 After students have gone through all the exchanges, end the conversation on an oral note. "What would you like to talk about now with your partner or group?" For the first time, students can converse out loud about their thinking. You will likely notice many of your students eager to elaborate on their written thoughts and to follow up on some of their comments. Finally, ask partners to share some of their conversation with the entire class and use this invitation to continue a large-group discussion about the topic and ideas from the text.

Advantages

- Written conversations provide students with valuable practice in verbalizing their thoughts about written texts.
- Students have an opportunity to comment upon, question, and summarize what they are reading and learning.
- Students are able to listen in on the thinking of their classmates and add their own take on the material.
- Students are afforded a way to socialize as they learn, interacting with their peers as they discuss their reading.

Reference

Daniels, H., Zemelman, S., & Steineke, N. (2007). *Content-area writing: Every teacher's guide*. Portsmouth, NH: Heinemann.

Reproducibles

Alphabet Brainstorming 194

Analogy Charting 195

Author Says/I Say 196

B/D/A Questioning Chart 197

Character Analysis Grid 198

Concept/Definition Map 199

Different Perspectives Graphic Outline 200

Discussion Web 201

Eyewitness Testimony Chart 202

Fact Pyramid 203

First Impressions Chart 204

History Change Frame Graphic Organizer 205

History Memory Bubble 206

I-Chart 207

Proposition/Support Outline 208

RAFT Role Definition Chart 209

Science Connection Overview 210

Story Map 211

Vocabulary Overview Guide 212

Word Family Tree 213

Alphabet Brainstorming

A	B	C	D	E	F	G

H	I	J	K	L	M	N

O	P	Q	R	S	T	U

V	W	X	Y	Z		

Source: Ricci, G., & Wahlgren, C. (1998, May). *The key to know "PAINE" know gain.* Paper presented at the 43rd Annual Convention of the International Reading Association, Orlando, FL.

Classroom Strategies for Interactive Learning (3rd ed.) by Doug Buehl © 2009. Newark, DE: International Reading Association. May be copied for classroom use.

Analogy Charting

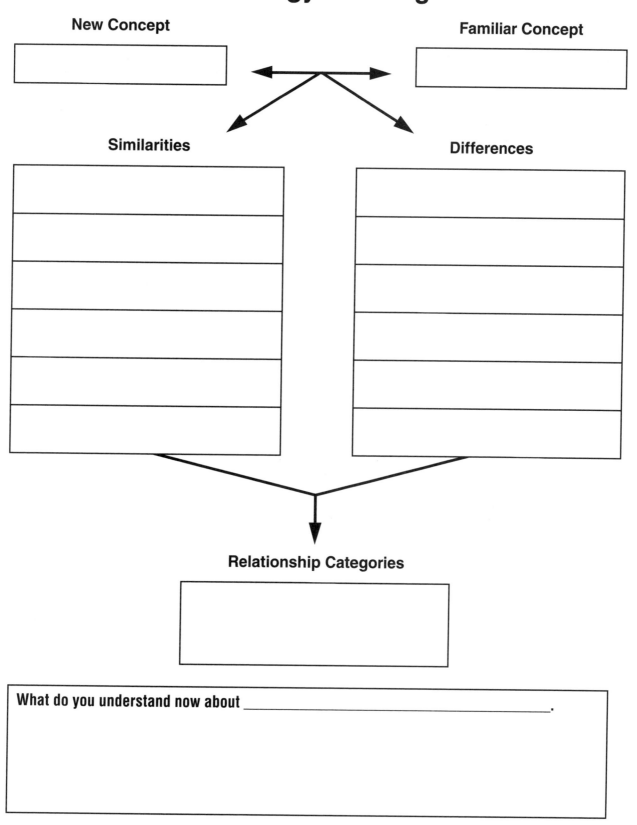

New Concept

Familiar Concept

Similarities

Differences

Relationship Categories

What do you understand now about _____.

Source: Buehl, D., & Hein, D. (1990). Analogy graphic organizer. *The Exchange. Newsletter of the International Reading Association Secondary Reading Special Interest Group, 3*(2), 6.

Author Says/I Say

I Wonder	The Author Says	I Say	And So

B/D/A Questioning Chart

What are you wondering?

Before Reading	During Reading	After Reading

What do you understand now that you didn't understand before?

Source: Laverick, C. (2002). B-D-A strategy: Reinventing the wheel can be a good thing. *Journal of Adolescent & Adult Literacy, 46*(2), 144–147.

Character Analysis Grid

1. What does the character do?

2. What does the character say or think?

3. How do others feel about the character?

4. How does the character change?

Conflict

5. Author's theme or point of view:

Concept/Definition Map

What is it?

What is it like?

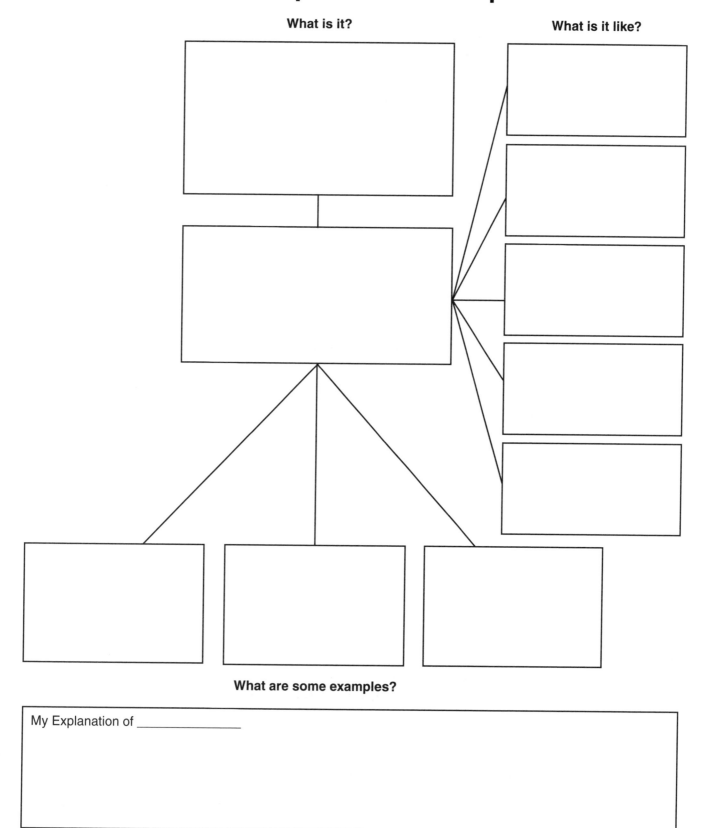

What are some examples?

My Explanation of _____

Source: Schwartz, R.M., & Raphael, T.E. (1985). Concept of definition: A key to improving students' vocabulary. *The Reading Teacher, 39*(2), 198–205.

Different Perspectives Graphic Outline

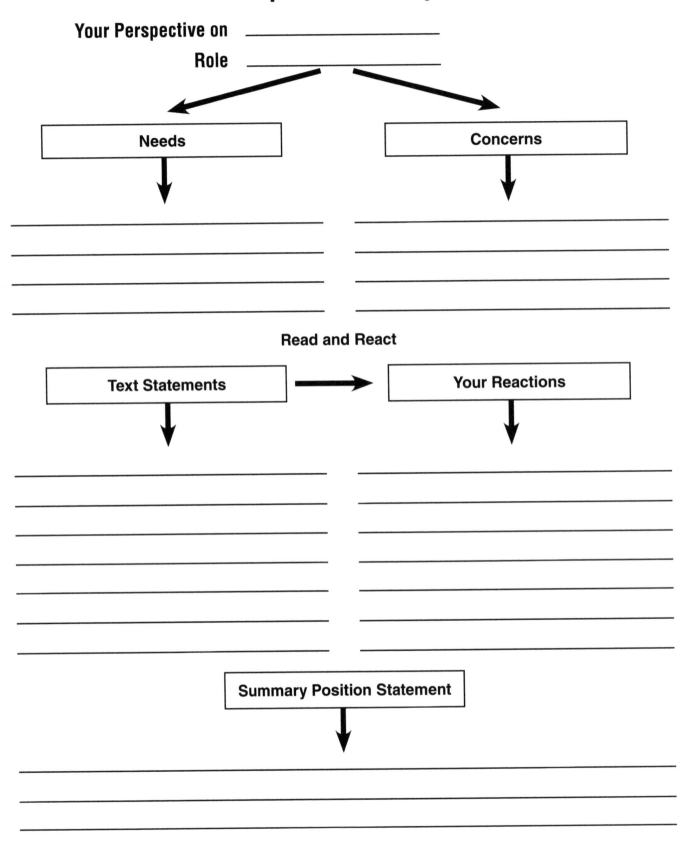

Your Perspective on _____

Role _____

Needs	Concerns

Read and React

Text Statements	→	Your Reactions

Summary Position Statement

Discussion Web

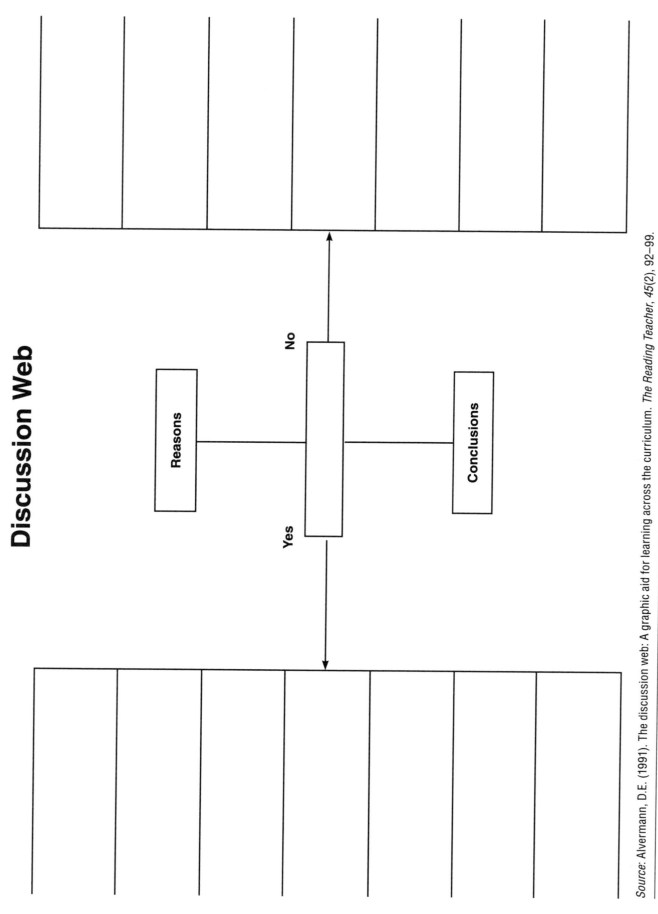

Reasons

Yes

No

Conclusions

Source: Alvermann, D.E. (1991). The discussion web: A graphic aid for learning across the curriculum. *The Reading Teacher, 45(2),* 92–99.

Classroom Strategies for Interactive Learning (3rd ed.) by Doug Buehl © 2009. Newark, DE: International Reading Association. May be copied for classroom use.

Eyewitness Testimony Chart

I Was There (and can describe...)	The Author's Words ("The author wrote...")	My Version ("I saw, heard, felt, experienced...")

Source: Buehl, D. (2008). First person reading. *OnWEAC*. Available online: www.weac.org/news/2007-08/feb08/readingroom.htm

Fact Pyramid

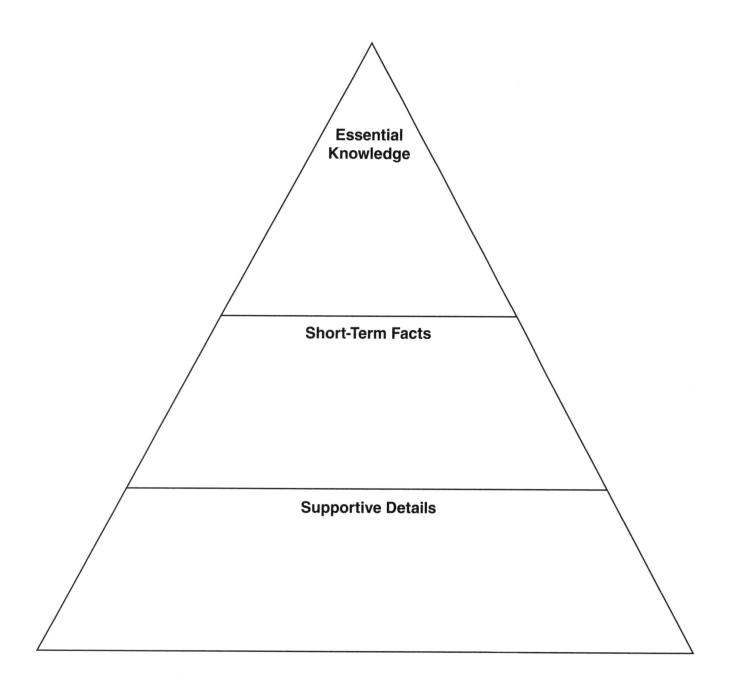

Essential
Knowledge

Short-Term Facts

Supportive Details

Source: Buehl, D. (1991). Fact pyramids. *New perspectives: Reading across the curriculum, 7*(6), 1–2. Madison, WI: Madison Metropolitan School District.

First Impressions Chart

The Author's Words		My Impressions
First		
Then		
Finally		

Source: Buehl, D. (2008). First person reading. *OnWEAC.* Available online: www.weac.org/news/2007-08/feb08/readingroom.htm

History Change Frame Graphic Organizer

Group	What problems did they face	What changes affected these people	What did they do to solve their problems?

Source: Buehl, D. (1992). A frame of mind for reading history. *The Exchange. Newsletter of the International Reading Association Secondary Reading Special Interest Group, 5*(1), 4–5.

History Memory Bubbles

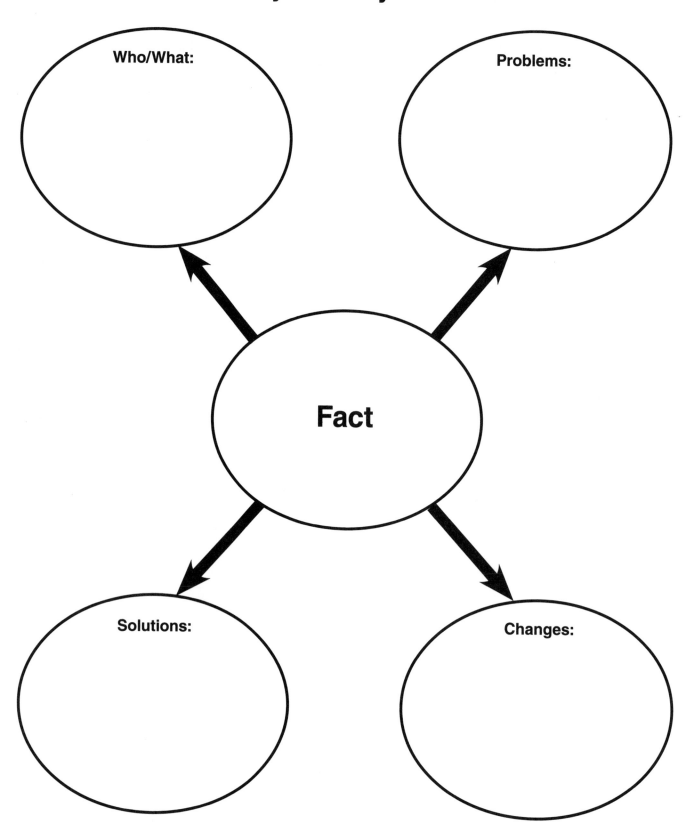

Source: Buehl, D. (1998). Memory bubbles: They help put information into context. *WEAC News and Views, 33*(7), 13.

I-Chart

Topic:	Q1:	Q2:	Q3:	Q4:	Other important information	New questions
What we know:						
Source:						
Source:						
Source:						
Summaries						

Source: Hoffman, J.V. (1992). Critical reading/thinking across the curriculum: Using I-charts to support learning. *Language Arts, 69(2)*, 121–127.

Classroom Strategies for Interactive Learning (3rd ed.) by Doug Buehl © 2009. Newark, DE: International Reading Association. May be copied for classroom use.

Proposition/Support Outline

Proposition:

Support:

1. Facts

2. Statistics

3. Examples

4. Expert authority

5. Logic and reasoning

Source: Buehl, D. (1992). Outline helps students analyze credibility of author's premise. *WEAC News & Views, 28*(1), 8.

RAFT Role Definition Chart

Personality—Who am I and what are some aspects of my character?	Attitude—What are my feelings, beliefs, ideas, concerns?	Information—What do I know that I need to share in my writing?

Science Connection Overview

What's familiar?

What topics are covered?

What are you wondering?

What will the author tell you?

Read and translate

Source: Buehl, D. (1992). The connection overview: A strategy for learning in science. *WSRA Journal, 36*(2), 21–30.

Story Map

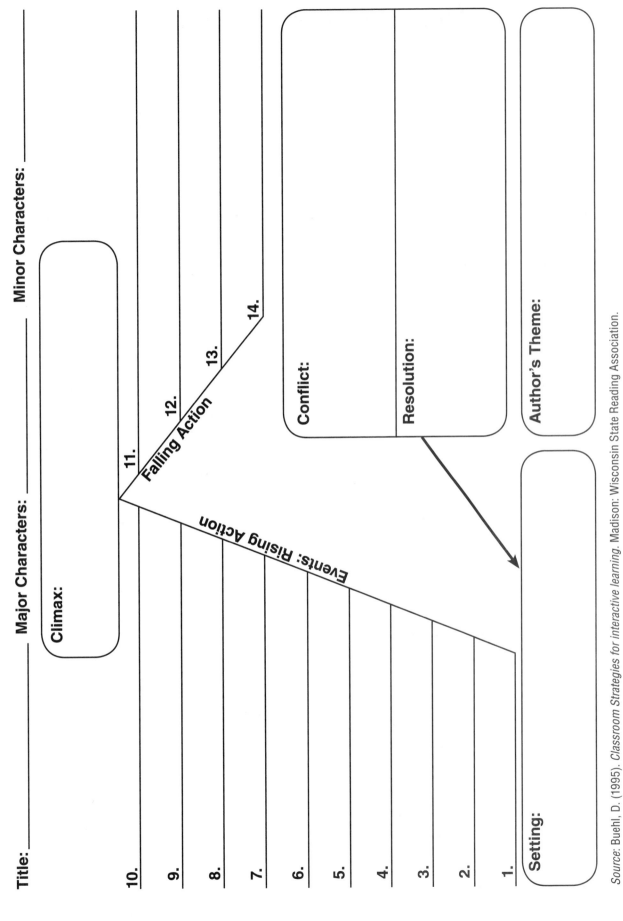

Title: _____

Major Characters: _____   **Minor Characters:** _____

Climax:

10.

9.

8.

7.

Falling Action

11.

12.

13.

14.

Events: Rising Action

6.

5.

4.

3.

2.

1.

Conflict:

Resolution:

Setting:

Author's Theme:

Source: Buehl, D. (1995). *Classroom Strategies for interactive learning.* Madison: Wisconsin State Reading Association.

Vocabulary Overview Guide

Clue:

Explain:

Use:

Clue:

Explain:

Use:

Clue:

Explain:

Use:

Clue:

Explain:

Use:

Clue:

Explain:

Use:

Clue:

Explain:

Use:

Note: Adapted from Carr, E.M. (1985). The vocabulary overview guide: A metacognitive strategy to improve vocabulary comprehension and retention. *Journal of Reading, 28*(8), 684–689.

Word Family Tree

| Ancestor (root word):

Which means:

Words that are relatives: | Pronunciation Key:

Memory Clue: | Words that are similar: |

Word:

| Explanation: |

| A sentence where you found this word: |

Who would say it? Pick three kinds of people who might say this word and write a sentence showing how they might use it.		

Source: Buehl, D. (1999). Word family trees: Heritage sheds insight into words' meaning and use. *WEAC News & Views, 35*(2), 14.